CW01160724

Approaches to Teaching the Novels of James Fenimore Cooper

Approaches to Teaching the Novels of James Fenimore Cooper

Edited by

Stephen Carl Arch

and

Keat Murray

Modern Language Association of America
New York   2022

© 2022 by The Modern Language Association of America
85 Broad Street, New York, New York 10004
ww.mla.org

All rights reserved. MLA and the MODERN LANGUAGE ASSOCIATION are trademarks owned by the Modern Language Association of America. To request permission to reprint material from MLA book publications, please inquire at permissions@mla.org.

To order MLA publications, visit mla.org/books. For wholesale and international orders, see mla.org/Bookstore-Orders.

The MLA office is located on the island known as Mannahatta (Manhattan) in Lenapehoking, the homeland of the Lenape people. The MLA pays respect to the original stewards of this land and to the diverse and vibrant Native communities that continue to thrive in New York City.

Approaches to Teaching World Literature 172

ISSN 1059-1133

Library of Congress Cataloging-in-Publication Data

Names: Arch, Stephen Carl, editor. | Murray, Keat, editor.
Title: Approaches to teaching the novels of James Fenimore Cooper / edited by Stephen Carl Arch and Keat Murray.
Description: New York : Modern Language Association of America, 2022.
Series: Approaches to teaching world literature, 1059-1133 ; 172 | Includes bibliographical references.
Identifiers: LCCN 2022017725 (print) | LCCN 2022017726 (ebook) | ISBN 9781603294201 (hardcover) | ISBN 9781603294843 (paperback) | ISBN 9781603294928 (epub)
Subjects: LCSH: Cooper, James Fenimore, 1789–1851—Study and teaching. | Cooper, James Fenimore, 1789–1851—Criticism and interpretation. | LCGFT: Essays. | Literary criticism.
Classification: LCC PS1438 .A67 2022 (print) | LCC PS1438 (ebook) | DDC 813/.2—dc23/eng/20220418
LC record available at https://lccn.loc.gov/2022017725
LC ebook record available at https://lccn.loc.gov/2022017726

CONTENTS

Introduction 1
    Stephen Carl Arch and Keat Murray

PART ONE: MATERIALS

Works 13
Biographies 15
Selected Recent Criticism 15
The Instructor's Library 19
Filmography 23
Critical Overview of Selected Feature Films 25
Additional Resources 33

PART TWO: APPROACHES

History and Culture

America's Historical Romance: *The Last of the Mohicans*
    to *Hamilton* 39
    Sarah Sillin

Cooper's Revolutionary Novels: Surface Reading and
    Grotesque American History 48
    Joseph J. Letter

Teaching *The Deerslayer* through Historical and Critical Debates 58
    Rochelle Raineri Zuck

Cross-Culturalism in *The Last of the Mohicans* 69
    Donna Richardson

Natural Environments

Collective Inquiry and Animal Studies in *The Pioneers* 80
    Keat Murray

Environmental Apocalypse and *The Crater* 92
    Matthew Wynn Sivils

Indigenous American Poetics in *The Prairie* 100
    Betty Booth Donohue (Cherokee Nation)

Language and Form

Interactive Identities: *The Last of the Mohicans* in English Literature
    Courses for Nonmajors   109
  Elaina Anne Frulla

Applying Pedagogies of Recovery to *The Pioneers*   119
  Lisa West

Narrative and Survival Strategies in *Satanstoe*   128
  Robert Daly

Mary Monson, Girl Detective: Cooper as a Mystery Writer   136
  Barbara Alice Mann

Language Diversity in Cooper's Novels   144
  Anna Scannavini

Visuality and Cinema

Wyandotté and American Scenery   153
  Michael Demson

Cooper's Early Work in a Media History Context   162
  Christopher J. Lukasik

The Social Power of Sentimental Lament: *The Last of the*
    Mohicans and Mann's Film Adaptation   169
  Paul Gutjahr

Teaching *The Last of the Mohicans* through Cinematic Adaptation   178
  David W. Hartwig

Cooper and Adaptation as Layered Cultural History   186
  Todd Nathan Thompson

Notes on Contributors   195

Survey Participants   199

Works Cited   201

Introduction

Stephen Carl Arch and Keat Murray

James Fenimore Cooper published thirty-two novels between 1820 and his death in 1851. Only a handful remain known to most instructors. And instructors who teach those few still-canonical novels understand that they present challenges to today's students. Cooper specialized in long novels, usually issued in three volumes for the British market, and shaped them to the demands of the American and British markets of that era. Students, however, often struggle with long novels. Cooper's plots are complex and often slow to develop, a virtue in a culture in which the novel was a major form of entertainment, but a drawback for students who today find instant entertainment in posts on *Instagram*, *Reddit*, and *Twitter* and in *YouTube* videos. Cooper wrote romances because he believed his readers, which included many women, expected a budding romance in the early chapters and a marriage at the end. Students are often suspicious of romance presented sentimentally and without irony. Cooper seems solidly part of the nineteenth-century establishment, and yet students find it difficult to engage with his high seriousness, which lacks the irony they find in Herman Melville, the idealism they find in Henry David Thoreau, the humor they find in Mark Twain, or the subversion they find in Harriet Jacobs. Teaching Cooper is a tough sell today.

We and our contributors believe that Cooper is a vital presence in Western literary traditions, especially those of the United States. In this collection, we offer instructors new methods for bringing Cooper's novels to life in the classroom. These innovative approaches offer ways to counter students' initial resistance to reading Cooper's hefty novels and empower students to engage the ideas that animate those novels—ideas relevant for young people today as we continue to struggle over the nature of democracy, the rights of marginalized peoples, and our relation to the natural world.

Cooper's Literary Career and Reception

Events in his life made Cooper intensely aware of class privilege. As a young man, he expected to inherit a fortune from his father, a land speculator and United States congressman who amassed substantial holdings in upstate New York at the end of the eighteenth century.[1] The fortune turned out to be almost worthless, however, and in his twenties Cooper suddenly had to learn how to make a living. Born in 1789, he had attended Yale University from 1802 to 1805 but was expelled before graduation for setting off a small incendiary device in a classmate's dorm room door. He had served in the merchant marine in 1806 and in the United States Navy from 1808 to 1810, but he had insufficient capital to succeed on his own as a merchant and did not wish to be a career naval officer. In the second decade of the century, he went from being a young single man who expected to become rich to being a married man with several young children and numerous debts from his father's land speculations. In a famous, perhaps apocryphal story, Cooper was reading a novel to his wife one day when he threw the book down in disgust and declared, *"I could write you a better book than that myself!"* (qtd. in Franklin, *James Fenimore Cooper: The Early Years* 248). Within months, he had completed and published his first novel, *Precaution*. Learning quickly, he next tried a more ambitious tale, *The Spy*, which was a huge success, and then another ambitious novel, *The Pioneers*, which was met with great acclaim and strong sales. His success seemed like magic. Nothing in his youth and education suggested that he wished to be a novelist. Nothing in the culture of the new United States suggested that a novelist could earn enough money to consider making a decent living from book sales. And yet Cooper had managed in three years to publish two bestsellers. He had invented himself as an author who lived off the productions of his pen.

Amid the vicissitudes of the United States and world economies over the next thirty years, Cooper would often struggle to make ends meet as a professional writer. Success was harder earned later in his life. Bills, debts, and public disputes often took a toll on his energy. In addition, the publishing industry was swiftly evolving, reading habits were changing, and readers' tastes were shifting. But over those years Cooper continued to make and remake himself as an author. During a seven-year sojourn in Europe starting in 1826, he met and befriended famous writers and politicians, including Walter Scott and the Marquis de Lafayette. There, and back at home in the United States in the 1830s, he inserted himself into political debates about democracy; the United States government's practice of displacing Native Americans, known as Indian Removal; slavery; economics; taxation; the United States Constitution; and authorship. In his writing he experimented constantly with content and with new kinds of stories, repeatedly setting forth what his contemporaries in the United States and in Europe took to be American themes: the frontier, the displacement or decimation of Native tribes, the ocean as a liminal space of possibility, and rugged individualism—as represented by figures like the pirate, spy, hunter, and settler, who go their own ways and move on restlessly in search of new beginnings.

Cooper's life and works are insistently modern and cosmopolitan. Cooper's novels are in conversation with those by contemporaneous writers like Honoré de Balzac in France and Charles Dickens in England. All three writers were fascinated with the rise of the modern city and its networks and bureaucracies. All three scrutinized the past to determine how it shaped the present and might shape the future. All three set fictional characters adrift in a changed and changing world and watched as they struggled to make sense of emerging Romantic ideas, shifting politics, and new technologies. Cooper's novels also resonate with the historical romances of Scott, the gothic novels of the Brontës, and the acute psychological analyses in the novels of Stendhal. Readers familiar with Cooper's novels will not be surprised to learn that Cooper knew many of these other writers personally, and that they read his work with the same interest and engagement with which he read theirs.

Cooper's most persistent theme was democracy, which his American readers often interpreted through the lens of the American Revolution and the promise of the young republic, but which Cooper understood as the proper inheritance of all rational, free-thinking peoples. When in the 1830s he wrote novels set in Europe about the common people's need for republican government and the aristocracy's resistance to political reform, many of his American readers were disappointed because he defended American principles through European examples. When in 1835 he wrote an allegorical satire about Europe and the United States featuring talking monkeys, they were bored. When in 1847 he wrote a speculative novel about colonization, settlement, and social reform on an imaginary Pacific island, readers hardly noticed and sales were lackluster. He was less an American writer in these and other works than he was a global writer. Democracy in the United States was a great experiment; it is where he experienced it. But he believed in a democratic future. The politics of a community capable of making or destroying itself was his great subject. He never ran out of material.

For complex personal, political, and cultural reasons, Cooper's literary reputation and book sales fluctuated in the 1830s, leading to a period later in the nineteenth century when the novels were dismissed, mocked, or forgotten. This trend began in the early 1830s, when Cooper decided to write those so-called European novels that disappointed many readers and when his outspoken views on politics created enemies in powerful places. To rectify the situation, the resilient author started the 1840s by resurrecting Natty Bumppo for two novels and, thus, reviving his popularity and critical acclaim for a time with a return to genres and motifs that had catapulted him to eminence in the 1820s. But in these and later novels of the 1840s, he sustained his commitment to social and political criticism, subtly tempering his critique in different kinds of narratives from his politically forthright novels of the 1830s. Indeed, throughout his prolific final decade, Cooper colored his production with invention—authoring a new trilogy, experimenting with first-person narration, blending romantic and realistic modes, and venturing into new genres, sometimes at the risk of sacrificing sales. Cooper's slip from prominence accelerated after his death in 1851: his novels began to seem old fashioned to readers becoming familiar with the realism of Gustave Flaubert and George Eliot and then later with the naturalism of Émile Zola, Henry James, Stephen Crane, and other writers. Cooper aided the decline of his popularity by insisting before he died that his family refuse to authorize a biography. The details of his life and career were therefore unavailable to most readers and were ignored or misunderstood by those who did have access to them. His politics were attacked by Whigs during his lifetime (Franklin, *James Fenimore Cooper: The Later Years* xvii–xviii), and later they were misread by readers unfamiliar with the controversies of the antebellum era. His works of nonfiction, as well as many of his novels, fell into obscurity. His impressive contributions to the profession of authorship in the United States were underappreciated and then forgotten. Only his character Natty Bumppo, or Leather-Stocking, lived on in popular culture.[2] While a small cadre of academic scholars published important books and articles on Cooper in the early and middle twentieth century, his reputation and stature continued to give way.

This collection of essays, however, builds firmly on the foundations of a major reassessment of Cooper's novels that began in the last quarter of the twentieth century. First, beginning in 1980, a group of Cooper scholars began to publish critical scholarly editions of Cooper's novels. Editions of twelve of the novels as well as five of Cooper's travel narratives appeared under the imprint of the State University of New York Press between 1980 and 1991. After a moribund period, another seven novels appeared under the imprint of AMS Press between 1999 and 2017. Today, with the renewed support of the State University of New York Press, editions of a number of Cooper's remaining novels are in various stages of production. For the first time ever, many of Cooper's novels and nonfictional works have been made available in trustworthy, carefully edited versions with authoritative historical and textual commentary. From its first volume, this large-scale editing project consistently revealed that Cooper was a careful artist, that he repeatedly engaged in innovative economic practices on his own behalf, and that he responded to changing tastes and market conditions with imagination, insight, and energy. He was not the sloppy artist whom Mark Twain made fun of in his injudicious parody, "Fenimore Cooper's Literary Offenses." He was instead a consummate artist who was often betrayed by his own handwriting, by the complexities of editing and typesetting in that era, by the need to negotiate and renegotiate contracts, and by the pressures of writing so much at one time. At one moment in 1837, for instance, Cooper had six full-length works in various states of production.

Second, in 2017 Wayne Franklin completed his two-volume biography of Cooper—*James Fenimore Cooper: The Early Years* and *James Fenimore Cooper: The Later Years*—the first to be based on documents long held by the Cooper family and the first to try to understand Cooper fully within the political, social, and economic context of his times. Franklin's magisterial biography has opened new lines of inquiry in Cooper studies about the author, his works, and his place in literary and cultural history. In Franklin's biography, readers can finally see how vital Cooper was to the literary landscapes of the United States and Europe in the first half of the nineteenth century. Franklin is especially insightful in revealing Cooper as a manager of his own business affairs who adapted to a publishing industry that remade itself over the course of his lifetime. Technologies changed, audiences changed, marketing changed, fads came and went, but Cooper survived and thrived. It is notable that of all the popular novelists in the United States in the 1820s, only Cooper managed successfully to negotiate new markets and new politics in the 1840s. He did so solely on his own initiative, writing at a quicker pace, searching for new markets, negotiating contracts, and purchasing reprint rights, understanding amid the new market forces at mid-century that artists were their own best business managers.

The scholarly editions of Cooper's works and Franklin's biography of Cooper have inspired new engagements with the novels. In recent scholarship, one can see more clearly now that Cooper anticipated many of the questions that engage us today, including those that revolve around race, immigration, gender, voting rights, and class resentment. For example, Dana Nelson argued in 2007 that the Leather-Stocking Tales raise provocative questions about friendship across racial, gender, and class differences in the antebellum United States. Reading Cooper's novels through the large body of scholarship on sentimentality, sympathy, affect, and friendship, Nelson argues that it is "far too reductive" (144) to associate sentimentality primarily with women authors: "Almost a decade before the nineteenth century's blockbuster sentimental novel, Harriet Beecher Stowe's *Uncle Tom's Cabin* (1851), Cooper preaches a message of interracial feeling" (143).

Jason Berger, to take another example, tapped into oceanic studies to investigate how Cooper charted the economic and social transitions of the emergent global capitalist markets in the antebellum period. Informed by the transatlantic studies of Ian Baucom, Cesare Casarino, Wai Chee Dimock, Peter Linebaugh and Marcus Rediker, and others, Berger in his 2012 book *Antebellum at Sea* analyzes the modification of spatial and political structures in the mid-nineteenth-century Atlantic world. Berger especially draws on Slavoj Žižek's reading of Lacanian fantasy to demonstrate how maritime narratives reshaped ideological coordinates, mediated desires, and complicated then-emerging forms of national identity. Novels by Cooper and Melville are his case studies.

And in 2012 Jerome McGann argued that Cooper has often been misread out of a desire to privilege art over the messiness of history. It is a "scandal" of Cooper studies that his work has been dismissed as mere romance (125). "Cooper's pervading greatness as an artist," McGann writes, "is a function of how he engages with the violence that suffuses 'the American Dream'" (130). Working against a tradition that associates Cooper with Indian hating and racist government policies, McGann reads Cooper as a critic of all easy political solutions. Cooper's novels, according to McGann, are designed to provoke critical reflection, often in ways that are uncomfortable for the reader. Whereas Scott imagines the reconciliation of historical forces in his novels, Cooper draws ever darker conclusions in his novels from the 1840s, in which he explores the past and critiques America's land seizures and economic exploitation. McGann has read deeply in European Romanticism and is able to see Cooper in a wider perspective, within the larger shifts we recognize as modernity. McGann aligns Cooper with a wide range of modern authors, from Lord Byron to Kathy Acker, who wrote to provoke more than to please.

This recent scholarship intimates the vibrancy of Cooper studies at this moment. Scholars have recently addressed topics as different as cross-dressing, ecocriticism, American privacy law, and racial passing. A large group of dedicated scholars (some of them represented in this collection) understand Cooper to be one of the central figures in nineteenth-century American literature,

Euro-American Romanticism, and the Victorian novel. In reading the results from our survey of literature instructors conducted during the development of this volume, we learned that Cooper's novels are most often taught in specialized courses in American literature or in general education survey courses of various kinds. Recent scholarship suggests that his novels could be more widely taught in introductory literary courses (as examples of superb narrative artistry), in history courses (as meditations on colonization, the policy of Indian Removal, westward expansion, and other topics), in courses on oceanic studies, gender studies, detective fiction, frontier fiction, the western, book history, aesthetics, and literary theory, to name just a few. We sense a large gap between current scholarship on Cooper's novels and the general understanding among many instructors of what Cooper was doing as an artist. We hope to demonstrate here in practical ways that Cooper's novels are timely, relevant, and even prescient for students living in a culture that is in dramatic flux, as was his in the antebellum period.

Teaching Cooper's Novels

Taken as a whole, this volume urges instructors to see the value in teaching Cooper's novels now. In part 1, we describe useful materials for instructors who teach the novels. In part 2, our contributors offer theoretical and pragmatic approaches to teaching individual novels or film adaptations in many different classroom environments.

As mentioned earlier, one practical problem of teaching Cooper now is that his forte was the long novel. When instructors teach the works of novelists such as Nathaniel Hawthorne, James, and Melville, of course, they can opt to use powerful and inventive short stories in place of long novels; but aside from two unmemorable early efforts, Cooper did not write short stories. (In the early part of his career, there was little money to be earned in writing short stories.) When instructors teach the works of Ralph Waldo Emerson, Margaret Fuller, and Thoreau, they can opt to use stand-alone poems or essays that introduce each thinker's main ideas; but Cooper did not write poetry, and his nonfiction works in history, biography, and travel are challenging even for specialists. It is true that Cooper's novels have sometimes been excerpted in literary anthologies (excerpts from *The Pioneers* and *The Last of the Mohicans* appear in the *Norton Anthology of American Literature*), but as passionate Cooper scholars we suggest that most attempts to teach Cooper's novels through excerpts contravene one of his primary goals, which was to force his readers to comprehend and evaluate complex political, moral, and social tales—to make judgments about human behavior, politics, and culture in the context of a long story.[3] Cooper had strong opinions on many subjects and was capable at times of lecturing his readers, but in general he expected them to grapple with the questions he was raising, not to passively and unquestioningly accept the answers provided by a character or the narrator. One oft-anthologized scene, for example, is the slaughter of the pigeons in chapter 22 of *The Pioneers* ([Beard et al.] 242–50). As a stand-alone scene, it introduces Cooper as an early environmentalist, critical of the "wasty ways" of many of the pioneers who misuse nature's bounty (248). Yet the novel frames that scene within a complex set of ideas and scenes about nature, law, ethics, and responsibility. In this early novel about settlement and the formation of national identity, Cooper offers no easy conclusion about how human beings should incorporate as a community and frame laws for self-governance. Students need to be encouraged to embrace a long novel like *The Pioneers*. And they need to be shown how to grapple with the novel as an extended meditation on the opportunities and problems of settlement. When instructors ask students to read that one scene in isolation, they encourage them to reduce the novel to the observation that Americans foolishly drove the passenger pigeon to extinction. To excerpt Cooper's work is often to deny students the larger challenge at the heart of Cooper's enterprise as a novelist.

While Cooper's novels require a substantial commitment of time in the undergraduate classroom, they engage in compelling ways many of the issues important to readers now. We have organized the volume to highlight connections between the varied approaches discussed by our contributors. Thus, the essays in "History and Culture" call attention to Cooper's extensive ruminations on how communities are formed, how individuals cooperate or exclude in order to form larger groups, how colonies become nations, and how nations become empires. Focusing on novels written in the 1820s and 1840s, the contributors in this section take up themes and problems that are central to nearly all of the novels Cooper wrote, but even more they grapple with how to make those themes and problems relevant for students.

The essays in "Natural Environments" highlight Cooper's remarkable prescience in understanding that colonization and settlement inevitably alter the landscape and sap natural resources. Cooper's pictures of colonization and settlement are never as simple as the myths of manifest destiny and westward expansion that were developed in the antebellum period or later in the nineteenth century, and that some readers claim to find in Cooper's novels. Cooper knew that settlers always yearn for a new beginning, but he understood as well that the land and the landscape are inevitably altered by human migrations and resettlement. Often they are irretrievably damaged. The contributors in this section try to shift the pedagogical focus to radically reframe Cooper's novels from different points of view.

The essays in "Language and Form" emphasize how attention to language and genre in Cooper's novels can benefit students in widely different contexts, from an introductory undergraduate course to a course on the detective novel to a master's course in foreign languages. According to our survey, instructors do not usually attempt to close read Cooper's long novels in a traditional manner, but the contributors in this section suggest that paying heightened attention to language, ambiguity, experience, and character types is a fruitful approach in the classroom, and they suggest quite different approaches to achieving that goal.

"Visuality and Cinema" is our concluding section on teaching the novels of Cooper. Early on, critics and artists recognized Cooper's ability to paint romantic scenes. This ability and the fame of novels like *The Last of the Mohicans* explain why nineteenth-century painters and twentieth-century filmmakers were drawn to his stories. The contributors in this section engage with the visual dimensions of Cooper's novels, and with how they were adapted by other artists. In the final three essays, by Paul Gutjahr, David Hartwig, and Todd Thompson, respectively, the focus narrows to film adaptations of Cooper's most famous story, *The Last of the Mohicans*. Gutjahr, Hartwig, and Thompson talk to each other in compelling ways about the three most famous film adaptations of that novel, but they offer distinct approaches to the novel and its three film versions in the classroom.

These seventeen essays offer ways in which Cooper's novels might be taught in general education courses, in courses for English majors, and in courses in a large handful of humanities fields: visual studies, film studies, media history, genre studies (e.g., the detective novel, dystopian fiction, and the western), and ecocriticism. Cooper's topics, subjects, and themes are quite diverse, and both the responses to our survey and the essays in this volume speak to the range of approaches that one might use to teach Cooper's novels.

When assembling the volume, however, we were struck by a number of commonalities in the approaches used by instructors who ask students to study Cooper's novels. One recurring idea in this volume is that Cooper challenges his readers to make judgments about human behavior. His texts are complex, ambiguous, and rich; and our contributors repeatedly suggest ways of bringing that complexity to students' attention at this historical moment, when forms of digital surface reading dominate our textual environment. A generation ago we first learned to surf the web, and now we flit from tweet to tweet and post to post; Cooper's novels often require a different set of reading skills, including a commitment to an extended narrative, comprehension of the large body of information (or the data set) contained in such a narrative, and an ability to form judgments about moral and political predicaments faced by characters, predicaments that have no simple answers. To get buy-in from students, some instructors emphasize the essential similarity between Cooper's texts and later texts (like the musical *Hamilton*) that students probably find more compelling. Others utilize ways of reading literary texts (e.g., horizontal reading and networked reading) that depend less on the New Critical close reading skills inculcated in literature students in the second half of the twentieth century. Indeed, one unspoken idea here is that a New Critical approach is probably not the best way of teaching a Cooper novel. His novels are well crafted, but not like Cleanth Brooks's well-wrought urn; instead, they depend on process, as characters respond to events in time and as readers grapple with complex situations that build upon each other. What seems at first to be a relatively simple setup in Cooper's novels always gives way to ambiguity and uncertainty. In *The Pioneers*, for example, the opening scene in which Natty Bumppo shoots a deer, and Judge Temple at the same moment inadvertently shoots Oliver Effingham, takes on more and more resonance as the plot develops. Students can come to grips with the scene's significance only at the end of the novel, when the rights of the settlers have been complicated by the rights of the Native Americans, by lawlessness, by class-driven anger, by the opinions of settlers not yet assimilated into the community, and by differing conceptions of natural law.[4]

Readers of this volume are invited to find other connections between these essays. They were written by passionate instructors who have thought long and hard about how to teach Cooper's novels and who have tried different approaches and theories in the classroom. They have discovered strategies that work. It is not a coincidence that Cooper himself wrote at a moment of deep political uncertainty, social upheaval, and technological change. Andrew Jackson has always served as a kind of shorthand for fundamental changes to the republic that some people embraced and others feared in the antebellum period. The questions that Jackson provoked in the age that has been named for him are at the heart of many of Cooper's projects: What is democracy? Who is an American? How do we decide what is right in a free society? These essays speak to the vitality of Cooper's novels at yet another moment of deep political uncertainty and technological change.

NOTES

[1] Cooper's father's story is brilliantly told in Alan Taylor's Pulitzer Prize–winning history, *William Cooper's Town*.

[2] In his 1850 preface to *The Deerslayer*, Cooper uses "Leather-Stocking" to refer to both the character Natty Bumppo and the five novels Cooper collectively called "The Leather-Stocking Tales" (*Deerslayer* [Penguin] 5). In this volume we use "Leather-Stocking," to be consistent with the form Cooper settled on in his preface, his final printed statement about the book series. However, works-cited-list entries for publications about the five novels retain the form employed by those publications, either "Leather-Stocking," "Leather-stocking," or "Leatherstocking."

[3] For an exception, see Matt Sivils's essay in this collection, which offers a thoughtful approach to teaching Cooper's late novel *The Crater* through excerpts.

[4] We refer here to Native Americans. In the essays that follow contributors use the terms *Native American*, *Indian*, and *Indigenous American*. This varied usage reflects an ongoing discussion, and contributors were encouraged to employ terms according to their own judgment.

Part One

MATERIALS

Works

During his thirty-year writing career, Cooper published more than forty books of fiction and nonfiction. Below are separate lists of Cooper's fiction and nonfiction arranged in the order of publication.

Fiction

James Fenimore Cooper was a prolific writer, and we list here his thirty-two novels; his novella, *Autobiography of a Pocket Handkerchief*; and his early slim volume of two short stories, *Tales for Fifteen*. Many of these works have been critically edited as part of the long-running project The Writings of James Fenimore Cooper (or the Cooper Edition) and published by the State University of New York Press or by AMS Press. Instructors wishing for background on the composition, publication, and reception of specific titles should consult the authoritative State University of New York Press or AMS Press edition, if one exists. Twenty-eight volumes have been published in the project, of a projected forty-two.

Most instructors are aware of the fact that Cooper linked the five Leather-Stocking Tales through the character of Natty Bumppo. But Cooper also wrote a trilogy of linked novels referred to as The Littlepage Manuscripts (*Satanstoe, The Chainbearer*, and *The Redskins*), two pairs of double novels (*Homeward Bound* and *Home as Found*, and *Afloat and Ashore* and *Miles Wallingford*), and three thematically related novels set in Europe (*The Bravo, The Heidenmauer*, and *The Headsman*). He set fifteen of his thirty-two novels on an ocean, a sea, or the Great Lakes. Instructors would do well to be cognizant of the broad reach of Cooper's imaginative endeavor.

> *Precaution: A Novel*, 1820
> *The Spy: A Tale of the Neutral Ground*, 1821
> *The Pioneers; or, The Sources of the Susquehanna: A Descriptive Tale*, 1823
> *Tales for Fifteen; or, "Imagination" and "Heart,"* 1823
> *The Pilot: A Tale of the Sea*, 1824
> *Lionel Lincoln; or, The Leaguer of Boston*, 1825
> *The Last of the Mohicans: A Narrative of 1757*, 1826
> *The Prairie: A Tale*, 1827
> *The Red Rover: A Tale*, 1828
> *The Wept of Wish-Ton-Wish: A Tale*, 1829
> *The Water-Witch; or, The Skimmer of the Seas*, 1830
> *The Bravo: A Tale*, 1831
> *The Heidenmauer; or, The Benedictines*, 1832

The Headsman; or, The Abbaye des Vignerons, 1833
The Monikins, 1835
Homeward Bound; or, The Chase, 1838
Home as Found, 1838
The Pathfinder; or, The Inland Sea, 1840
Mercedes of Castile; or, The Voyage to Cathay, 1840
The Deerslayer; or, The First Warpath, 1841
The Two Admirals: A Tale, 1842
The Wing-and-Wing; or, Le Feu-Follet: A Tale, 1842
Autobiography of a Pocket Handkerchief, 1843
Wyandotté; or, The Hutted Knoll: A Tale, 1843
Afloat and Ashore; or, The Adventures of Miles Wallingford, 1844
Miles Wallingford, 1844
Satanstoe; or, The Littlepage Manuscripts: A Tale of the Colony, 1845
The Chainbearer; or, The Littlepage Manuscripts, 1845
The Redskins; or, Indian and Injin, 1846
The Crater; or, Vulcan's Peak, 1847
Jack Tier; or, The Florida Reef, 1848
The Oak Openings; or, The Bee-Hunter, 1848
The Sea Lions; or, The Lost Sealers, 1849
The Ways of the Hour: A Tale, 1850

Nonfiction

Cooper's nonfiction is generally less well-known than the writer's fiction, but Cooper wrote extensively in a number of genres including travel writing, history, biography, and cultural and political theory. His five volumes of travel writings and *Notions of the Americans* have been critically edited in the Cooper Edition. *The American Democrat* was republished several times in inexpensive paperbacks in the twentieth century. Some of the shorter works listed here are available online through the James Fenimore Cooper Society (see "Additional Resources" below). Cooper's letters were collected first by his grandson and then more extensively in a six-volume critical edition by James Franklin Beard.

Notions of the Americans: Picked Up By a Travelling Bachelor, 1828
Sketches of Switzerland, 2 vols., 1836
Gleanings in Europe: France, 1837
Gleanings in Europe: England, 1837
Gleanings in Europe: Italy, 1838
The American Democrat; or, Hints on the Social and Civic Relations of the United States of America, 1838
The Chronicles of Cooperstown, 1838
History of the Navy of the United States of America, 2 vols., 1839

History of the Navy of the United States of America: Abridged, 1841
Ned Myers; or, A Life before the Mast, 1843
Lives of Distinguished American Naval Officers, 1846
New York; or, The Towns of Manhattan, published posthumously, 1864
The Letters and Journals of James Fenimore Cooper, 6 vols., 1960–68

Biographies

The standard and essential biography of Cooper is Wayne Franklin's two-volume life, *James Fenimore Cooper: The Early Years* and *James Fenimore Cooper: The Later Years*, based on archival materials unavailable to earlier biographers and crafted in the light of contemporary research on Cooper's fiction. Franklin's biography supersedes all previous biographical scholarship, correcting and enriching our understanding of Cooper's life and work. The short biographies by Robert Long and by Donald Ringe (*James Fenimore Cooper*) are still useful, as is Stephen Railton's psychological study (*James Fenimore Cooper*). Earlier biographies by Thomas Lounsbury, Robert Spiller, and James Grossman are dated.

Selected Recent Criticism

Propelled by research on the Cooper Edition and by Franklin's authoritative biography, recent criticism grounds Cooper's novels in the sociocultural politics of nation, empire, race, democracy, gender, sexuality, and affect. One good general resource for understanding Cooper's novels is Leland Person's *A Historical Guide to James Fenimore Cooper*. Person's guide features broad and insightful essays by John P. McWilliams, on women and gender in Cooper's novels; by J. Gerald Kennedy, on Cooper's criticisms of America; by Dana D. Nelson, on sympathy in the novels; and by Barbara Alice Mann, on the novels' depictions of race. Also included is a short biography of Cooper written by Franklin, a useful overview of Cooper's oeuvre by Person himself, and a substantial bibliographic essay by Jeffrey Walker. Walker cogently discusses many of the critical works on Cooper published through the beginning of the twenty-first century, hence we have not duplicated that sort of survey here. Instead we focus on a handful of key book- and article-length critical studies published since the turn of the century.

Walker also edited two important collections of essays on Cooper's works. For *Reading Cooper, Teaching Cooper*, he commissioned essays from nineteen Cooper scholars. Most of the essays focus on reading Cooper's works through various lenses such as gender and sexuality, satire, and race. These lenses can inform an instructor's pedagogy, but few of the essays offer concrete suggestions on how to teach Cooper's fiction. Only the essay by John McWilliams is straightforwardly concerned with pedagogy, and even then his essay is more anecdotal than it is useful for instructors ("*Pioneers*"). For his volume *Leather-Stocking Redux; or Old Tales, New Essays*, Walker commissioned eleven new essays on the Leather-Stocking Tales. These essays take on a range of topics that ground Cooper's novels in antebellum contexts, including race, gender, the grotesque, and the author's publishing history.

For background on themes, patterns, and key ideas in the novels of Cooper and his contemporaries, instructors can consult volume 5 of *The Oxford History of the Novel in English, The American Novel to 1870*, edited by Kennedy and Person, which also includes a chapter on Cooper by Franklin ("James Fenimore Cooper: Beyond Leather-Stocking"). Likewise, *The Cambridge History of the American Novel*, edited by Leonard Cassuto, Clare Virginia Eby, and Benjamin Reiss, contains useful essays on topics central to Cooper's fiction as well as Sandra Gustafson's essay on Cooper and the idea of the Indian ("Cooper"). Many critics mistakenly cast Cooper as an apologist for Jacksonian federal policies, but in *The Oxford Handbook of Nineteenth-Century American Literature*, edited by Russ Castronovo, Robert Levine argues in his essay on *The Deerslayer* that by the final Leather-Stocking tale Cooper was an outright critic of White racist violence and the seeming course of White empire. (For more on the inaccurate casting of Cooper's politics, see Rochelle Zuck's essay in this volume.)

Jerome McGann has written a useful general reframing of Cooper's fiction. He argues against purely aesthetic readings of Cooper's novels, demonstrating instead that Cooper calculatedly left his novels open to interpretation, hoping thereby "to provoke critical reflection" rather than aesthetic satisfaction (124). Cooper's novels engage with pressing sociohistorical problems of their time, as well as with recurring issues of nationalism, individualism, and agency. McGann shows that the art of Cooper's novels is in their critical provocation, not their beauty as well-wrought urns (see Brooks).

Critics are interested in Cooper's prescience around questions central to democracies. Jeffrey Insko, for example, reads Cooper's novel *The Pioneers* within the context of an emerging and messy discourse around the right to privacy. He argues that modern philosophical and legal conceptions of privacy are fraught with the same problems as those that animate Cooper's novel. Similarly, Castronovo reads *The Pioneers* in the context of the consolidation of the security state as it emerged in the nineteenth and twentieth centuries. For Castronovo, the novel discloses how nature, property, and consent were becoming "settled" conceptual categories alongside the settlement of the "wilderness" ("James Fenimore Cooper" 690). Gustafson studies deliberative democracy in the early republic. In her chapter on Cooper's "deliberative" novels (*Imagining* 167–79), including *The Last of the Mohicans*, she reads Cooper as querying the limits of state power, partisanship, religion, and violence. She reads Cooper with and against William Apess's *Indian Nullification*, comparing White- and Native-written perspectives on the failure of deliberation and the seemingly inescapable turn to violence.

Other critics are interested in grounding Cooper's fiction specifically in the questions of the author's era. Bill Christophersen reads all five Leather-Stocking novels in their specific sociohistorical contexts, emphasizing how Cooper and his project changed from the 1820s to the 1840s. Cooper resurrected Natty Bumppo after a thirteen-year hiatus in 1840, Christophersen argues, to "ask, in effect, whether the common man might not redeem a country that had, Cooper believed, lost its republican backbone" (ix). Chad May reads the Leather-Stocking Tales as a search for a form that could encompass and contain the traumas of the nation's origins. He argues that Cooper repeatedly attempts to mitigate the nation's traumas but just as repeatedly fails in his attempts. It is in those failures that Cooper actually succeeds, however, because in them Cooper exposes the insuppressible force and complexity of historical trauma. Nancy Armstrong and Leonard Tennenhouse propose that Cooper's novel *The Last of the Mohicans* maps an imaginative territory for the emergence of an American tradition that is both descended and distinct from the British tradition. They claim that Cooper in 1826, at that moment of cultural nostalgia, imagined the nation's originators as a heterogeneous assortment of stateless people whose political future was still up in the air. In the indeterminacy of the Seven Years' War, as depicted in *The Last of the Mohicans*, the British encounter with Native Americans reformulated the question of which European power would prevail in North America into a question of how British colonists would acquire mastery of the wilderness.

Joseph Letter also reads Cooper's fiction through the lens of time. He looks to Walter Benjamin's understanding of the ruin as "an allegorical figure that represents the process of historical decay" (34) to explain Cooper's conflicted temporal sensibility in *The Spy*. The novel's images of suffering soldiers—including Harvey Birch—are ruins that disrupt linear narratives of progress prevalent in American culture and mark the uncertain emergence of a national ethos in the 1820s. Like Christophersen and like Armstrong and Tennenhouse, Letter tries to map Cooper's unique and complicated relation to the quickly shifting politics of Cooper's time.

Geoffrey Sanborn explores Cooper's attitude toward racism and prejudice through a study of his 1833 novel, *The Headsman*. He argues provocatively that Cooper's novel about the family of a public executioner in Switzerland is an allegory of racial passing ("James Fenimore Cooper"). In his book-length study of Cooper and Herman Melville, Sanborn reads *The Last of the Mohicans* and *Moby-Dick* in the light of antebellum cross-cultural encounters between Europeans and the Maori. Seen in the light of those encounters, Magua becomes a complex figure, certainly less of a villain than traditionally imagined, and Cooper is revealed to be thinking in his most famous novel more about conflicts concerning social status—such as between chiefs and commoners—than about race (*Whipscars*).

Cooper is often read through the lens of physical space and the nineteenth century global remapping of nation, trade, and cross-cultural encounters. Oana Godeanu-Kenworthy reads Cooper and his contemporary, the Canadian author John Richardson, as creole authors negotiating various real and ideological frontiers. Godeanu-Kenworthy shifts the focus from Cooper as a nationalist author, reading him instead as a settler-colonist trapped in a state of betweenness that was neither colonial nor national. Andy Doolen studies Cooper's contribution to the articulation of United States expansionism and empire through his Leather-Stocking Tales. In looking at what he calls "cartographic texts" that map the expanding empire, Doolen challenges scholarship that reads Cooper's novels as "noxious artifacts of white racism" (11, 152). He argues instead that *The Prairie*, for example, demonstrates a deep ambivalence toward expansionism and slavery. Doolen considers the expanding empire on land, while Jason Berger uses a Lacanian framework to understand the complex work of fantasies of the sea in the nineteenth century. Like Sanborn (*Whipscars*), Berger focuses on Cooper and Melville, but he uses the lens of oceanic studies to think about the cultural work of narratives like Cooper's *The Pilot* and *The Crater*.

Patricia Roylance tracks a nineteenth-century American fascination with "imperial eclipse narratives" that recount episodes when one great world power declined and was overtaken by another (2). She argues that these historical moments of imperial conflict act as spatiotemporal contact zones for authors to articulate anxieties about the present and future of America. She looks at Cooper's novels *The Water-Witch* and *The Bravo*, which juxtapose rising republicanism in the United States with a declining Venetian oligarchy, but in which Cooper also voices concerns about an emergent Whig class that, he feared, was seeking control in the United States.

Critics are interested in reading Cooper's fiction in the context of female authorship. Barbara Mann studies the influence of Jane Austen on Cooper. She notes that it was well known from the start that Cooper's first novel, *Precaution*, owed a debt to Austen, but Mann demonstrates other unexpected connections between the two writers' novels, among them their use of sexual allusion, strong sororal pairings, and complicated thinking about race (*Cooper Connection*). Signe Wegener reads Cooper's novels in the context of the emerging cult of domesticity in the antebellum period. She compares and contrasts Cooper's fiction to that of Susan Warner, Lydia Maria Child, Catharine Maria Sedgwick, and others to illuminate the origins of domestic fiction (*James Fenimore Cooper*). Shirley Samuels compares *The Last of the Mohicans* to Sedgwick's *Hope Leslie* and Child's *Hobomok*, arguing that legal contracts about land and about the shedding of blood in the early republic rely on the hidden terms of female bodies ("Women"). Ezra Tawil studies Cooper's Leather-Stocking Tales and *The Wept of Wish-ton-Wish*, Child's *Hobomok*, and Sedgwick's *Hope Leslie*, arguing that interiority and emotion—or sentiment—emerge in novels of the 1820s as key elements of racial identity. Seen in this light, these frontier romances are precursors to novels like Harriet Beecher Stowe's *Uncle Tom's Cabin* and Melville's *Benito Cereno*.

Especially because of *The Pioneers*, Cooper has long been read as an early environmentalist. Matthew Sivils, in his study of the American environmental imagination, reads three novels by Cooper, *The Pioneers*, *The Prairie*, and *The Crater*, as major developments within American environmental fiction. He places them in dialogue with other contemporary works (including visual art) reaching back to the revolution and forward to Ralph Waldo Emerson and Henry David Thoreau. John Hay, in his study of nineteenth-century postapocalyptic fantasies, reads Cooper's *The Last of the Mohicans* and *The Crater* as critiques of American exceptionalism and settler colonialism.

Following Franklin, Susan Ryan studies Cooper's entire career in the context of emerging conceptions of authorship in the nineteenth century. She uses the decline of Cooper's reputation in the 1830s and its recovery in the 1840s and 1850s to demonstrate the instability of reputation and of literature itself as "property" at mid-century (27). Franklin himself explores the connections Cooper maintained while in Europe with writers and artists like Samuel Taylor Coleridge, Washington Allston, Horatio Greenough, and Samuel F. B. Morse ("James Fenimore Cooper and American Artists").

The Instructor's Library

Cooper's immense popularity in the nineteenth century meant that many of the writer's bestsellers went through multiple printings and editions during and after Cooper's lifetime, which resulted in the introduction of faults (or corruptions) and the circulation of many variant texts. Although Cooper regularly corrected his own manuscripts, those of his amanuenses, and proof sheets pulled from presses, textual errors have been traced to all steps in production and to any combination of factors—his handwriting, his proofing oversights, amanuensis errors, compositor mistakes, printer interventions, unauthorized reprints, and so on. Cooper also sometimes oversaw revised versions of his novels, either individually or in multivolume sets, and these revised versions complicate the textual history of the individual novels. As a result, many versions of his works available on the market today are descended from flawed editions or unauthorized reprints and repeat the variants and problems from their parent editions.

Since the 1970s, textual scholars involved with the Cooper Edition have been producing editions of Cooper's works that document and resolve substantive differences between versions of the same text. As of 2022, twenty of Cooper's thirty-two novels, as well as his five travel narratives, have been published by the State University of New York Press or AMS Press as part of the Cooper Edition, each volume with a complete scholarly apparatus including the documentation of variants. As the Cooper Edition moves toward completing the author's oeuvre, instructors can reap the benefits of the finished volumes, which have been approved by the Modern Language Association Committee on Scholarly Editions.

The Cooper Edition includes the following novels (in order of their original publication by Cooper): *The Spy: A Tale of the Neutral Ground*, edited by James Elliot, Lance Schachterle, and Jeffrey Walker; *The Pioneers; or, The Sources of the Susquehanna: A Descriptive Tale*, edited by Schachterle and Kenneth M. Andersen; *The Pilot: A Tale of the Sea*, edited by Kay Seymour House; *Lionel Lincoln; or, The Leaguer of Boston*, edited by Donald Ringe and Lucy Ringe; *The Last of the Mohicans: A Narrative of 1757*, edited by James A. Sappenfield and E. N. Feltskog; *The Prairie: A Tale*, edited by Elliot; *The Red Rover: A Tale*, edited by Thomas Philbrick and Marianne Philbrick; *The Water-Witch; or, The Skimmer of the Seas*, edited by Thomas Philbrick and Marianne Philbrick; *The Bravo: A Venetian Story*, edited by Schachterle and Sappenfield; *Homeward Bound; or, The Chase: A Tale of the Sea*, edited by Stephen Carl Arch; *Home as Found*, edited by Arch; *The Pathfinder; or, The Inland Sea*, edited by Richard Dilworth Rust; *The Deerslayer; or, The First Warpath*, edited by Schachterle, Kent Ljungquist, and James Kilby; *The Two Admirals*, edited by Donald Ringe, Sappenfield, and Feltskog; *The Wing-and-Wing; or, Le Feu-Follet: A Tale*, edited by Schachterle and Anna Scannavini; *Afloat and Ashore; or, The Adventures of Miles Wallingford*, in two volumes, edited by Thomas Philbrick and Marianne Philbrick; *Wyandotté; or, The Hutted Knoll: A Tale*, edited by Thomas Philbrick and Marianne Philbrick; *Satanstoe; or, The Littlepage Manuscripts: A Tale of the Colony*, edited by House and Constance Ayers Denne; and *The Chainbearer; or, The Littlepage Manuscripts*, edited by Schachterle and Elliot.

Of course, these editions are not priced for the classroom, nor do undergraduate students usually need to consult the extensive apparatus in editions like these. However, instructors may wish to consult the authoritative scholarly edition for information about the text they plan to teach. If they prefer, they could teach from a digital facsimile of a first edition available through a variety of sources like HathiTrust. For novels that have not yet appeared in a scholarly edition, such as *The Ways of the Hour*, instructors are advised to locate a facsimile of the first edition in e-book or paperback.

When a scholarly edition is available, we strongly recommend that instructors select for students an affordable paperback that reprints the Cooper Edition's established text. Failing that, we recommend an edition that explains an editorial decision to reprint one version of the text over another. There are sound reasons, for example, for choosing to teach the 1826 edition of *The Last of the Mohicans* rather than the revised 1831 edition. But the editor of the chosen volume should be clear and upfront about those reasons, as should instructors with their students. Below are the affordable paperback or e-book editions we recommend for classroom use, some of which are cited in this volume's essays. These editions either reprint the Cooper Edition's established text or provide a good justification for reprinting one version of the text over others.

The Library of America has published four volumes dedicated to Cooper. These hardback and e-book editions are outside the price range of most undergraduate classrooms, but with the generous amount of material in each volume, they could certainly be used in graduate courses. They include *The Leatherstocking Tales*, volumes 1 (*The Pioneers, The Last of the Mohicans,* and *The Prairie*) and 2 (*The Pathfinder* and *The Deerslayer*), edited by Blake Nevius and published in 1985; *Sea Tales:* The Pilot, The Red Rover, published in 1991; and *Two Novels of the American Revolution:* The Spy *and* Lionel Lincoln, edited by Alan Taylor and published in 2019. All of the Library of America editions use the texts established by the Cooper Edition. They do not include introductions by contemporary scholars.

Cooper's most-taught novels are of course the Leather-Stocking Tales. All five of the tales are available in reasonably priced paperback editions from Belknap Press: *The Pioneers*, with an introduction by Robert Daly; *The Last of the Mohicans*, with an introduction by Franklin; *The Prairie*, with an introduction by Domhnall Martin Mitchell; *The Pathfinder*, with an introduction by Franklin; and *The Deerslayer*, with an introduction by Tawil. All use the texts established by the Cooper Edition.

All five tales are also available from Penguin Classics in reasonably priced paperback editions that use the text established by the Cooper Edition:[1] *The Pioneers*, with an introduction by Ringe;[2] *The Last of the Mohicans*, with an introduction by Richard Slotkin; *The Prairie*, with an introduction by Nevius; *The Pathfinder*, with an introduction by House; and *The Deerslayer*, with an introduction by Donald E. Pease.

Cooper's first Leather-Stocking tale, *The Pioneers*, is also available as an inexpensive stand-alone paperback edition from the Library of America, with an introduction by Alan Taylor.

Cooper's second Leather-Stocking Tale, *The Last of the Mohicans*, is his most popular and thus is available in five dependable and relatively inexpensive classroom editions. Four use the text established by the Cooper Edition: the Belknap Press edition, the Penguin Classics edition, a Modern Library edition with an introduction by Leslie Fiedler, and an Oxford University Press edition edited and with an introduction by John McWilliams. The Modern Library edition is also available as an e-book. A fifth option is the edition published by Broadview Press, edited and with an introduction and contextual materials by Paul C. Gutjahr, which reprints the 1826 edition but offers a clear rationale for that decision.

The Prairie and *The Pathfinder* are available in dependable paperback editions only from Belknap Press and Penguin Classics.

Cooper's final Leather-Stocking tale, *The Deerslayer*, is available from Belknap Press, from Penguin Classics, and in a Modern Library edition with an introduction by Leslie Fiedler.

Signet Classics has published editions of *The Pioneers*, with an introduction by Max Cavitch; *The Last of the Mohicans*, with an introduction by Richard Hutson and an afterword by Hugh C. MacDougall; and *The Pathfinder*, with an introduction by John Stauffer and an afterword by Thomas Berger, but those editions do not use the Cooper Edition texts and do not offer rationales for their choice of text, and so we do not recommend their use in the classroom. The Signet Classics edition of *The Pioneers*, for example, reprints a Riverside edition of the novel from 1872, which was itself printed from the plates of an 1859 edition. That edition was based on Cooper's final revised edition of the novel published in 1851. However, between the first appearance of the novel in 1823 and that final revised edition lay nearly a dozen reprintings and one revision (in 1832), any of which may have introduced errors. Students rarely need to know such information, but the texts established by the Cooper Edition correct transmission errors that can impede students' reading of Cooper's novels.

Bantam Classics offers what are among the cheapest paperback editions on the market, but these editions lack both a rationale for their choice of text and a note that explains which version their reprint is based on. The Bantam Classics edition of *The Last of the Mohicans* has an introduction by A. B. Guthrie, Jr., but *The Deerslayer* has no introduction. Similarly, Dover Publications offers editions of *The Last of the Mohicans* and *The Deerslayer* that lack introductions, textual notes, bibliographies, and any other supporting materials.

Barnes and Noble Classics has published paperback editions of *The Last of the Mohicans*, with an introduction by Railton; *The Deerslayer*, with an introduction by Bruce L. R. Smith; and *The Pathfinder*, with an introduction by Kevin J. Hayes. In addition to introductions, these editions include notes, bibliographies, and other supporting materials; however, they do not include explanations for the choice of text. Still, they are perhaps a better choice than the bare but very cheap editions by Dover Publications.

At this time, very few of Cooper's other novels are available in dependably edited paperback or e-book editions. *The Spy* is available from Penguin Classics as a paperback and an e-book edited by Franklin. Franklin reprints the edition of the novel illustrated by F. O. C. Darley and published by W. A. Townsend in 1859, with corrections of some obvious mistakes; his edition preceded the publication of the AMS Press authoritative edition in 2002. State University of New York Press has recently reprinted *The Spy* in paperback to celebrate the bicentennial of Cooper's first bestseller. This edition is perhaps priced out of the undergraduate classroom market.

Cooper's novel *The Crater; or, Vulcan's Peak* was edited by Thomas Philbrick for the Belknap Press in 1962 and is still available as an e-book, but it too is priced out of the undergraduate classroom market. Given rising concerns about global warming, Cooper's novel that features geological catastrophism should be back in print.

Some of Cooper's political writings are available from two conservative presses. Bradley J. Birzer and John Willson collected three of Cooper's nonfiction texts in their hardback volume The American Democrat *and Other Political Writings*, reprinting first editions with fidelity. And the Liberty Fund has reprinted in paperback the 1931 Alfred A. Knopf edition of Cooper's 1838 treatise, *The American Democrat*, with an introduction by H. L. Mencken. The Liberty Fund volume is reasonably priced.

Filmography

Cooper's novels have sparked dozens of film and television adaptations. The author predicted that his literary legacy would rest primarily on the Leather-Stocking Tales, and that prediction has proved true for film and television, as well as in the study of literature. With the exception of *The Spy*, all screen adaptations of Cooper's works are based on the tales featuring Natty Bumppo. All five Leather-Stocking novels have been adapted since the early twentieth century, with *The Last of the Mohicans* and *The Deerslayer* having been most often remade for screen audiences. Like Cooper's books, films and television programs based on the author's novels have been produced internationally and have held great appeal in the United Kingdom, Russia, Germany, Italy, Romania, and other European countries. Film historians generally agree that the 1920, 1936, and 1992 adaptations of *The Last of the Mohicans* are the most popular of the many film versions of Cooper's tale to date. The 1992 film version was nominated for many international cinema awards. Also among the Cooper adaptations is the Emmy award–winning PBS miniseries for children *The Leatherstocking Tales*, produced for WQED in Pittsburgh, Pennsylvania. Yet the majority of adaptations of Cooper's works have received rather tepid critical responses, in which reviewers frequently note that filmic media struggle to capture Cooper's imagination so richly inscribed on the page. We note that at the time of this writing, a new television series adaptation of *The Last of the Mohicans* is in production at HBO.

The below list of films and television adaptations of Cooper's novels was compiled primarily from information provided by Martin Barker and Roger Sabin; Alan Goble; Edward Harris; and Michael Pitts.

1909	*Leather Stocking*, directed by D. W. Griffith, Biograph Studios
1911	*The Last of the Mohicans*, directed by Pat Powers, Motion Picture Company
1911	*The Last of the Mohicans*, directed by Theodore Marston
1911	*The Last of the Mohicans*, directed by Edwin Thanhouser, Edwin Thanhouser Company Films
1911	*The Pathfinder*, directed by Laurence Trimble, Vitagraph
1911	*In the Days of the Six Nations*, Republic Motion Picture Manufacturing Company
1911	*The Deerslayer*, directed by Laurence Trimble and Hal Reid, Vitagraph
1914	*The Spy*, directed by Otis Turner, Universal Film Manufacturing Company
1920	*The Last of the Mohicans*, directed by Maurice Tourneur and Clarence L. Brown, Maurice Tourneur Productions
1920	*Der Wildtoter* (*The Deerslayer*) and *Der Letzte der Mohikaner* (*The Last of the Mohicans*), directed by Arthur Wellin, Luna-Film; parts 1 and 2 of *Lederstrumpf* (*Leatherstocking*)

FILMOGRAPHY

1923	*The Deerslayer* (an American release of the 1920 *Der Wildtoter*)
1924	*Leatherstocking* (ten-episode film serial), directed by George B. Seitz, Pathé Exchange
1926	*The Last of the Mohee-cans*
1932	*The Last of the Mohicans* (twelve-episode film serial), directed by B. Reeves Eason and Ford Beebe, Mascot Films
1936	*The Last of the Mohicans*, directed by George B. Seitz, RKO-Pathé Studios
1941	*The Pioneers*, directed by Albert Herman, Monogram
1943	*The Deerslayer*, directed by Lew Landers, Republic Cardinal Pictures
1947	*The Last of the Redmen* (released as *The Last of the Redskins* in the United Kingdom), directed by George Sherman, Columbia Pictures
1947	*The Prairie*, directed by Frank Wisbar, Screen Guild Productions
1948	*The Return of the Mohicans* (condensed film of the 1932 serial)
1950	*The Iroquois Trail*, directed by Phil Karlson, United Artists
1952	*The Pathfinder*, directed by Sidney Salkow, Columbia Pictures
1957	*The Deerslayer*, directed by Kurt Neumann, Twentieth Century Fox / Regal Films
1957	*Hawkeye and The Last of the Mohicans* (thirty-nine-episode series), directed by Sam Newfield and Sidney Salkow, Television Programs of America / Canadian Normandie Productions
1962	*Along the Mohawk Trail, The Red Man and the Renegades, The Long Rifle and the Tomahawk*, and *The Pathfinder and the Mohican* (television films edited together from 1957 series)
1965	*Uncas, El Fin de Una Raza* (*Uncas, the End of a Race*; distributed in Italy as *L'ultimo dei Mohicani* [*The Last of the Mohicans*]), directed by Mateo Cano, International German / Balcazar / Cineprouzione
1965	*Der Letzte Mohikaner* (also distributed as *The Last Tomahawk*), directed by Harald Reinl, International German / Balcazar / Cineprouzione
1966	*Der Wildtoter*, directed by Richard Groschopp, Deutsche Film-Aktiengesellschaft
1967	*Chingachgook: Die Grosse Schlange* (*Chingachgook: The Big Snake*), directed by Richard Groschopp, Deutsche Film-Aktiengesellschaft
1968	*Die Lederstrumpferzählungen* (*The Leatherstocking Tales*; a four-part television miniseries), directed by Pierre Gaspard-Huit, Serbiu Nicolaescu, and Jean Dréville, Deropa Films
1969	*Ultimul Mohican* (*The Last Mohican*), directed by Jean Dréville and Sergiu Nicolaescu, Deropa Films
1971	*The Last of the Mohicans* (released in the United States in 1972), directed by David Maloney, BBC
1973	*Hawkeye, The Pathfinder* (miniseries), directed by David Maloney, BBC
1975	*The Last of the Mohicans* (animated television series), directed by Chris Cuddington, Hanna Barbera Productions
1977	*The Last of the Mohicans*, directed by James L. Conway, Schick Sunn Classics

1978	*The Deerslayer*, directed by Richard Friedenberg, Schick Sunn Classics
1979	*The Leatherstocking Tales* (four-part miniseries), directed by Nick Sgarro, Metropolitan Pittsburgh Broadcasting / PBS WQED
1981	*The Spy* (radio play), directed by Timothy Jerome, NPR
1987	*Sledopyt (Pathfinder)*, directed by Pavel Lyubimov, Soviet Union
1992	*The Last of the Mohicans*, directed by Michael Mann, Twentieth Century Fox
1994	*Hawkeye: The First Frontier* (twenty-two-episode television series), directed by Brad Turner et al., Stephen J. Cannell Productions
1996	*The Pathfinder*, directed by Donald Shebib, Hallmark Home Entertainment
2004	*L'ultimo dei Mohicani* (twenty-six-episode animated series), directed by Guiseppe Lagana, Mondo TV / RAI

Critical Overview of Selected Feature Films

The following discussion surveys the critical reception of the three most popular and influential film adaptations of *The Last of the Mohicans*, released in 1920, 1936, and 1992.

The Last of the Mohicans, *1920 (71 minutes)*

Maurice Tourneur and Clarence L. Brown's 1920 silent film *The Last of the Mohicans* was the first feature-length adaptation of Cooper's novel and has generally garnered commendations since its release. In 1995, the Library of Congress recognized the film as a culturally significant artifact and deemed it worthy of preservation on the National Film Registry. Now in the public domain, the film is available for classroom use through various websites.

Over the past several decades, assessments of the 1920 picture by film historians and commentators have waxed positive. In 1978, William Everson deemed the film "a masterpiece" (151); in 1996, Barker and Sabin described the film as "a work of genuine beauty and power" that "has passed into undeserved oblivion" (72, 75); in 2001, Bertil Österberg wrote that the film is generally considered "the best film version of Cooper's story" (161); and in 2013, Pitts praised the "[w]ell made silent version of the James Fenimore Cooper novel" (180). David Sterritt has remarked that the 1920 film is a successful first effort to adapt Cooper's novel to a feature-length film, calling it "a beautifully shot silent movie." The cinematography of the film set it apart from its contemporaries and has impressed filmgoers for a century. The vistas so richly preserved on film were shot in California at Big Bear Lake and the Yosemite Valley in the Sierra Nevadas.

Instructors might find early reviews helpful to put the film in the context. In January 1921, *The New York Times* issued measured compliments for the "agreeable surprise" in "the rehashing of an old story" in the film. Like Cooper's novel, the composition of the film's scenery is praised for evoking "pure delight" and creating "suspensive melodrama" in the dynamic between the scenery and human action (Review 87). The review writer was the first in a long procession of critics who were dazzled by what Österberg describes as the film's "brilliant photography of extraordinary natural settings" (161). Creative decisions by the directors Tourneur and Brown and by the photographers Philip Dubois and Charles Van Enger have since been lauded by Patrick Keating, who identifies in selected scenes a lighting effect resembling the eighteenth-century painter Joseph Wright's practice of hiding a light source in the middle of a table to illuminate the facial expressions of seated personages (65). Other emerging cinematographic innovations implemented by Brown included the use of panchromatic stock, creating the illusion of sunlight through mist, the simulation of heavy rain, and a perambulating camera (Barker and Sabin 67). For *The New York Times*, one illusion failed miserably in the otherwise "extraordinary picture": miscasting White actors to play "Indians." The film is "seriously marred" when actors playing Indians get too close to the lens (Review).

Harriette Underhill's review of the "perfectly thrilling picture" in *The New-York Tribune* tempers its assessment with mordant derision, especially for the film's inept portrayal of Native Americans. Bringing "Cooper's masterpiece" to the screen is "a colossal undertaking," says Underhill, but that feat is undercut by a parade of action with "beautiful girls and battles and massacres and Indians" that she likens to an unruly New Year's Eve celebration. Like *The New York Times*, *The New-York Tribune* disparages the depiction of "un-Indian-like Indians" on the screen. Poor choices were made to cast the White actors Albert Roscoe as Uncas and William Beery as Magua, but worse is the lack of perceptible difference between the good and bad Indians, especially when they grapple, says Underhill, because "Indians all look alike in a fight."

Quite telling about *The New York Times* and *The New-York Tribune* reviews is the omission of Natty Bumppo, played by Harry Lorraine, from their commentary, which is for good reason: Natty, called Hawk-eye in the film, does not command the spotlight. The reviews follow the film's emphasis on the relationships between the Mohicans and the Munro sisters, with the focus on the rivalry between the Mohican Uncas and the Huron Magua for Cora Munro. The focus on this triad of characters left scenes involving Hawk-eye and Chingachgook on the cutting-room floor (Horak 14). Both reviewers admit having only a hazy recollection of the novel, which helps to explain their inattention to Natty and the fact that neither one flinches at the film's invention of a Captain Randolph. The presence of Randolph is particularly important for giving racism a face in the film, for it is this traitor who objects to Cora's interest in a Native American man. Even so, the 1920 adaptation of *The Last of the Mohicans* exceeds the 1936 and 1992 adaptations in propagating racist tropes, most obviously in mischaracterizing the Mohicans' foes, the Hurons, as a "drunken, dangerous and primitive" people whose violent behavior reads as "almost subhuman" (Edgerton 1). Yet, of the three major film adaptations discussed here, Tourneur and Brown's 1920 film strays the least from events in the novel and the relationships between its principal characters.

Another element of the 1920 film that distinguishes it from later popular adaptations is its inclusion of the rivalry between Uncas and Magua for Cora's favor. Rather than modify the burgeoning love relationships in Cooper's novel, the 1920 film dares to depict a strong love between a Native American man and a White woman, though without suggesting Cora's biracial ancestry. Barker and Sabin argue for the importance of contextualizing the 1920 film by viewing it alongside two films by D. W. Griffith, *Leather Stocking* and *The Birth of a Nation*, the latter of which was an epic "paean to the Ku Klux Klan," which stoked racial division in the postbellum United States (73). For contemporary audiences, both Griffith's *The Birth of a Nation* and Tourneur and Brown's *The Last of the Mohicans* registered the influence of social Darwinism and racist ideologies that cast Whites as an intellectually and genetically superior race. A clear difference between the two films is that Griffith sees racial divisions as unbridgeable, whereas Tourneur and Brown glimpse a possibility for peaceful coexistence among races in America, symbolized by Cora and Uncas lying hand-in-hand in death at the bottom of a cliff (Barker and Sabin 73–75).

The Last of the Mohicans, *1936 (91 minutes)*

George Seitz's 1936 adaptation of Cooper's *The Last of the Mohicans* was Seitz's second effort to adapt Cooper's book to film, following the director's 1924 ten-episode serial *Leatherstocking*. Philip Dunne and John L. Balderston wrote an original script that was subsequently reworked by writers hired by the producer Edward Small. When the film hit the screen, Dunne was disappointed to find that the product was "a pallid ghost [of the] full-blooded screenplay" he and Balderston had written. The film was sapped of the vitality of the original screenplay, writes Dunne, which richly combined "adventure and excitement with ... some respectable poetry in the love story between the patrician English girl and the young Mohican brave" (35). Dunne's emphasis on the romance between Cora and Uncas, a relationship that the finished film subordinates to the plot featuring the characters Alice, Natty, and Heyward, opens questions about the changes made to the 1936 adaptation.

The 1936 film featured three well-known film actors in lead roles: Randolph Scott as Hawk-eye, Binnie Barnes as Alice, and Henry Wilcoxon as Heyward. Casting Barnes as a brunette Alice and creating a rivalry between Natty and Heyward for Alice are two of the film's significant departures from the novel and the 1920 film adaptation, the latter of which emphasizes the plight of Cora and Uncas at the hands of Magua. *The New York Times* reviewer was not receptive to this difference in the 1936 film, asserting that the film studio RKO committed a "clear heresy" for getting Hawk-eye involved in a romance and, more generally, for "play[ing] fast and loose with the favorite fictional character of our youth" (J. T. M.). Conversely, a reviewer for *Variety* complimented the film's "surprising fidelity" to the novel and identified the film's accentuation of love stories as something done "quite naturally" (*"Last of the Mohicans"*). The *Variety* reviewer was also delighted with Scott's "virile interpretation [of] the scout" Hawk-eye, which does not go "overboard at any time" and which puts Hawk-eye closer to the center of the action than the 1920 film does (*"Last of the Mohicans"*).

For his film, Seitz modified Cooper's story by making Hawk-eye a rebellious American, a pronounced change that later resurfaces in Michael Mann's 1992 adaptation of *The Last of the Mohicans*. The confluence in Seitz's film of Hawk-eye's antiauthoritarian attitude and defiance of European hegemony yields a "strong undercurrent of American skepticism" about the validity of European rule and law (Edgerton 4). Patriotic themes were incorporated into advertising campaigns for the film, which included theater handbills promoting "the hand-to-hand struggle for a nation still unborn!" (qtd. in Österberg 170).

Anticipation of the film's release was heightened by orchestrated efforts among businesses and theaters to plug the film. A slew of articles in fall 1936 issues of *The Film Daily*, for instance, document Loew's nationwide campaign to publicize the film for its chain of cinemas ("Chamber"; "Jack Chalman's 'Mohicans' Campaign"; "Martin Burnett's 'Mohicans' Campaign"). Loew's theaters in cities across the United States worked with regional merchants, magazines, newspapers, department stores, restaurants, and educational organizations to promote the film with advertisements, pamphlets, study guides, exhibits, costumes, parades, and prizes to lure families to the film. The avalanche of advertising tactics helped to make the film a national blockbuster that bettered a major competitor at the box office, Charlie Chaplin's *Modern Times* ("Martin Burnett's 'Mohicans' Campaign" 11).

The 1920 film set a formidable standard for the 1936 feature film, particularly in its scenery and depiction of Native Americans. The 1936 film's title card, reproduced by the American Film Institute, notes that filming occurred at two California sites, one in Sherwood Forest and one at Cedar Lake in the town of Big Bear Lake, to set the action amid valleys, lakes, and forests that resemble eighteenth-century New York (*"Last of the Mohicans* [1936]"). Unlike the 1920 film's casting of White actors as Indians, which received scathing reviews, Bruce Cabot is praised by *The New York Times* for playing Magua "as evil a Huron as you ever pictured him" (J. T. M.), while Chingachgook, played by Robert Barrat, and Uncas, played by Phillip Reed, are overshadowed by the plot revolving around Alice and her competing beaux. Yet the 1936 film's representation of Native peoples leaves much room for improvement. Not only were White actors cast in Native American roles, but the film also homogenizes the diversity of American indigenous cultures by using what Edgerton calls "Hollywood shorthand" for screen "Indians": wigs, feathers, war paint, smoke signals, grunts, whoops, and other marks of the White man's Indian (7).

The film's depiction of scalping was of particular interest to the research director Edward Lambert, who, according to the American Film Institute, consulted Remington Schuyler's painting *Custer's Last Stand* for its multiple tableaux of scalping. Lambert believed that "authentic" representation would bolster the film's reception and obviate critics' questions about faithfulness to colonial history ("*The Last of the Mohicans* [1936]"). To what degree Schuyler, a purported authority on Native American history and a pulp magazine illustrator, accurately depicted Native war practices begs interrogation. Nonetheless, promoters made violence emblematic of the film's content, as violent acts were featured in posters and cited in film reviews. The Huron attack on the British surrendering Fort William Henry to the French was extended in the film and, according to *The New York Times* review, "even more ghastly than [the attack Cooper's] original text cited" and "by far the bloodiest, scalpingest morsel of cinematic imagery ever produced" (J. T. M.).

Barker and Sabin's chapter on American mythology in early adaptations of *The Last of the Mohicans* ends with a claim ready-made for students analyzing the 1920 and 1936 films:

> [P]erhaps the most striking new meaning [the 1936] version of *Mohicans* offers is of the wilderness, and urban and industrial development. If the Tourneur/Brown version starkly contrasts the world of the Indians and the English . . . , this version puts Hawkeye at the center of a new vision: a vision of the future in which, in truth, there is little place for wilderness. Its value is only in what it can become. . . . [Hawk-eye] tells [Cora] that he imagines cities being built at the end of every new trail he blazes: "I wonder if you can imagine what it feels like to be the first." This is a New Deal version of the frontier. (92)

Barker and Sabin argue that Seitz's revival of frontier mythology articulates both Hollywood's emergent cultural function as a "dream factory" and the American yearning for a reassuring alternative to the political extremes that gained traction during the Great Depression (85).

One of the largest Hollywood productions of the time, Seitz's 1936 film *The Last of the Mohicans* was the most magnificent adaptation of Cooper's 1826 novel until a new film, derived in part from the screenplay for Seitz's film, premiered fifty-six years later.

The Last of the Mohicans, *1992 (112 minutes)*

Michael Mann's 1992 film adaptation of *The Last of the Mohicans* was a major box office success and has since enjoyed sustained popularity in home entertainment. In its opening weekend, the film grossed almost $11 million and eventually earned more than $75 million in ticket sales in the United States. Sales of DVDs and Blu-ray disks of the film in 1992, expanded editions in 1999 and 2001, and a director's definitive cut in 2010 show the ongoing appreciation for Mann's historical romance. Lured by Cooper's magnificent story and the steamy on-camera union of Daniel Day-Lewis as Nathaniel Poe, or Hawk-eye, and Madeleine Stowe as Cora, audiences have been captivated by the film's depiction of colonial communities and imperial warfare, representation of Native Americans, and grand panoramic scenery and powerful musical score. Since its release, the film has been cited in American film histories and genealogies that trace its lineage to earlier adaptations and mark it as a forebear of later films, such as *The Revenant*.

Predictably, critical commentary about the film varies greatly in gauging the cinematic experience of the film, its cultural work, and its casting decisions. Michael Sragow says the adaptation is "a thrilling foray into the American wilderness ... that boasts an epic story to match its stunning images." Janet Maslin's otherwise scathing review admits the critic found the film "riveting" for its "keen sense of natural spectacle" and its attempt to render Native language and material culture on film. Similarly, in his close scrutiny of the film's historical inaccuracies, Ian Steele praises the casting of Native actors in Native roles, despite the tribal and linguistic discrepancies of those portrayals. Barker and Sabin likewise note Mann's "evident quest for authenticity" in attempting to present ethnographic details of Mohicans and Haudenosaunee peoples (114). Patrick Brantlinger acknowledges Mann's pursuit of historical detail and material authenticity, even as the director's obsessive concern for detail blinds him to the racial themes of what Brantlinger argues is an inherently racist novel. Words of praise for the merits of Native actors are generally reserved for Wes Studi, the Cherokee actor who plays Magua. Maslin lauds Studi, as does John Simon, who briefly stays his characteristic vitriol to speak kindly of Studi's performance of the "malign Magua with appropriate ferocity" (62). Andy Pawelczak, a critic for *Films in Review*, concurs with Simon about Studi but questions the director's choice for casting Russell Means as Chingachgook and keeping the outspoken activist "silent" in his role. That the Mohican sagamore is little more than a "shadowy protective spirit," says Pawelczak, undercuts the power of his elegiac speech at the close of the movie (404). Conversely, in the mix of his high praise for various dimensions of the film, Ian Nathan writes that casting Means as Chingachgook lends "real credibility" to the film and signifies "a knowing endorsement to Mann's delivery of tribal conflict in the burgeoning Americas." To Jacquelyn Kilpatrick, the high visibility of Native characters in the film misleads audiences to think Mann's production gives ample time to Native voices and perspectives, but the reality is that Native characters speak very little in the film; instead, Native perspectives are usually delivered through White characters, especially Hawk-eye (*Celluloid Indians* 95).

The film's representations of Native Americans have received mixed reviews. To what degree the film perpetuates or resists Indian stereotypes and misrepresentations of a vanishing race is disputed, as critics and scholars spar over the film and its intersections with Cooper's novel and previous film adaptations.

Among other things, the film's employ of Native actors, its inclusion of an indigenous language (Munsee Delaware), and its attention to Native material culture in a trade economy have garnered broad appreciation. Some Native Americans, including the actors themselves, see progress in the film's depiction of American Indians. Studi says he had to navigate the limitations of Indian stereotypes in playing Magua if the prospect of shedding them were to be realized: "I'm a Cherokee, myself, and we're just as different from the Hurons as the Serbs are from the Bosnians. . . . But in the movie business, an Indian is an Indian, I'm afraid. It's a sad thing about human nature that we are the way we are, that we stereotype all people so. I'd like to see it improve" (qtd. in King). Means sees playing Chingachgook as an opportunity to educate audiences about "a time when Indians and whites were separate but equal, and they intermingled and wore each other's clothes." That the renowned activist saw his character as "three-dimensional" prompted him to accept the role that, in his view, advances the veracity of Native images in commercial films (*"The Last of the Mohicans* Press Kit"). Additionally, Means and Studi do not read Magua as the stereotypical bad or bloodthirsty Indian but as a multidimensional character. Studi further believes Magua is relatable to all audiences, who will "see that he has reasons, that it makes him feel better to act ruthless" (qtd. in Arnold D1). In this way, Studi and Mann preserve facets of Cooper's Magua by giving him a clear motivation for committing violence against Colonel Munro, who is played by Maurice Roëves in the film. Moreover, Means sees Studi's Magua as groundbreaking: "Magua, the bad Indian in this film, for the first time in history, has a good reason for being bad . . . [and] he's intellectually superior to his French counterpart," General Montcalm, who is played by Patrice Chéreau in the film (*"The Last of the Mohicans* Press Kit").

Writing for Library of America's website, Sragow extols Mann's film as a "provocative revision" of Cooper's 1826 classic novel, concluding that "Hawkeye's and Cooper's admiration for the Mohicans' way of life—their blend of pragmatism and chivalry, and their genius at warfare, hunting, and navigating their environment—emerges stronger than ever in Mann's version of the tale." Still, the film perpetuates deeply ingrained misrepresentations of Native culture. For instance, the Comanche anthropologist Barbra A. Meek's linguistic analysis of Native dialogue in the film details how Mann's adaptation continues the industry's reliance on a staple of the White man's Indian, "Hollywood Injun English" (93).

Mann's invented romance between Hawk-eye and Cora and Mann's whitening of Cora by erasing her biracial identity are plot interventions often appraised in reviews and scholarship. The "romantic subplot that would have made Cooper blush," writes Maslin, gives audiences reason to patronize the latest attempt to breathe new life into the writer's "stupefying" classic novel. Pawelczak roasts Mann and Day-Lewis for making Hawk-eye "a sexy wood sprite" (403) in a "deliriously romantic" love scene that positions viewers to identify with the "ecstatic Cora." (404). The *Rolling Stone* reviewer Peter Travers questions the wisdom of Mann's decision to erase Cora's identity as a biracial woman of color and to transfer her affections from Uncas to Hawk-eye. To Brantlinger, Mann's invented romance is a crucial device for "the erasure of Cooper's racism" in the interracial romance at the heart of the novel (25). In Brantlinger's view, the film "perfects Cooper's novel" by envisioning the "inevitable extinction" of Native people through the lens of sentimental racism, which, the critic reasons, perceives nothing racist in the historical processes that sought to effect extinction (24). Jeffrey Walker agrees that Mann's film expunges some racial themes from Cooper's story, but he differs markedly from Brantlinger on the novel's presentation of miscegenation, racism, and history, which together form "the essential theme and flavor of Cooper's classic tale." Conceding that some alterations to Cooper's plot are justified for a modern audience, Walker argues that "Mann's decision to turn *The Last of the Mohicans* primarily into a love story" does a great disservice to Cooper's novel and to filmgoers ("Deconstructing" 107). The notion that Cooper's novel does not explore racial themes and forces in history is squarely refuted, Walker shows, in the 1826 novel itself, in contemporary reviews of the novel, and in recent decades of Cooper scholarship. Lacking an understanding of the novel, which is one of the film's main sources (the other main source being Seitz's 1936 film adaptation), leads some critics to misreading the nexus between the book and the film adaptation, particularly in regard to race and history. Critics who rail on Mann's film tend to have difficulty extricating their own readings from Mark Twain's satirical appraisal of Cooper's work. The reviews of Mann's film by Roger Ebert, Maslin, Simon, and Brantlinger, for instance, build their critiques on Twain's satirical gag, giving credence in turn to Twain's piece as literary criticism rather than as the amusing gem it is.

The conversation about Mann's film is rich with commentary that dissociates the movie from its primary sources to investigate auteur theory and the adaptation's filmic techniques. Barker and Sabin, for instance, discuss Mann's characteristic use of extended close-ups and "awkward silences" to complement dialogue and to create the film's "powerful mix of moods" (117, 109). If there is an attempt at mythmaking in the film, Barker and Sabin write, that attempt fails, and so do critics who try to abstract a coherent myth from the film. Rather, the film features liminal figures—a staple of Mann's work—in Hawk-eye and Cora, who denounce greed, exploitation, and the systemic ills of British colonialism in favor of a "rich humanism" in a new nation (116).

Cora's role in Mann's adaptation has received a significant share of critical attention, much of which untethers the film from its sources. Barker and Sabin argue that Mann's ethnographic research is evident not only in the film's depiction of Native American material culture but also in the cultural gap that separates Cora and Hawk-eye, a gap that narrows for Cora when Hawk-eye relates a Mohican story of the cosmos (114). In their book on women in film, Ralph Donald and Karen MacDonald offer a similar take on Cora. For them, the invented romance highlights in Cora the qualities of a "Hawksian woman," a term an anonymous reviewer used to describe female leads in Howard Hawks's films who are "consequential, self-assured, and even at times superior to the hero" (qtd. in Donald and MacDonald 113). Alan Woolfolk's essay on the film's depiction of an emergent American revolutionary spirit puts Cora in the center of the action, arguing that her "awakening democratic sympathies" displace the aristocratic privilege of her upbringing and, thus, prepare her to permanently depart the British aristocratic social hierarchy and to make a home with Hawk-eye (218). Jonathon Rayner reads Cora's evolution as a key element of a film production that implicitly questions the Hollywood formula promulgating "traditional forms of male authority" while, in some ways, adhering to them (111). As the film challenges the authority of a king and of his military officers, it employs Cora and, to a lesser degree, her sister Alice, played by Jodhi May, and the frontier woman Alexandra Cameron, played by Tracey Ellis, to question patriarchy in the figures of fathers, husbands, and male suitors as the women assert their will and fend for themselves without male protectors. Rayner reads in Cora the clash, in Gavin Smith's words, between "marginal individualism and mainstream culture" that Smith identifies in Mann's Hawk-eye (77).

With the exception of Seitz's 1936 film, no adaptation of *The Last of the Mohicans* has enjoyed the popular appeal, critical attention, and cultural impact of the 1992 film. Mann's version is now positioned as the standard for most consumers who have seen a film adaptation of *The Last of the Mohicans*. As has been true at least since 1920, film adaptations of Cooper's novel are more firmly lodged in the public's cultural consciousness than the novel is. And if the past is prologue to the future, the novel will likely undergo more filmic interpretations: Cooper's tale still has much more to tell.

Additional Resources

We are grateful for the feedback to our online survey provided by sixty college-level instructors who regularly teach Cooper's novels. Their responses assisted in the development of this volume and suggested many of the resources listed in part 1.

Survey respondents frequently mentioned the need when teaching Cooper's novels to provide students with historical background on contemporaneous events like the Missouri Compromise, the emergence of the Whig Party, and the Indian Removal Act. Instructors may wish to consult one of the many overviews of the Jacksonian period, such as those by Daniel Howe and by Sean Wilentz, or one of the many specialized studies on those topics.

Respondents often mentioned the need to provide students with historical maps. Instructors may consult online databases like the David Rumsey Historical Map Collection, housed at the Stanford University Library.

Many respondents mentioned teaching nineteenth-century visual artworks alongside Cooper's novels, and in particular painters and paintings of the antebellum period. Several essays in this collection discuss Cooper and the visual arts. The painter Thomas Cole was mentioned most often by respondents, and there are many print sources that discuss his friendship with and artistic connections to Cooper. Instructors can consult his paintings online, especially on the website of the Thomas Cole National Historic Site (www.exploretho mascole.org) and on the website of the New-York Historical Society. Several respondents teach Cole's 1836 "Essay on American Scenery" alongside Cooper's novels and Cole's paintings. The essay is readily available online. Respondents also mentioned teaching the works of other painters of the Hudson River School, including Washington Allston and John Vanderlyn. Several instructors make use of online materials from the New-York Historical Society Museum and Library. Some universities and colleges subscribe to Artstor Digital Library, which has a large database of publicly accessible images for classroom instruction, and some respondents reported using it as a teaching resource. The website of the Fenimore Art Museum in Cooperstown, New York, is also a rich resource for images of the Cooper family, Cooperstown, and nineteenth-century American art.

Information on Cooper's manuscripts and on published and forthcoming critical editions of his works can be found on the website *The Writings of James Fenimore Cooper*. The American Antiquarian Society online project *James Fenimore Cooper: Shadow and Substance* provides useful information on Cooper's manuscripts, images of Darley's famous illustrations of Cooper's novels, and reflections by editors of Cooper's novels and travel books. The James Fenimore Cooper Society website, developed and maintained for many years by Hugh MacDougall, is dated technologically but still a useful resource for information on Cooper, his novels, out-of-print materials, Cooper scholarship, and many other odds and ends. Conference papers from panels on Cooper at the American Literature Association going back to its founding in 1989 are published on the site, as are conference papers from the biannual international conferences on Cooper held at the State University of New York, Oneonta, starting in 1978. Since 1989, the society has published Cooper scholarship, reviews, and news in its periodicals, which in 2017 were combined into one biannual publication, *The James Fenimore Cooper Society Journal*.

Respondents indicated that they use a wide range of approaches to teach Cooper's novels. Most often mentioned were critical race studies, gender studies, postcolonial studies, ecocriticism, indigenous studies, and New Historicism. Multiple respondents cited Greg Garrard's edited collection of essays on ecocriticism, Levine on temporality and race, Doolen on imperialism and the United States empire, and Kilpatrick ("Keeping") on the film adaptations of *The Last of the Mohicans*. Respondents who teach indigenous studies often cited Robert Berkhofer, John P. Bowes, Philip J. Deloria, and Paul Chaat Smith and Robert Allen Warrior. According to many respondents, works by Benedict Anderson, Homi K. Bhabha, Toni Morrison, Eric J. Sundquist, and Jane Tompkins are persistently useful.

NOTES

[1] Four of the publishers that offer paperback editions of Cooper's novels—Penguin Classics, Modern Library, Signet Classics, and Bantam Classics—are imprints of Penguin Random House.

[2] An edition oft-cited by the respondents to our survey of instructors when this volume was in development.

Part Two

APPROACHES

HISTORY AND CULTURE

America's Historical Romance: *The Last of the Mohicans* to *Hamilton*

Sarah Sillin

According to George Dekker, "The sheer range of races and conditions that [James Fenimore] Cooper sometimes brought together in a single narrative . . . was unprecedented in serious fiction. Of course that range was also, if you like, distinctively American" (85). As Dekker's remarks suggest, literary scholars have long asked how historical romances construct a sense of American identity by representing interracial encounters. To explore this question, critics have considered the array of romances that fictionalize early American history and that explore how ideas of race and racism shaped the country. James Fenimore Cooper's work remains a touchstone in these discussions, even while scholars ask if Cooper is the guide we want to this past. As Robert Levine argues, "[O]ver the past two decades it has become a tenet of U.S. literary studies that Cooper's Leatherstocking series supported and enabled Indian Removal, gloried in an emerging white U.S. empire, and trafficked in essentialist notions of race." By contrast, Levine asserts, there is a need to recognize the "conflict and critique" within the Leather-Stocking series (165). Ezra Tawil makes a related case that Cooper's novels and frontier romances more broadly "helped to redefine 'race' for an emerging national culture" (2).[1]

These debates inform my upper-level undergraduate course America's Historical Romance. The course asks students how historical romance narratives portray American identity by reflecting on the country's history of international and interracial relations. Beginning our course with *The Last of the Mohicans*, we engage critiques of Cooper's work and the possibility that the novel critiques race relations in the United States. Indeed, knowing that scholars continue to debate the text's meaning fosters my students' interest in considering these questions. We ask who, in Cooper's fiction, helps shape colonial America? At the close of this romance, who remains to lead the country? And how did the questions that shaped Cooper's work likewise drive historical romances written in later decades?

The Last of the Mohicans treats the French and Indian War as the backdrop to a fictional kidnapping plot. Set near Lake George in 1757, the story unfolds in the days leading up to and following the British loss of Fort William Henry to the French. In the chaos of battle and retreat, the Huron Magua pursues revenge against the British Colonel Munro, who has publicly whipped him for intoxication. In retaliation, Magua kidnaps Munro's daughters, Cora and Alice. However, a small band of allies forms to rescue them, including the White colonial Americans Duncan Heyward and Natty Bumppo and the Mohicans Chingachgook and Uncas. These friends save Alice (Duncan's love interest), but they cannot save Cora. Both she and Uncas die in the novel's final skirmish. As this summary suggests, the plot centers on vengeance and rescuing damsels in distress. Cooper explores the skills and virtues—including marksmanship, navigation, and self-sacrificing courage—that the Native Americans and colonial Americans need in order to prove their worth to one another in this world.

Despite these conventional themes, when my students begin reading the novel, they are often baffled by the lack of context in its fictionalization of historical events and by the initial lack of information about the characters. Yet the text's potential to disorient readers proves generative for introducing students to the historical romance genre. Even as this and other historical romances position readers to reconsider the relation between America's past and present, clear definitions of what makes someone an American remain elusive. Thus first I map out Cooper's characters and plot for the class, then we explore how the opening confuses us by rendering the American landscape and the characters' identities unfamiliar. In subsequent classes, we consider which characters seem to embody American virtues and which seem marked as foreign. Cooper's romance becomes useful background for examining later historical romances (loosely defined) that rethink race relations and international encounters in the United States: among them are Catharine Maria Sedgwick's *Hope Leslie*, María Amparo Ruiz de Burton's *Who Would Have Thought It?*, Charles Chesnutt's *The House behind the Cedars*, and Lin-Manuel Miranda's *Hamilton: An American Musical*. This essay relates the questions that guide our discussions of *The Last of the Mohicans* and inform our interpretation of *Hamilton* as a historical romance, and it includes students' responses from the first iteration of the course.

How Cooper Disorients Readers

As my students are unfamiliar with historical romances, we begin by discussing the genre's conventions. Claiming leeway to reimagine the past, writers of this genre blur history and romance as their fictional characters experience historical moments that resonate with the writers' own eras. American historical romances often entwine military action with a courtship plot. Thus they explore what qualities characters need to survive the conflict and to forge an American family based on affinity. Given my interest in how the genre constructs racial identity, we also consider Dekker's claim that Cooper's portrait of interracial encounters is a particularly American feature of his romances (85). *The Last of the Mohicans* suggests America gives rise to interracial relations, for instance, when Cooper portrays how the White, southern colonial American Duncan survives the French and Indian War while protecting his White, Scottish lover, Alice, by forging alliances with the scout Natty and his Mohican allies. Further, we consider how the preface promises to elucidate depictions of race in the novel, as Cooper argues that "there is so much obscurity in the Indian traditions . . . as to render some explanation useful" and that "[f]ew men exhibit greater diversity, or . . . antithesis of character, than the native warrior of North America" (5).[2] Insisting on the complexity of Native American identities, he claims authority to help readers grasp this knowledge and so to understand interracial relations.

Yet the preface's explanation underscores that the opening chapters do little to resolve ambiguities of character or to clarify the historical conflict that shapes this tale. Thus I summarize the French and Indian War for the class and circulate a list of characters with short descriptive phrases from the novel. For example, the list notes that Natty is also called Hawk-eye and La Longue Carabine (the Long Rifle) in the novel and that he is a colonial American scout for the British and longtime friend of Chingachgook; the novel's narrator asserts Natty's "sturdy honesty," other characters know him for his marksmanship, and he often proclaims that he has "no cross in his blood" (Cooper, *Last* 30, 35). Students noted that viewing a list of characters in advance resonates with how we encounter plays, including works by Shakespeare to which Cooper often alludes in the novel. And providing these overviews lets students concentrate on how Cooper sets the stage and how each character enters the story.

We closely examine the first chapter, which opens near Lake George and describes Cooper's heroines, one of his heroes, and his central villain. Yet this summary makes the chapter sound rather more straightforward than it is. Thus I ask students to jot down notes about what makes these pages obscure. Students have commented on a variety of elements: from the detached narrative voice in the chapter to its comma-laden sentences. But several students observed that Cooper portrays "North America," in his terms, as a "peculiar," "danger[ous]," and exhausting "wilderness." Further, he does not state the lake's British name. Instead he locates it "near [Lake Champlain's] southern termination" and recounts how different colonists have viewed the lake. Whereas "Jesuit missionaries" used its waters to "perform the typical purification of baptism" (Cooper *Last* 11), he explains, "the less zealous English thought they conferred a sufficient honour on its unsullied fountains, when they bestowed the name of their reigning prince." Only in a footnote does Cooper clarify that these descriptions refer to Lake George (11–12). In examining this dense chapter, we draw from arguments like Jerome McGann's that "aesthetic and formal concerns are secondary [for Cooper], a means to . . . 'elucidate the history, manners, usages, and scenery, of his native land'" (129). Such criticism is an affirmation to students who are not drawn to Cooper's style, and it invites the class to analyze how the form of the novel and its cultural commentary shape each other.

Given that Cooper's novel opens with obscurity—in both its subject and its style—I ask students what we need to know to make sense of the setting. Cooper engages histories of European imperialism alongside romantic portraits of American wilderness. He frames America's landscape as distinctive in its beauty, while insisting that this beauty renders the country politically and spiritually significant to Europeans. Why does the entwining of romantic and imperialist discourses matter? Some students saw tensions between celebrations of a pure natural environment and fascination with imperial conquest, while others noted that Europeans could justify colonialism by romanticizing an American landscape. In turn, we considered whether the romance suggests that European empires do not belong in America or perhaps that the American colonists are uniquely equipped to navigate these two worlds.

The novel's focus on European colonialism also fosters discussion of why we might read the novel as commenting on American identity. I invite students to look for moments when the text connects this past to Cooper's era. For instance, the preface suggests that Natty's experiences of colonial America and the frontier "furnish a witness to the truth of those wonderful alterations which distinguish the progress of the American nation" (Cooper, *Last* 7) even as Cooper describes the Lake George region in the colonial period as largely undeveloped. Thus he suggests that the history he envisions reveals the growth of American identity, while he also highlights the significance of a place that remains part of his present.

To theorize how the novel constructs American identity, we analyze its connections to American art and culture in Cooper's time, including Thomas Cole's *Landscape with Figures: Scene from "The Last of the Mohicans"* and *Scene from "The Last of the Mohicans": Cora Kneeling at the Feet of Tamenund*. These paintings can surprise us if we expect representations of the romance to focus on its characters. Cole instead portrays a grand setting that dwarfs the people in it. Yet my class found that Cole's interpretation of the novel was related to their own. He, too, envisions wilderness that threatens to obscure human beings. One of my students compared the landscape in these paintings to a stage and led us to speculate about how the environment cloaks characters and yet lends drama to their actions. By threatening to overwhelm the characters, does the landscape reveal something about them?

In considering how Cooper defines these figures, my class was struck by his choice to omit names when first introducing characters. Without naming Alice or Cora, the first chapter describes their horses' equipage and the high rank it signals; the narrator then compares the younger, fairer, artless Alice to her "raven"-haired, "rich blood[ed]," and suitably modest elder sister, Cora (*Last*

19). We debate the effects of this introduction. By leaving the women unnamed here, the novel could be signaling the malleability of their identities. Does entering an American wilderness free them from British designations? Do they, like Lake George, take on new identities as they encounter new people? Yet Cooper details the sisters' appearance, age, and status before naming them. Are these aspects of their identities immutable? Rather than encourage my class to reach a consensus, I suggest to them that the opening chapter raises questions that will structure the rest of our reading: How stable or fluid is identity in this romance? And how does an American environment influence such identities?

Race and Identity in Cooper

To contextualize for the class why American identity might have seemed unstable in the early national era, I assign an excerpt from Katy Chiles's *Transformable Race* (1–30). Chiles familiarizes students with climate-based theories of race, shifts in racial thinking, and literature's role in imagining how environment influenced nations and races. As Chiles focuses on eighteenth-century literature, her work also leaves room for students to analyze how historical romances engage these ideas. How, we ask, do these texts treat individual characters as symbols who embody their communities or nations and shape the future? What role does race play in shaping the characters and their views of the world? For example, Cooper explores how Duncan's origins in a southern colony influence his character by depicting both Duncan's devotion to Alice and unspoken repulsion toward Cora's Black heritage.

Asking how Cooper's characters become symbols of the nation or of communities within it leads us to discuss what's at stake in reenvisioning the French and Indian War. Many students remarked that they expected stories about American identity and the American past to focus on more familiar conflicts, like the Revolutionary War. Our conversation in class prompted them to rethink the opening chapter of the novel, which asserts America's distinctiveness as well as its connections to Europe. They noted that focusing on the French and Indian War lets Cooper return to this theme throughout the romance thereby implying that America can be geographically distinct from Europe without becoming isolated. By portraying the conflicts between French and British forces, as well as among Native American tribes—including the Abenaki, Algonquian, Catawba, Cherokee, Iroquois, Lenape, Mi'kmaq, Ojibwa, Ottawa, Shawnee, and Wyandot—Cooper implies that colonial Americans had to learn to navigate transnational politics. Even as he suggests that Europeans found the land "peculiar" (*Last* 11), he insists that the settlers' experiences marked America as a location whose history was worth recalling.

Relations between communities that circumscribed the Atlantic basin shaped the French and Indian War, and these relations in turn become sources of strength in Cooper's romance. My class suggested that Cooper values characters like Uncas and Cora, who are marked as racially and culturally foreign to the White American characters in the novel. Uncas deftly anticipates potential enemies, while Cora bravely negotiates with Magua and displays selfless concern for her would-be protectors. One of my students described how much easier she found it to identify with Cora than with Alice. After all, Cora is more active, from caring for Alice to leaving a trail that Duncan and Natty can follow when Magua kidnaps the sisters. This readerly identification merits attention, since the historical romance plays on such attachments to foster readers' sense of connection to earlier generations. Moreover, Uncas's and Cora's presence in the novel highlights that the White colonial American characters, Duncan and Natty, forge deep affinities with people who have different racial and national identities. Through this diverse band of friends, Cooper implies that colonial Americans matter to a circum-Atlantic community.

Our analysis in class of how Cora and Uncas contribute to the romance led us to focus on two familiar but critical questions in our final discussion: What are the effects of Uncas's and Cora's deaths, and why do readers often identify this story as racist when it has a Native American protagonist and a heroine of Black West Indian and White Scottish lineage? My class connected these questions by noting that Uncas neatly fits the trope of the noble savage, and we can read in Cora the trope of the tragic mulatta. Students who were surprised by these characters' fates, given their heroism, found it useful to read their demise in relation to the novel's other Native American and biracial characters. They debated whether these deaths reflect a desire to acknowledge the country's international and interracial origins while positioning the White characters as parents to future generations.

One student wondered whether we were imposing presentist views of racism on the past: for instance, by presuming that readers in Cooper's era would recognize racism as such. Thus in class we analyzed textual evidence of how the characters view race. My student who identified strongly with Cora and was frustrated by her death and exclusion from the novel's imagined future turned our attention back to the scene where Munro describes her heritage. After misunderstanding which of his daughters Duncan wants to marry, the White Scottish Munro discloses that Cora's West Indian mother is "descended, remotely, from that unfortunate class, who are so basely enslaved to administer the wants of a luxurious people!" (Cooper, *Last* 159). Here characters disagree about race: Munro and Duncan offer conflicting perspectives on Cora's identity. Both recognize the pervasive racism that suggests Black heritage could disqualify Cora from the White hero's affections. Yet Munro grows "fiercely" demanding at the prospect that Duncan might "scorn to mingle the blood of the Heywards, with one so degraded" as Cora. In response, Duncan begs, "Heaven protect me from a prejudice so unworthy of my reason!" Internally, though, he possesses "such a feeling" and is relieved to learn that his beloved Alice's mother is White (159).

To analyze whether the novel challenges Duncan's racism, we compare the two men's opinions. Munro defends Cora against Duncan's prejudice. Yet my class argued that he depicts the "degrad[ation]" of slavery as a problem largely for its effects on White people. He characterizes slavery as a "curse entailed on Scotland, by her unnatural union with a foreign and trading people." Munro describes unions between different peoples (the Scottish and English) as "unnatural," much as the narrator hints that Duncan's reaction against an interracial union with Cora may be natural. Cooper writes that Duncan's response is "deeply rooted as if it had been engrafted in his nature" (159). The simile is ambiguous. If these racist feelings are "rooted" in Duncan like a plant, are they natural? Yet if they are "engrafted," are they an external influence on his "nature"? While Duncan is discomfited that his anti-Blackness might alter his relationship with Munro, the romance is fuzzier on whether Duncan should or can resist this ideology.

In class we analyze not only what characters say about race but also who gets to comment. Trying to uncover how Cora views her racial identity reveals a startling lack of evidence, as Cooper's novel primarily emphasizes how slavery and racism affect White men. Moreover, while Munro and Duncan interrupt their conversation to address their impending loss of the fort, they do not revisit the subject of race. Cora's subsequent death lets these White male characters evade their vexed views of race and slavery.

Of course, many of the questions we discuss in class about race and identity in *The Last of the Mohicans* are familiar. Students thus join broader scholarly conversations on these subjects and assess their continued relevance. For instance, do debates over how the deaths of Black people are represented in the media today give us new understandings of the novel's funeral scene for Uncas and Cora? Can we see why this scene—which mourns characters of color even as it kills them off—might have appeared progressive in Cooper's era? If Cooper's decision to kill off these characters reflects a desire to locate American racial diversity in the past, where might we see such desires at work today? Students who choose to write research essays on this text investigate how Cooper's novel resonated with debates over race in Cooper's era by engaging literary scholarship by Tawil and by Levine as well as histories of slavery, the French and Indian War, and the United States government policy of Indian Removal.

The Historical Romance Genre Today

Our class discussion of who constitutes America in *The Last of the Mohicans* launches our conversation about nineteenth-century historical romances more broadly, which concludes with a turn to a twenty-first-century work, Miranda's *Hamilton*. I argue that Miranda's hip-hop musical fits into the historical romance genre and suggests its ongoing resonance. Despite the marked differences between these texts, reading them together highlights that diverse writers have persistently grappled with how race and racism influence who can be American. Of course, listening to the original Broadway cast recording of *Hamilton* can seem like a non sequitur after a semester of nineteenth-century romances. But like *The Last of the Mohicans*, *Hamilton* emphasizes how individual characters shape American identity on the battlefield and in the bedroom. And the musical likewise briefly alludes to slavery and reflects on the bonds between circum-Atlantic communities that shaped American history. King George's song "You'll Be Back" underlines the United States' significance to the British Empire after the Revolutionary War. *Hamilton*'s most extended reflection on race, though, lies in its casting of performers of color as the founders and in its use of hip-hop to relate the story of the American Revolution. When listening to the musical, students developed compelling interpretations that connected and distinguished Cooper's and Miranda's popular narratives of American identity.

Notably, some students struggled to express why it matters that *Hamilton* casts performers of color as the founding fathers. To reframe this discussion, I asked students to talk about a time when they read a book and then imagined who should be cast in a movie adaptation of it or saw a movie and disagreed with its casting. We had earlier examined how Michael Mann's film adaptation of *The Last of the Mohicans* reinterprets the novel in its screenplay and casting choices. Students' examples highlighted that our sense of who should play whom reveals what traits we think characters embody and which actors we believe evoke them. Students also cited recent critiques of films that whitewash characters, including the response to Emma Stone's role as a Hawaiian and Asian character in *Aloha*. Connecting the two discussions, my class speculated whether casting predominantly White actors in films reinforces assumptions that people of color cannot embody particular qualities.

Our conversation offered an entry into analyzing *Hamilton*'s casting choices. The casting of Christopher Jackson as George Washington, Daveed Diggs as Thomas Jefferson, and Leslie Odom, Jr., as Aaron Burr attests to these actors' consummate talent as performers while addressing Broadway's historical scarcity of roles for people of color. Moreover, students noted that if the musical associates characters like Washington with dignity and statecraft, then casting Jackson and other performers of color in these roles implies that they can embody such a trait and skill. Whereas *The Last of the Mohicans* imagines its young characters of color dying as they help to protect the White American family, *Hamilton*'s artists of color embody the founders' legacies. Students likewise highlighted how the show's use of hip-hop demonstrates that African American and Latinx musicians have developed rich modes for relating narratives about American identity.

I should note that my aim in these discussions is not to establish *Hamilton* as an ideal example of progressive art against which to measure Cooper's work. One student helped to clarify this in a class presentation in which she shared Lyra D. Monteiro's review of *Hamilton*. Monteiro argues that, while it creates new opportunities for performers of color, the show risks eliding Black people's presence in revolutionary America. The presentation engaged other students in this cultural debate, as they considered whether the musical further enshrines the founding fathers. Some argued that Miranda addresses the founders' abuses of power, for instance through mention of Sally Hemings. Meanwhile, others suggested that historical romances like *Hamilton* evoke nationalism through a loving fascination with the past, even when such stories criticize histories of exclusion and oppression.

We likewise explore *Hamilton*'s reception and racial politics by watching clips from *Hamilton's America: A Documentary Film*. In interviews with the performers of *Hamilton*, the film briefly acknowledges their ambivalence about the founders. Diggs (who originated the roles of the Marquis de Lafayette and Thomas Jefferson) remarks that Jefferson wrote "this incredible document . . . that we all believe in," but "he sucks" (qtd. in Kornhaber). Diggs elicits a laugh from my students, as his understated comment refuses to pay homage to the founding father merely for his storied status. We also consider the range of politicians who appear in the documentary, from George W. Bush to Elizabeth Warren. Noting how these disparate public figures regard Alexander Hamilton and the musical reminds us that their perspectives are interpretations, too.

Hamilton concludes by emphasizing this openness to interpretation in the song "Who Lives, Who Dies, Who Tells Your Story?" This final number invites us to reconsider who is unable to live on in the nation, from Cooper's Uncas and Cora to Miranda's Hamilton. Further, the song asks listeners to reflect on the power that diverse writers and leaders claim by narrating history. Recognizing this power lets us consider the appeal of the historical romance genre for writers—whether in the nineteenth century or today—who wish to reinvent the past and decide which events define America, to whom the past belongs, and who belongs in the future of the nation.

NOTES

[1] To deepen students' understanding of the historical romance genre, instructors might also assign Rans, who argues that *The Last of the Mohicans* "deconstruct[s]" the historical romance's conventions in "express[ing]" its "massive historical criticism" (118). To explore disparate perspectives on Cooper's racial politics, students could examine Christophersen's reading of the novel as a critique of the Missouri Compromise; Axelrad's assertion that the novel treats the loss of Uncas, Cora, and their potential interracial marriage as "an American tragedy" (53); and Rifkin's argument that the novel naturalizes the White conjugal household and pathologizes Native kinship structures to legitimize the expansion of the United States.

[2] This and subsequent passages from Cooper's *The Last of the Mohicans* are from the 1986 Penguin Classics edition.

Cooper's Revolutionary Novels: Surface Reading and Grotesque American History

Joseph J. Letter

Teaching Cooper's novels to students is difficult. For many of them, his prose appears arcane, and the narratives are hard to discern. But students commonly face such challenges in nineteenth-century literary texts, not just in Cooper's, and the extent of these challenges is related to how students read today. Without polemicizing, I want to offer an approach to teaching Cooper that makes the current problems of historical disconnection visible to student readers. I mean here undergraduates not majoring in English, the students one generally sees in introductory survey courses, although I believe the pedagogy would be appropriate for courses that majors or graduate students might take. I generally allow three weeks of class time to cover each of Cooper's lengthy Revolutionary novels, and I roughly divide those three weeks into three pedagogical units. While most introductory courses only allow enough time to read one of Cooper's novels, for the sake of breadth and symmetry I will briefly discuss three Revolutionary texts: *The Pilot*, *The Spy*, and *Lionel Lincoln*.

The Pilot, *The Spy*, and *Lionel Lincoln* are novels that overtly address the history of the Revolution, and as such, they stipulate a dialogical relation between two narratives, a fictional one designed by Cooper and a historical one collectively generated by historians. That basic dialogue between fiction and history is ubiquitous in the three novels but often remains invisible to students until they are taught to recognize it. What adds special interest to this intertextual dialogue is that it was already apparent when Cooper was composing. At the time, the national narrative was under construction, and most readers, including Cooper himself, knew people from the former generation who had participated in the war. The presence of Revolutionary veterans suggested a fundamental tension between living memories of events and written records of them, a tension that was critical to the success of Revolutionary novels as a genre. And this genre (or subgenre of the historical novel) indeed flourished throughout the antebellum era. Cooper, and the many other Revolutionary historical novelists who followed him, developed narratives that drew on the memories of veterans or on oral legends about the war that had become attached to particular local sites. Such legends reflected deep ambivalence about a war that, at least on the local level, had been a civil conflict that turned neighbors against one another, and, therefore, these local legends often ran counter to the historical narrative of the Revolution as the heroic origin of the nation.

As their titles suggest, these three novels by Cooper depict individual, sometimes anonymous heroes whose actions take place within or alongside the official historical narrative of the Revolution. In effect, the novels responded to official history by qualifying the master narrative of national progress. The common people who had fought and died for the country were quickly fading from memory by the 1820s, but their stories persisted in local legends, in which figures and sites were broadly representational of common folk identity associated with a pre-Enlightenment, communal ethos.[1] I refer to this form of representation as grotesque history, first, because it evokes a buried or secret past (as in *grottoesque*, meaning cavelike), and second, because for students it is easily visible in the surface features of grotesquely exaggerated settings and characters in the three novels by Cooper.

The term *grotesque* has a complex history in art and literature, but basically it refers to scenes and figures that are depicted in hyperbolic ways. In other words, the grotesque pushes physical boundaries and reasonable limits, and as a result it becomes apparent on the surface of texts. For student readers it lends itself to what Stephen Best and Sharon Marcus have described as "surface reading." Surface reading includes an array of critical strategies that focus on literal features or meanings in a text, as opposed to interpretive or symptomatic readings that locate meaning beneath the surface of a text. I believe surface reading holds great value for addressing the disconnection from literary texts that student readers experience. By "surface," Best and Marcus mean "what insists on being looked at rather than what we must train ourselves to see *through*" (9).

For students, the grotesque surface features of characters and settings in Cooper's Revolutionary novels become sites for engaging the intertextual relation between history and fiction, and we explore these relations in the three pedagogical units, each of which uses a distinct temporal frame of reference and which together function like a triptych. These units stress a comparative, nonlinear approach that guides students horizontally from Cooper's texts to historical contexts. Like the panels in a triptych, the temporal frames used in these units can stand alone, but when they are taught alongside one another, students are encouraged to see multiple articulating relations between the frames.

Reading the Present as a Surface in The Pilot

The first pedagogical unit addresses the present as a surface by highlighting for students the immediacy of their own experience reading Cooper's narratives, even when they struggle to engage with those narratives. Failures of engagement suggest key differences between the reading contexts of students today and of readers in Cooper's time, and thus careful attention to disjunctions in the reading experience can mark specific textual sites for further analysis. The present is both connected to Cooper's era and disconnected from it, and this dual relation generates in students an appropriate ambivalence toward any reading of Cooper's texts. Thus, to begin, students are asked to identify places in Cooper's texts that connect with their own experience or, conversely, to identify places that explicitly alienate them from the narrative. Often this is as simple as recognizing places that they know or have visited or historical figures that they have heard of. Frustrated students can identify particular words or phrases that appear arcane to them. In both cases, though, the present becomes an overtly acknowledged frame through which the texts are engaged. In classical rhetoric, such a frame would be called an appeal to the text's *kairos*: the ways that the text accounts for the immediate details of the reader's place and time. Kairos altogether resists the fallacy of transparency in prose by marking the literal points of relation between reader and text; furthermore, it establishes a critical reading process for students that allows individuals to engage at their own level.[2]

In *The Pilot* Cooper reflects on the ironies of selective memory in national history by dramatizing a distinctly modern problem, the pursuit of fame. The title character, who is based on John Paul Jones, is driven by an obsessive desire to make a name for himself, and that desire is contrasted with the heroic service of anonymous American seamen in the narrative. Despite Jones's tremendous skill as a sailor and bravery as a warrior, his personal desire for renown outweighs any noble sacrifice he makes to the American cause, and when his naval vessel's mission to raid the coast of England fails, the pilot insists that his involvement be forgotten and his name never mentioned (426). Jones readily acknowledges that in his native land of England he may be remembered as a traitor and a pirate, but he believes he has chosen the right side of history. As he says, "The picture must be drawn by the friends of the hero as well as by his enemies! Think you there are not pens as well as swords in America?" (363). For Cooper, Jones's personal character surely registers ambivalence; nevertheless, for student readers today Jones's desire to craft a public reputation or persona has strong resonance with their experiences of social media. Jones's narrow pursuit of fame at all costs speaks to the kairos of Cooper's novel and becomes a starting point for engaging other aspects of the narrative.

The behavior of the pilot contrasts sharply with that of another heroic figure in the novel, Cooper's fictional mariner Long Tom Coffin, and through their surface characterizations, both poles of the literary grotesque are enacted. While the pilot remains shrouded in mystery, a figure of concealment in the narrative, Coffin is larger than life, a grotesque giant whose physicality sharply contrasts with the pilot's mysterious behavior and secret identity. And these surface contrasts represent Cooper's thematic conflict in the novel. The pilot is based on a distinctly modern historical figure, one whose personal motives were hidden from history, but Coffin is a fictional composite whose hyperbolic character reveals the forgotten communal culture of common American sailors.

The surface descriptions of both the pilot and Tom Coffin suggest their contrasting functions within the narrative. Only the navy captain Munson and his second in command, the romance hero Edward Griffith, know the pilot's true identity, and they are sworn to secrecy. Thus, the pilot, who wears no uniform, remains aloof and anonymous throughout the novel, even as he directs his American ship, *The Ariel*, through storms and battles. The pilot's historical identity is effectively represented as being internalized through his secrecy and anonymity, while Long Tom Coffin's composite identity is externalized through hyperbolic features and actions that surely fit the grotesque. Tom Coffin towers over the other sailors in both his physical form and personality and at one point kills the captain of a British ship by harpooning him to the mast (203). Yet, in the end, like the thousands of forgotten heroes that he stands for, Coffin sacrifices his own life: he throws the novel's second romance hero, Richard Barnstable, into a lifeboat and then straps himself to the mast of *The Ariel* as it sinks beneath the surface of the sea; his body is never found (285–88).

What makes *The Pilot* such an interesting starting point for students is the accessibility of its structural contrasts. The plot is easily divided between a land-based traditional romance, involving Griffiths and Barnstable, and Cooper's innovative story of life at sea. Quite literally, the two settings represent two genres, the older conventional romance narrative focused on a quest to rescue kidnapped lovers and a new one that Cooper invents, the historical novel of maritime adventure. Like a contemporary remix of a familiar popular song, *The Pilot* moves between two distinct literary realms, and the contrasting settings make the surface features of the two genres wholly visible to student readers. Moreover, Cooper's awkward conjunction of forms also makes apparent the transitional moment in which Cooper was writing. The novel presents an ideological clash between a traditional representation of the past, literally manifest in the structural features of the abbey and nearby ruins where the land-based narrative is set, and a new democratic conception of historical consciousness represented by the transnational domain of the sea and further reinforced by the pilot's assertions that democratic liberty is a human, not a national, right. As the pilot notes, "I was born on this orb, and I claim to be a citizen of it. A man with a soul, not to be limited by the arbitrary boundaries of tyrants and hirelings" (151). The narrative surface of *The Pilot* invites reflection on the accuracy of historical narratives, an issue that parallels the debates about truth in media representations that students recognize today. Examining the narrative surface encourages them to make connections between the text and their present, whether in class discussions or in short written reflections, that can serve as an excellent starting point for critically reading Cooper's work.

Grotesque History in **The Spy**

In a triptych the central panel is the largest and is therefore the primary focal point, and that point of focus also applies to the second pedagogical unit on Cooper's Revolutionary novels. This unit accounts for the boundary between fiction and history within the text of the novels, especially *The Spy*. The temporal frame of reference for this unit is Cooper's moment of production in the early 1820s, and the class uses that frame to consider how Cooper's fictional narrative both agrees and disagrees with the official historical accounts of the Revolutionary era that are woven into the narrative. More specifically, this unit addresses the deeply ambivalent space between purely fictional characters and settings and historical persons and places. This liminal space is grotesque in its fusion of oddly contradictory concepts (like fiction and history) and in the hyperbolic surface features of characters and settings that draw students' attention to ideological assumptions about what is normal or real. Whereas readers of histories might readily accept that George Washington was a historical figure, and readers of romances might accept that a fictional hero should be gallant and handsome, grotesque characters and settings deliberately strain credulity, forcing readers to consider the liminal nature of historical novels. For students, discerning the boundary between fiction and history invokes another form of engagement and opens an enormous range of possible readings that raise important questions about narrative structure. Thus, after having considered the present in the first unit, students now analyze their assumptions about history, a process that often begins with straightforward examples like the case of George Washington in *The Spy*. In the novel Washington first appears as a mysterious disguised figure who uses the pseudonym Harper, and only later is he revealed as the historical personage, but this foreshadowed doubling frames all the most important instances of grotesque liminality in the novel. Students of course know Washington as a historical figure, but it is his symbolic function as a national father that makes his role essential to the narrative. Furthermore, because he first appears in disguise, he becomes a literary foil for the title character, the spy Harvey Birch, who is the grotesque obverse of Washington's historical symbolism. As Washington is gradually revealed to be the father of the nation, Birch, a common man but the narrative's true hero, descends into tragic anonymity, drawing out a narrative irony that students can analyze. For instructors, the goal is to guide that analysis by drawing students' attention from the grotesque surfaces that have been identified in the novel toward broader historical contexts.

The character of Birch was apparently based on an actual person named Enoch Crosby. Since Cooper had no direct knowledge of Crosby, he based the character on stories he had heard from John Jay, who was the father of his boyhood friend William Jay. John Jay had overseen the American spy network on the Westchester neutral ground, an area between the fronts of the British and American armies during the Revolutionary War. In the same way that Long Tom Coffin is a hyperbolic and composite representation of common American seamen in *The Pilot*, in *The Spy* Birch is a representative figure, an agglomeration of stories about forgotten local heroes from the neutral ground. Such stories were hidden from official histories because of their deep ambivalence with respect to American or British allegiance and the meaning of neutrality during the Revolutionary War, but they persisted in apocryphal relation to the national narrative, a relation that can inform students' analysis of *The Spy*.[3]

The boundary between history and fiction is never a neat line dividing official accounts from fictional invention; rather, like the neutral ground itself, it is a broadly grotesque terrain that calls historical narratives into question. Spies were perfect figures for this grotesque history because they suggested the ambivalent relation between concealed local histories and official versions of the Revolution as a master narrative of the nation's origins. By examining how the descriptions of grotesque figures like Harvey Birch relate to narrative events, students make visible the latent complexities of American history. Thus, instructors can serve as guides who encourage careful reading of the narrative surface and point students beyond the frame of the narrative toward historical connections that reveal a network of local histories.

Throughout *The Spy* Birch takes on various disguises and operates in the shadows, so much so that he becomes indistinguishable from the local landscape of Westchester County, repeatedly disappearing among the rocks and trees. In his various disguises—as a Yankee peddler, an Irish woman, and a Puritan zealot—Birch's true identity as an American patriot remains concealed. And yet, from the periphery of the narrative, often quite literally at the furthest limit of the scenic frame, he orchestrates every key turn in the novel's plot. His grotesque narrative function permeates the more traditional romance plot that builds toward the marital union of the patriot heroes Peyton Dunwoodie and Frances Wharton, a union that is delayed until Birch can free Frances's brother, Henry Wharton, from false imprisonment as a British spy.

The novel's climactic scene reveals the true identity of both Birch and Washington (Cooper, *Spy* [Franklin] 355–63). It occurs in Birch's secret hut on a mountain overlooking the neutral ground. Only Frances has noticed the site, which is built around a cave. Upon arrival she looks in its single window to see Harper and, shortly thereafter, Birch himself. In a strange fusion of their narrative functions, Harper meets with Birch in the hut then goes into the cave, reemerging in full uniform as Washington; meanwhile, Birch swears Frances to secrecy about his own true identity as an American spy. Before descending from the mountain, Birch shatters the window that had revealed his secret, literally and figuratively closing off any historical access to himself, while Washington leads Frances down, telling her, "[Y]ou are my child: all who dwell in this broad land are my children, and my care" (362). For students, the hut scene marks the birth of Washington as the nation's father, even as the character's grotesque history of disguise and involvement in espionage complicates that narrative.

The Spy concludes thirty-three years later when Birch encounters Frances and Peyton's son, Wharton Dunwoodie, during the War of 1812. Young Wharton is the perfect composite of his parents, the ideal romance hero of the new American nation, while Birch is battered and old. At the Battle of Lundy's Lane, Wharton storms a redoubt and helps the Americans claim victory over the British and the Canadians, but in the aftermath he discovers Birch's anonymous body among the dead. Thus, the novel's final grotesque scene depicts the conflict over historical representation in American history. Wharton Dunwoodie, the aristocratic landowner, shines as the romantic symbol of the new nation, while on the ground lies the grotesque remains of the spy, whose only legacy is a paper note, signed by Washington, acknowledging his secret service to the country.

For instructors, the pedagogical goal of the second unit is to guide students toward the reckoning with American history that Cooper depicts in the final scene of *The Spy*. In the dialectic between this text from the past and a present reading of it, students move from a kairotic connection between the text and their own present toward questioning their assumptions about national history and how those assumptions compare with Cooper's representation of history. Instructors can facilitate this critical move by assigning short outside readings (discussed in note 3) that illuminate the contrast between local and national history and by asking students to write brief responses.

History as Master Narrative in Lionel Lincoln

None of the authors who wrote Revolutionary novels had been participants in the Revolution. Instead, Cooper and other novelists from the second and third generations after the founding of the United States relied on narrative accounts from historians that they blended with local oral legends and eyewitness accounts. Because of this fusion of two ideologically distinct genres—written narrative history, as developed by Enlightenment historians like Edward Gibbon, David Hume, and William Robertson, and oral legends and accounts, which were considerably more ambivalent about events—historical novelists were compelled to address the theoretical problem of history as an unstable text. As Sacvan Bercovitch argues in *The Rites of Assent*, written Revolutionary histories, beginning with those written by patriot historians such as David Ramsay and Timothy Dwight, and thereafter those by the great narrative historians of the Romantic era (George Bancroft, William Prescott, and Francis Parkman), were focused on establishing a national identity that consolidated thirteen separate stories of colonial insurrection into a single narrative of the nation's origins (170–73). By contrast, oral Revolutionary legends and first-person accounts typically featured local geographic sites, like Faneuil Hall in Boston, the Liberty Bell in Philadelphia, or the tulip tree in Westchester where the British spy Major John André was captured. This third pedagogical unit on Cooper's novels asks students to consider the conflicted relation between Revolutionary histories as a national master narrative and Cooper's grotesque retelling of historical events. This unit takes a comparative textual approach that highlights the ideological contrasts between the national master narrative and local histories that were omitted from that narrative or forgotten over time.

Cooper's last specifically Revolutionary novel, *Lionel Lincoln; or, The Leaguer of Boston*, exemplifies the contrast between official history and the historical novel because it attempts, more than any of Cooper's other works, to resolve the problems caused by America's break with the colonial past. Although twentieth-century historians like Bernard Bailyn and Gordon S. Wood stressed the ideological origins of the Revolution, most recent scholars agree that the war had never been a clear ideological fight over taxation without representation, and the many civilian claims of neutrality during the war further complicate attempts to define the conflict in binary terms. Familial generational conflict, especially children breaking from parental rule, became the dominant metaphor for the historical separation from England.[4] In Revolutionary novels, romance plots were adapted to fit that metaphor; thus, in the typical Revolutionary romance, an older Loyalist father arranges to marry off his daughter to a British officer (usually the villain) but is ultimately foiled because the daughter patiently resists until she can be united with her true love, a dashing American patriot. Contrived and overtly conventional, such romance plots hold little interest for student readers, but in their specific surface adaptations to local histories they reveal fascinating conflicts with the national narrative.

In *Lionel Lincoln* Cooper adapts the typical romance narrative by fusing it with a gothic plot involving a quest undertaken by Lionel to learn his true family history, which is closely connected to the history of Boston. The motif of an arranged marriage is still present, but it recedes as the avarice of Lionel's colonial merchant family is revealed to be the true motive behind the union. By reading against the grain of romance, students can see how Old World gothic meets the new American grotesque in *Lionel Lincoln*, specifically through a clash between Lionel's aristocratic feudal past and the rapacious modernity of colonial Boston. As the novel progresses, the pestilential atmosphere of besieged Boston during the Revolution becomes more oppressive. The narrative culminates with a midnight marriage followed by a grotesque series of deathbed scenes that explain Lionel's true history. In quick succession, the protagonist discovers that his aunt had arranged his marriage to solidify claims to his family fortune, that he has a lost brother in Boston whose mental and physical growth was stunted and who has died of starvation and smallpox, and finally, that his father is an insane Revolutionary leader who has escaped from an asylum in England (354–56).

Ironically, despite the attention Cooper paid to national history in his other novels, *Lionel Lincoln* was the only novel that he called "historical" (6), but that very description reveals the confused boundary between history and fiction at the time of the novel's composition. He had intended for *Lionel Lincoln* to be the first of a series called the Legends of the Thirteen Republics, but when the novel failed to interest the reading public, he abandoned the project (Ringe and Ringe xv). Cooper had devoted himself to historical research about the time and place of the narrative, consulting numerous historical accounts of the Battles of Lexington, Concord, and Bunker Hill, and he had even traveled to Boston to see the locations that he would describe in the novel. Students can be encouraged to do research on the Internet comparing historically significant places to their representations in Cooper's novel.[5] Such places are often described in great detail within historical novels and in many cases still exist today as visible ruins or remnants of the historical past. That is, their surface features, both in the text and in our present, make the problems of national history apparent to students.

For example, Boston sites like Faneuil Hall and the Province House appear in *Lionel Lincoln* and provide a wealth of historical context for initiating class discussion. Furthermore, the local historical narrative centers on two locations, the home of Madame Lechmere, where Lionel stays, and the oddly gothic warehouse where his brother, Job Pray, lives. Cooper had investigated both locations carefully and then altered them in ways that are deeply suggestive. What he calls the Lechmere mansion was based on the Clark-Frankland House, the home of Jonathan Sewall, the Loyalist attorney general of Massachusetts during the Revolutionary era. But the name Lechmere (which is still ubiquitous in the Cambridge area and can be researched online by students) deliberately resonates with Boston's merchant trade, including the slave trade, thus intensifying Cooper's thematic emphasis on class issues as the true cause of Revolutionary violence. The troubling contrast between colonial splendor and common life in Boston is further intensified in the novel by the grotesque description of the abandoned warehouse, replete with gothic towers and confusing passageways, which was based on a building called the Triangular Warehouse on Merchants Row (a structure that was razed in 1824 as Cooper was writing the novel; Ringe and Ringe xvi). As a setting, the empty warehouse represents the physical consequences of the siege of Boston, and it is also the place where Lionel learns about his lost brother and his insane father, both of whom die there. Having students research key sites in Cooper's narrative may prompt them to question the actual causes for the American Revolution. What many students may have perceived earlier as a military conflict led by the founding fathers can now be seen as a complex confrontation between a corrupt colonial system and the people who suffered under it. In Cooper's novel, at least, history is not hidden, buried, or repressed; rather, it is illuminated in the details of the narrative surface.

Unfortunately, Cooper's failed experiment with *Lionel Lincoln* as the first in a series of novels about the Revolution in the thirteen colonies suggests that the progressive master narrative of the nation had already triumphed by the 1820s. Rather than a gothic story about the aberrant psychology of a colonial leader and the avarice of his merchant family leading to violent revolt, most American readers preferred the romance narrative focused on youthful love and patriotic devotion to ideals. The literary trope of a younger generation rejecting arranged marriage in favor of romantic love fit with the elitist progressivism of heroic national history. Gaining familiarity with the modern master narrative of American history allows students to make distinct contrasts between the surfaces of Cooper's texts and the historical assumptions that inform their contexts. Although *The Spy*, *The Pilot*, and *Lionel Lincoln* ultimately celebrate the national narrative, they also surely complicate its foundational premises. By giving voice to grotesque local histories, Cooper and other Revolutionary novelists preserved the legacy of the Revolution as a people's war. For students, Cooper's Revolutionary novels not only challenge them to develop a critical reading process but also persist as physical reminders that not all of the American past was a golden age.

NOTES

[1] See Bakhtin for more on the connection between communal folk identity, its links with local geography, and the adaptation of the grotesque in the Western literary tradition.

[2] See Spratt and Draxler; Wilson about using the concept of presentism as a means of teaching engagement with historical texts. But note that presentism carries a pejora-

tive connotation, especially among historians, because it suggests anachronism, whereas kairos focuses on the surface contexts that shape meaning and directly appeals to the immediacy of one's present rhetorical situation as both distinct from and connected to former moments or eras.

[3] For instructors, myriad resources exist for exploring local historical legends and accounts from the Revolutionary era. Historical society newsletters, local newspapers, and books by antiquarians are freely available online. Crosby gave an account of his own exploits that was published in 1828 as *The Spy Unmasked* (Barnum); furthermore, numerous recent historians have written about the deep ambivalence of the Revolution, most notably Nash.

[4] See Samuels, *Romances*, for more on the family romance as a national allegory.

[5] For more advanced students, Donald Ringe and Lucy Ringe's historical introduction to *Lionel Lincoln* (and indeed all the historical introductions to the State University of New York Press editions of Cooper's works) offers an excellent guide for comparing Cooper's narrative to the writer's historical source texts. But the third pedagogical unit in this course does not require that level of historicization.

Teaching *The Deerslayer* through Historical and Critical Debates

Rochelle Raineri Zuck

James Fenimore Cooper is widely considered to be the preeminent American novelist of the early nineteenth century. Dubbed "the American Scott," Cooper used the Romantic style popularized by Walter Scott to describe American themes, settings, and characters (Dekker 34). In creating the hero of the Leather-Stocking Tales, Natty Bumppo, Cooper created a vision of the American hunter and frontiersman that would spawn many literary imitations throughout the nineteenth and twentieth centuries. While *The Last of the Mohicans* is perhaps the best known of the series today, thanks in no small part to the 1992 film adaptation, *The Deerslayer* was heralded by D. H. Lawrence as "the most fascinating Leatherstocking book." Lawrence called this novel, the last of the Leather-Stocking Tales to be published but the first in terms of the series' chronology, "a gem of a book" (87). Indeed, *The Deerslayer* has much to offer general readers and students alike.

Yet anyone who wishes to incorporate Cooper's work into the undergraduate, and perhaps even the graduate, classroom needs to reckon with a few issues. First, Cooper's novels are long. The Penguin Classics edition of *The Deerslayer*, the edition used in this essay, comes in at 548 pages. Instructors cannot expect undergraduate students to read the book in a week. Nor can they easily excerpt it, because of Cooper's writing style, which privileges thick description and plots that unfold slowly over many chapters. Moreover, instructors cannot easily turn to short fiction to give students a small dose of Cooper. Unlike other canonical nineteenth-century novelists such as Nathaniel Hawthorne and Mark Twain, Cooper did not write much short fiction, and those short stories that he did write under the pseudonym Jane Morgan differ greatly from many of his longer novels in both content and style. The second issue to consider when teaching Cooper's novels is their accessibility. Students often find it difficult to relate to them from an aesthetic perspective, and many of them would agree with Stephen Railton's assessment that "Cooper, in fact, is one of the few great nineteenth-century American writers who never seems 'modern.'" While highlighting Cooper's tremendous popularity in his own time, Railton suggests that "his aesthetic assumptions, his prose style, and the conventions of character and narrative to which he subscribed are too irretrievably outdated" for his works to ever "enjoy a vogue." While Cooper may never regain his former popularity, Railton proposes that modern readers, "after some adjustment of their expectations and a little practice with Cooper's syntax, could still read eight or ten tales with real pleasure" ("James Fenimore Cooper" 74). The challenge for instructors is how to help students make these adjustments and how to find points of entry into Cooper's works so that students might appreciate at least one of the novels produced by one of the nineteenth century's most important writers.

Focusing primarily on *The Deerslayer*, this essay moves beyond a New Critical approach that privileges close reading and aesthetic appreciation and instead introduces students to one of the key points of debate related to *The Deerslayer* and to the Leather-Stocking Tales writ large: Cooper's representations of Indigenous peoples and the extent to which the novels are complicit in justifying their dispossession of their lands by the United States government during the antebellum period, a process known as Indian Removal. There are other debates that could be explored, for example, those concerning the novel's treatment of Judith Hutter and the work's style (or what Mark Twain dubbed the literary offences committed in *The Deerslayer* ["Fenimore Cooper's Literary Offenses"]), but focusing on Cooper's representations of Indigenous peoples also allows for discussions of gender, sexuality, and literary style. In what follows, I discuss strategies for introducing students to nineteenth-century debates about Indigenous sovereignty and land rights and to contemporary scholarly debates about Cooper's engagement with these issues before turning students' attention to the novel itself. I then highlight sections of *The Deerslayer* that are particularly germane to these conversations. Once students have a grounding in some of the points of contention and have read the novel themselves, they write a position paper in which they offer their perspective on Cooper's portrayal of Indigenous peoples and on whether his novels should be read as an endorsement of Indian Removal. While I devote much of this essay to strategies for the undergraduate classroom, I also offer some suggestions for how this approach to Cooper could be adapted for graduate students.

The goals of this approach, one that uses historical-critical debates as a lens through which to view a particular novel, are to introduce students to one thread of scholarly conversation about Cooper's *Deerslayer* alongside their own reading of the novel and to help them formulate their own positions. Such an approach draws on *They Say / I Say*, by Gerald Graff and Cathy Birkenstein, a frequently assigned book that seeks to help students frame their written academic work as part of an ongoing scholarly conversation, and Graff's essay "Disliking Books at an Early Age." Graff recounts in that essay how his own relation to literature changed when, during his junior year of college, an instructor introduced his class to the debate about the ending of Twain's *The Adventures of Huckleberry Finn*: Does the ending undercut the rest of the novel's critical stance on racism and slavery by making light of Jim's efforts to free himself from bondage? Is the novel itself racist or does it expose and critique the racism of Jim and Huck's society? Graff recalls that being introduced to this debate gave his reading of the novel a sense of focus and "personal engagement" (39) even though the novel's characters and setting were distant from his own life experience. Given the challenges of asking undergraduate students to identify and analyze a scholarly conversation, read a lengthy nineteenth-century novel, and articulate and support an arguable thesis position, I outline here a strategy for modeling the process for students by guiding them to a particular conversation and helping them think through the various perspectives that could be argued.

Teaching Academic Writing through The Deerslayer

The assignment for this unit on *The Deerslayer* is a four-to-six-page position paper related to Cooper's representations of Indigenous peoples in the novel, and the parameters of the paper reflect Graff and Birkenstein's vision of writing as entering a broader "conversation" (20). By assigning a topic, instructors can identify one such conversation and, either by assigning critical texts or summarizing some of the critical positions, help students appreciate the various perspectives in this debate. Working with the templates in *They Say / I Say*, which model key rhetorical strategies for effective academic writing, students can learn to introduce, support, and challenge the views of others and to express their own arguments. The goals of the paper are for students to summarize and analyze critical perspectives, compose their own persuasive argument that responds to the broader critical conversation, analyze representations of Indigenous peoples and issues surrounding sovereignty and land rights in *The Deerslayer*, and demonstrate their understanding of the rhetorical moves outlined by Graff and Birkenstein in *They Say / I Say*. Some instructors might argue that structuring the assignment in this way makes it too formulaic and prevents students from using their creative thinking skills to develop a unique topic.[1] While I agree that such an assignment would likely be too restrictive for students in a graduate course, directing undergraduate students toward a particular conversation rather than asking them to find one on their own decreases the cognitive load for students who are already reading a lengthy novel, presumably one of a series of books assigned in the course. And as Graff and Birkenstein suggest, by assigning templates, instructors can also make visible for students the kinds of rhetorical moves academic writers make when writing a critical essay. Thus, in addition to requiring students to understand a facet of Cooper's work more deeply, the assignment requires them to demonstrate their ability to engage in critical debates and compose persuasive written arguments that speak to the interests of a particular academic audience.

A course designed for graduate students (or perhaps a senior seminar or capstone) could adapt this approach. Rather than having the instructor summarize the critical conversation in such a course, students could engage more directly with secondary sources. After reading *The Deerslayer*, students would be asked to complete a collaborative literature review focused on the critical debate over what Levine has called "Cooper's implication in U.S. empire building, particularly the project of Indian Removal" (164). To complete the review, students would be placed in groups of three to five (depending on the size of the class), and each group would be assigned one article or chapter that takes a position on the topic of Cooper, empire building in the United States, and Indian Removal. Group members would read the critical piece and work together to prepare a summary of that critic's position on the subject, which they would then contribute to a shared document that becomes an annotated bibliography of all the works of criticism under examination in the class. In a subsequent class period, student groups would be rearranged so that each group contains a member who has read and annotated each of the articles. These groups would, in turn, discuss the key issues and points of contention in each article so as to understand the scholarly debate more fully. The class would then reconvene to discuss students' readings of *The Deerslayer* in the light of the critical debate and how and to what extent their initial impressions had been confirmed or challenged or had become more nuanced. Such an exercise mirrors the process that students would then use for their own independent critical essays but leaves space for them to pursue their own topics of interest.

Indian Removal and Literary Context for The Deerslayer

A starting point for the class's exploration of nineteenth-century debates about the sovereignty and land rights of Indigenous peoples is the 1831 Supreme Court case *Cherokee Nation v. Georgia*, the 1835 Treaty of New Echota, and the forced relocation of the Cherokee Nation from its homelands east of the Mississippi in what became known as the Trail of Tears. The legal battles between the Cherokee Nation and the state of Georgia lie at the center of nineteenth-century debates about Indigenous sovereignty and land rights, not because the Cherokee were the only Indigenous people to face forced dispossession, but because of the amount of publicity their case generated. To get a grounding in this history, students could listen to "The Treaty," an episode of the podcast *This Land*, hosted by the Oklahoma journalist and Cherokee citizen Rebecca Nagel, which offers an engaging account of this period in Cherokee history and of the various forces that led to the signing of the Treaty of New Echota and the Trail of Tears. As one episode of a broader story about the case that was eventually decided in 2020 in *McGirt v. Oklahoma*, "The Treaty" also suggests the continued relevance of questions about Indigenous sovereignty and land rights and the stakes involved. Instructors can also point students toward the episode "The Ruling," which analyzes the Supreme Court's determination that large sections of eastern Oklahoma are and have historically been Indigenous lands.[2] Assigning the podcast creates an opportunity to discuss how nineteenth-century representations of Indigenous peoples and their legal struggles over sovereignty and land continue to resonate today. To supplement the podcast, students could read excerpts from *Cherokee Nation v. Georgia* (Peters 2–38, 159–64), in which attorneys and justices of the Supreme Court debate whether Indigenous peoples are capable of forming a nation and what the relation of that nation is to the state of Georgia and the United States, a debate that lands finally on John Marshall's notion that Indigenous peoples constitute "domestic dependent nations" (Peters 161). Then students could be directed to online archives such as the Library of Congress research guide "Indian Removal Act: Primary Documents in American History" and "American Indian and Alaskan Native

Documents in the Congressional Serial Set, 1817–1899," available through the University of Oklahoma College of Law Digital Commons, to find and analyze a primary source related to Indian Removal.

In addition to helping students explore the legal and political debates about Indian Removal, instructors could also briefly survey the nineteenth-century literary landscape that surrounded *The Deerslayer*, which, as Wayne Franklin notes in his recent biography of Cooper, relates directly to Cooper's representations of Indigenous peoples and complicates readings of Cooper as an ardent and explicit proponent of Indian Removal. Franklin asserts that Cooper wrote *Deerslayer* as a response to and a correction of popular understandings of the earlier books in the series and, in particular, of the character Natty Bumppo: "The novel not only finished the series of books—it clarified Cooper's views and enacted them with unmistakable conviction" (*James Fenimore Cooper: The Later Years* 268). Cooper was motivated to issue this corrective, Franklin suggests, by Charles Fenno Hoffman's novel *Greyslaer: A Romance of the Mohawk* and by Robert Montgomery Bird's *Nick of the Woods; or, The Jibbenainosay*, both of which feature characters who resemble Natty Bumppo except for their vitriolic hatred of Indigenous peoples and violence toward them (268–74). Cooper, according to Franklin, sought to defend his own literary reputation against those like Bird, who challenged what they saw as overly positive depictions of Indigenous peoples in the Leather-Stocking Tales (272), and the reputation of Cooper's hero, who was being reimagined in figures like Hoffman's Balt as a violent "Indian hater" (268). Franklin highlights that both Hoffman and Bird were Whigs (unlike Cooper, who was a Democrat) and links their "use of the hunter as a figure of white American expansion" not with "ordinary white settlers . . . but rather those [interests] of the urban capitalist who stood to benefit from land sales and increased commercial activity." Thus Cooper, who engaged in a series of legal disputes with Whig editors in the late 1830s and 1840s, may have had political as well as artistic reasons for revisiting the figure of Natty Bumppo in *The Deerslayer* (Franklin 274).

Representations of Indigenous Peoples in The Deerslayer

There are several key moments in *The Deerslayer* that are germane to an analysis of Cooper's representations of Indigenous characters. The first is the 1850 preface to the novel, in which Cooper summarizes some of the criticisms levied against the Leather-Stocking Tales. He writes, "It has been objected to these books that they give a more favorable picture of the red man than he deserves."[3] To answer these objections, Cooper asserts that it is the prerogative of fiction writers, particularly those who "aspire to the elevation of romances," to offer readers "the *beau-idéal* of their characters" (*Deerslayer* 8). Anyone who expects "that the red man is to be represented only in the squalid misery or in the degraded moral state that certainly more or less belongs to his condition, is, we apprehend, taking a very narrow view of an author's privileges" (8–9).

When discussing this preface, it is important for the class to analyze Cooper's use of the term "red man" and to consider both the offensiveness of this term in contemporary parlance and a historical view of its use. Students could look up the term in the *Oxford English Dictionary* to gain a general sense of its history and could find other examples of nineteenth-century works that employ it. As a parallel, instructors could point out that during the nineteenth-century African colonization movement, African Americans such as David Walker embraced the word *colored* (rather than *African*) as a means of asserting their claim to an American identity and resisting the movement's campaign to remove free Black Americans from the United States and send them to West Africa (Yingling 324–25).[4] Did any nineteenth-century Indigenous writers use the term *red man*, or was this solely a term applied by Whites to Indigenous peoples?

Another important point to consider is that the most racist and violent views in the novel are ascribed not to its hero, Natty Bumppo, but to Harry March (also known as Hurry Harry), who is in many ways framed as an unsympathetic character. Students reading the novel should weigh the extent to which it supports or challenges March's perspectives. March is said to have "all the antipathies and prejudices of a white hunter, who generally regards the Indian as a kind of natural competitor, and not infrequently as a natural enemy" (Cooper, *Deerslayer* 49). March's views on Indigenous peoples are clearly expressed in the third chapter of the novel, in which he asserts the following: "But, this is what I call reason. Here's three colours on 'arth: white, black, and red. White is the highest colour, and therefore the best man; black comes next, and is put to live in the neighborhood of the white man, as tolerable and fit to be made use of; and red comes last, which shows that those that made 'em never expected an Indian to be accounted as more than half human" (50–51).

March's attitudes toward scalping line up with this sense of the subhuman status of Indigenous peoples. March likens scalping to "cutting the ears of wolves for the bounty, or stripping a bear of its hide" (50) and points, as he does repeatedly in the novel, to the bounty paid by colonial authorities for scalps (50–51, 87–88). He also repeatedly classifies Indigenous peoples (and the French) as akin to animals (44). His views are translated into action when he and Thomas Hutter go in search of the Huron camp with the intent of scalping any women and children they find there. Instructors can ask students how readers are invited to feel about March and Hutter and the views March holds. An analysis of March's character would yield some textual evidence of his positive traits: "Hurry, in the main, was a good hearted, as well as good natured fellow" (54). The novel highlights his good looks, height, and strength (20–21, 54, 92–93), and both Hetty and Judith express romantic interest in him at times in the novel (69, 96, 534), although Judith ultimately refuses to marry March in chapter 21 and declares her preference for Deerslayer (572). March's positive traits seem to be far outweighed by negative ones, however. March commits one of the novel's most shockingly violent acts when he kills a Huron woman as a response to being held captive for his and Hutter's efforts to scalp Huron women and children (317–18). He is boastful and at times cruel, mocking Natty for his looks in the third chapter (53–54) and judging Judith throughout the novel for what he perceives to be her vanity and her sexual improprieties (26–28, 55). Reviewing these scenes in class for evidence of March's character opens up an opportunity for students to talk about the representation of Judith, why Natty refuses to marry her, and constructions of gender, female sexuality, and virtue in the novel.[5] Chapters 30 and 31, in which both Captain Warley and Natty reject the idea of marrying Judith, are especially relevant to such a discussion.

March's perspective on Indigenous peoples is countered by Natty's own, which holds that all races have been made by God and that all have different "gifts." Natty espouses a kind of cultural relativism, particularly when it comes to scalping, suggesting that while it is a practice employed by Indigenous peoples, for Whites to do it would be wrong and would constitute a violation of their "gifts" (50). For Natty, the act of scalping, like interracial romantic relationships, is a threat to his sense of himself as a White man. While both March and Thomas Hutter point to the fact that Indigenous peoples take scalps as a justification for the colonies' payment for scalps and their own actions, Natty subscribes to the idea (which he says he learned from Moravian missionaries) "Do as you *would* be done by" (89). He refuses to participate in March and Hutter's attack on the Huron camp. Natty's views on scalping are highlighted in chapter 7, when after shooting Le Loup Cervier (Lynx), he promises not to scalp him and dismisses the idea of claiming a bounty. He asserts, "White I was born, and white will I die; clinging to colour to the last, even though the King's Majesty, his governors, and all his councils, both at home and in the colonies, forget from what they come, and where they hope to go, and all for a little advantage in warfare" (125). Natty's remarks here frame his decision not to take scalps as a move meant to preserve his Whiteness, suggesting his discomfort with certain forms of hybridity, a point he makes explicitly in chapter 15 when he tells Judith, "I hold it is wrong to mix colours, any way except in friendship, and services" (267). He reiterates these points when he refuses to marry Sumac. Students could be asked if such statements communicate something of the same sense of racial hierarchy that March espouses, particularly when considered in the broader context of the novel's representations of Indigenous characters, such as the narrator's reference to Rivenoak as a "rude being of the forest" and the Hurons who accompanied him as "children of the forest" (243).[6] Yet elsewhere Natty contradicts March's racist ideas and appeals to a sense of common humanity: "I look upon the red man to be quite as human as we are ourselves, Hurry. They have their gifts, and their religion, it's true, but that makes no difference in the end, when each will be judged according to his deeds, and not according to his skin" (59). Students should consider to what extent readers are invited to agree with Natty's perspectives and whether there are instances (such as when Natty kills the eagle in chapter 25 and rejects Judith in chapter 32) in which his judgment might be questioned.

It is also helpful to remind students of the trope of the vanishing Indian—the idea that American Indians were destined to disappear from North America, leaving it open for settlement by White Americans—and to point them toward an example of the trope such as Rivenoak's remarks in chapter 27 in which the character, like Tamenund in *The Last of the Mohicans*, forecasts the effects of White settlement on Indigenous peoples and their territorial sovereignty. Addressing Natty, Rivenoak states:

> You are a man whose fathers came from beyond the rising sun; we are children of the setting sun; we turn our faces towards the Great Sweet Lakes, when we look toward our villages. . . . We love most to look in that direction. When we gaze at the east, we feel afraid, canoe after canoe bringing more and more of your people in the track of the sun, as if their land was so full as to run over. The red men are few already; they have need of help. (471)

Set in the year 1740 but written a century later, *The Deerslayer* frames Indigenous peoples as already diminished and needing "help." The ensuing massacre of the Hurons by British troops using bayonets, in which Hetty is killed alongside Huron women and children (521–35), underscores the dangers to which Rivenoak alludes and casts the English as the agents of "vengeance" and "savage warfare" (522), statements that trouble what in the nineteenth century would have been a commonly accepted binary of White civilization and so-called Indian savagery. While the novel earlier describes in graphic terms the scalped head of Thomas Hutter (354), it obscures the aftermath of the massacre, claiming that "[h]appily for the more tender-minded and the more timid, the trunks of trees, the leaves, and the smoke had concealed much of that which passed, and night shortly after drew its veil over the lake" (523). Students should consider the implications of the novel's reluctance to describe the scene and whether shrouding the scene in nature allows the reader a certain freedom to elide the killing of Huron men, women, and children by the English soldiers. This scene opens up questions about the novel's position on Indigenous land claims and whether it participates in discourses of the vanishing Indian that naturalize the dispossession of Indigenous peoples.

Contemporary Scholarship on Cooper and Indigenous Peoples

Once students have some historical context on the removal of Indigenous peoples from their lands and have begun to read the novel itself, it is time to turn to the scholarly debate about the extent to which Cooper's Leather-Stocking novels can be seen to reflect or even to have shaped public opinion about Indigenous sovereignty and Indian Removal. Given the length of *The Deerslayer* and the challenges of fitting it into a syllabus alongside other materials, instructors may need to summarize the positions that scholars have taken on Cooper and Indigenous peoples unless they plan to focus the course on Cooper's works. Numerous scholarly books and articles deal, to some extent, with Cooper's representations of Indigenous peoples and the writer's engagement with nineteenth-century legal and political discourses on Indigenous land rights. I highlight a few works that will help students to appreciate some aspects of this scholarly conversation and to consider their own arguments for their position papers.

Over the last thirty years, a number of scholars have read Cooper's Leather-Stocking novels as both reflecting and shaping nineteenth-century legal and political discourses that sought to bolster White Americans' land claims and to promote the notion of the vanishing Indian. Theresa Strouth Gaul offers a cogent summary of this line of argument in "Romance and the 'Genuine Indian,'" asserting that there was a "collusion between literary policy and national polity during the period immediately preceding the passage of the Indian Removal Act of 1830." She highlights what she sees as the "dominant critical image of Cooper . . . as a prime perpetuator of the myth of the 'vanishing Indian'" (159). Lora Romero argues that Cooper's *The Last of the Mohicans* was one of about forty novels published between 1824 and 1834 that depict an inevitable decline of Indigenous peoples, a phenomenon she describes as a "virtual 'cult of the Vanishing American'" (35). In *The Insistence of the Indian*, Susan Scheckel links Cooper with Chief Justice John Marshall, framing the two as engaged in a shared project of cementing Anglo-American land rights at the expense of Indigenous peoples. Scheckel's reading of *The Pioneers* suggests that, "[l]ike Marshall, Cooper attempted to create a narrative that would legitimate American claims in the face of the nation's Revolutionary origins and the Indians' prior claims" (19). Joshua Bellin's *The Demon of the Continent* positions the publication of *The Last of the Mohicans* in 1826 within the time of Indian Removal, connecting Cooper's novel with the policies and actions of Presidents James Monroe and Andrew Jackson (158). Referring to *The Last of the Mohicans*, Bellin writes that Cooper's efforts to mythologize Indigenous peoples functioned to support a broader national agenda: "the need to create a history free of Indian people, a history that, even as it translated Indian narratives into the source of its own liberty, could claim an immediate relation to a land from which its translations necessarily distanced it" (169). Philip Fisher observes, "Cooper writes *The Deerslayer* in 1840 at the moment of the conclusion of Jacksonian Indian Removal" (36). Thus, a number of scholars have read Cooper as complicit, by virtue of both the content of his novels and the timing of their publication, in the removal of Indigenous peoples from their lands and the perpetuation of ideas of manifest destiny and the vanishing Indian, linking Cooper with major legal and political figures such as Marshall, Monroe, and Jackson.

Robert Levine challenges this line of argument in "Temporality, Race, and Empire in Cooper's *The Deerslayer*." He writes:

> Arguments about Cooper's implication in empire building, particularly the project of Indian Removal, tend to deploy overdetermined critical

> strategies of temporal juxtaposition and homology that take as a given that literary history and the history of expansionism can best be understood, not as a complicated zigzag within a deep and uneven time frame, but as a simple (and symbiotic) chronological unfolding. (164)

Levine argues that his point "isn't that Cooper was a progressive reformer who actively worked for Indian rights, but that the connections most commentators insist upon between cultural context and Cooper's novels have become rigidified to the point that we are virtually unable to see conflict and critique in the Leatherstocking series" (165). One such conflict or tension that Levine highlights relates to the bounties that both the French and English offer for scalps in *The Deerslayer*. While Natty "initially speaks of racial gifts in relation to a providentially ordered nature," he becomes critical of colonial authorities for adopting the practice of scalping and offering bounties (170). Levine also highlights the function of Hist-oh!-Hist (also known as Wah-ta!-Wah) in the novel as a "critic of the violence, racism, and hypocrisy undergirding white empire" (173) and the laudable qualities of Rivenoak. Levine concludes by reminding readers of Cooper's friendship with the Ojibwe writer, minister, and activist George Copway (Ka-ge-ga-gah-bowh), who was a staunch opponent of Indian Removal. Copway wrote the following to Cooper after visiting him in Cooperstown in 1850: "Of all of the writers of our dear native land, you have done more justice to our down trodden race than any other author. . . . By your books the noble traits of the savage have been presented in their true light" (qtd. in Levine 176). Levine makes the point that Copway had likely read *The Deerslayer* and would have been unlikely to offer such high praise of Cooper's oeuvre if he had seen the book as supporting Indian Removal (176). Levine suggests that "within the constraints of his somewhat typically nineteenth-century vision of the Indians, Cooper raises significant questions about Indian policy, and, in a larger sense, about the nature of white empire on the North American continent" (165).

Whether instructors summarize this critical debate for students or ask them to engage scholarly sources directly, giving students a sense of what scholars have to say about Cooper's representation of Indigenous peoples and the writer's engagement with federal Indian policy and with debates over land and sovereignty offers them a point of entry into an ongoing debate whose stakes transcend the pages of an individual novel. The approach outlined in this essay invites students to read *The Deerslayer*, consider key aspects of its historical and critical context, and take a position within an established field of debate, rather than to read the novel and find meaning on their own within its pages. As Graff reflects on his experiences reading *The Adventures of Huckleberry Finn*, "Exposure to that debate [over the novel's ending] made me less of an outsider, provided me with a social community that gave my reading stimulus and direction. . . . Relation to a community made the intimacy of literary experience possible" (43). Fostering this sense of community, I would suggest, is one way to help students appreciate Cooper's novels and hone their academic writing skills.

NOTES

[1] Here, I am following Graff and Birkenstein's advice (78–91) about putting a "naysayer" in the text (78).

[2] I am indebted to my colleague Brianna Burke for drawing my attention to this podcast.

[3] Such criticisms were made by, among others, Lewis Cass, who served as secretary of war under President Andrew Jackson and thus was tasked with carrying out Jackson's plans for Indian Removal. In an article about Cooper for the *North American Review*, Cass writes, "His Uncas, and his Pawnee Hardheart . . . have no living prototype in our forest. They may wear leggings and moccasins, and be wrapped in a blanket or a buffalo skin, but they are civilized men, and not Indians" (376). For more on contemporary reviews of Cooper's novels, see Dekker and McWilliams.

[4] African American periodicals such as the *Colored American* also embraced the term *colored* for this reason; see Yingling 324–25.

[5] For scholarly perspectives on Judith Hutter, see, for example, Baym; Person, "Cooper's Queen."

[6] For a reading of Natty as a "mixed blood," see Mann, "Man."

Cross-Culturalism in *The Last of the Mohicans*

Donna Richardson

James Fenimore Cooper's *The Last of the Mohicans* is a difficult text to teach to undergraduates, not least because it can be read as an apology for colonialism.[1] I have argued at length, however, that such an interpretation underemphasizes the complex ways that Cooper adapts his contemporary British influences (Richardson 221–23). When teaching the book in an Anglo-American survey course for sophomores, as well as to adult learners with similarly limited historical and literary background knowledge, I have found that presenting Cooper's novel through its use of the discourse developed by these British influences not only makes the novel accessible but also demonstrates that Cooper constructively addresses many of the issues central to contemporary criticism.

Critics have noted Cooper's description in the novel of Magua as "[t]he Prince of Darkness, brooding on his own fancied wrongs" (*Last* 284),[2] and they have acknowledged that Cooper is comparing Magua to John Milton's Satan and the displacement of Native American culture to the biblical fall of Adam and Eve.[3] However, Cooper does not, as his interpreters suggest, use a few straightforward allusions to Milton's *Paradise Lost* to imply that Native Americans in the novel deserve their metaphorical expulsion from Eden by the European incursion because they are excessively vengeful. If he did, the logic of the comparison would indeed be regressive, casting the Europeans in the role of Milton's God. But Cooper's extensive, ironic references to the biblical fall owe as much to Samuel Taylor Coleridge and even to the atheistic Percy Bysshe Shelley and Mary Shelley as to Milton. Cooper implies that both Europeans and Native Americans are inevitably in a fallen condition more like that of Babel than Eden, in the sense that every culture participates in the collective sin of ethnocentrism. Even the most enlightened characters in the novel take pride in their "unmixed" ethnicity (*Last* 33); Cooper puns repeatedly on this desire to be "without a cross" (274), suggesting that this desire is the primary impediment to the characters' participating in a cross-racial society. Cooper further implies that the Europeans have aggravated this inevitable sin of pride by trying to play God, imposing their values and institutional practices as if they were divinely sanctioned absolutes, thereby provoking the justifiable rebellion of Magua, the novel's equivalent to Milton's Romantic Satan. When even the best of the Europeans cannot avoid implication in this sinful pride, none of them can make the Christlike sacrifices that could redeem their values; ironically, the only person in the novel who can make such a sacrifice is neither Christian nor European.

I introduce this approach to reading *The Last of the Mohicans* in the context of Romantic revisions of Milton by having students focus on a quotation from Cooper's introduction to the 1831 edition of the novel. In describing what he sees as the character of Native Americans, Cooper makes a criticism that he also applies to Europeans, or "nations of higher pretensions": like these nations, "the American Indian gives a very different account of his own tribe or race from that which is given by other people. He is much addicted to over-estimating his own perfections, and to undervaluing those of his rival or his enemy; a trait which may possibly be thought corroborative of the Mosaic account of the creation" (6). In saying this failing of Native Americans may be "corroborative of the Mosaic account of the creation," that is, Genesis, in which original sin features prominently in the Christian tradition, Cooper identifies this failing with original sin and expands the reach of that sin from individuals to entire cultures. If students have studied Milton, they may be asked how Milton depicts the sin of Satan; if not, the instructor can point out how Milton depicts what Satan represents as all the more attractive because Satan exhibits the qualities of a Greek epic hero — in his resistance to the perceived injustice of a stronger power and his determination to bear suffering in the name of restoring his own rights — but he also asserts his own power and idea of justice as more righteous than any other. The cultural version of such sin is the ethnocentricity Cooper characterizes as the act of overestimating the "perfections" of one's own "tribe or race."

After this introductory class discussion, I divide discussion of the novel into six parts, roughly corresponding to four or five classes. These discussions focus on those debates between characters in the novel in which Cooper invites readers to confront the differing perspectives on the causes and consequences of the American fall.

The Original Sin of Ethnocentricity

For our next class discussion, I pose the following questions to spark student engagement with the issue of ethnocentricity at the beginning of *The Last of the Mohicans*.

> Many writers described the New World as an Eden whose noble savages hadn't been corrupted by European civilization and where it might have been possible to create a more innocent, possibly more multicultural society closer to nature. How is the behavior of European characters in the New World described in the first paragraph of *The Last of the Mohicans*? How does their encounter with a seemingly more natural world and its people affect their behavior?
>
> What biblical and other references does Cooper make in describing the way Europeans have renamed the Lake of the Horican? What values do these new names for the lake signal? In the first dialogue (20–27), how willing and able is each character — David Gamut, Magua, Alice, Heyward, and Cora — to speak other languages and understand other cultures?

> As the Europeans journey into the wilderness, what do they learn are the shortcomings of their own customs? What do they learn from Hawk-eye and the Mohicans about Native American cultures and languages? What do the Mohicans and Hawk-eye learn about Christian values from Cora at Glens Falls?

There is no potential for an Edenic relationship in the opening of the novel. Native peoples are barely mentioned; instead, we learn that Europeans have brought their territorial conflicts with them to the New World, instigated by "the cold and selfish policy of the distant monarchs of Europe," and all they have learned from the "practiced native warriors" are the "patience and self-denial" to be even more destructive than they were before (Cooper, *Last* 11). In an evocation of Babel, the Europeans linguistically impose their values on the landscape, naming Lake Horican Lake George, after the English ruling monarch, King George II, and Lac du Saint-Sacrement (Lake of the Holy Sacrament), after the French practice of converting the Native Americans to Christianity. The opening encounter between the music teacher David Gamut and Magua shows both characters unable and unwilling to understand the first thing about the other's language and culture, and in a subsequent conversation among European characters about Magua's reliability, only Cora questions their distrust of a guide "because his manners are not our manners, and . . . his skin is dark" (21).

The journey of Heyward's party to Fort William Henry is an ironic version of the induction of Europeans into a more primitive culture popularized by Walter Scott's historical novels. Most of what the Europeans discover during their journey to the fort in *The Last of the Mohicans* is the inadequacy of their cultural values, especially Heyward's chivalry and the delicacy of upper-class femininity embodied by Alice. They learn from their multicultural guide, Hawk-eye, that although no culture may be free from ethnocentricity, the language of Native Americans is freer from the curse of Babel, as exemplified in Hawk-eye's comment about Chingachgook, the serpent in this savage garden, who may be violent but whose language is not satanically deceitful:

> the Christian fashions fall far below savage customs in this particular. The biggest coward I ever knew was called Lyon. . . . With an Indian 'tis a matter of conscience; what he calls himself, he generally is—not that Chingachgook, which signifies big sarpent, is really a snake, big or little; but that he understands the windings and turnings of human natur, and is silent, and strikes his enemies when they least expect him. (57)

In turn, Hawk-eye and the Mohicans learn from the example of Cora's Christian courage at Glens Falls. While the warriors prepare to go down fighting when they run out of ammunition, Cora asks them to leave the weaker members of the party behind to save themselves and then to rescue them later. While

Chingachgook sees the natural reason in her self-sacrifice and leaves, Hawk-eye is moved by Cora's "spirit of Christianity" as well as by the "reason" in her self-sacrifice (78).

The Essence of Ethnocentrism: Pride in Being "without a Cross"

But witnessing Cora's courage does not prevent the conventional hero, Heyward, from preferring Alice even after he sees how much better Cora would be as a mate in the New World. This choice, which he makes without knowing of Cora's mixed-race descent, shows how deeply ingrained are his prejudices about gender, which lead him to favor a passive admirer of his chivalric protection rather than an independent woman who questions his conduct. His inability to exceed his cultural boundaries is not, however, only a limitation of a conventional European descendant. It is foreshadowed by the first of several debates in the novel that are centered on the fall of Native Americans, Hawk-eye and Chingachgook's discussion of how the Mohicans lost their land (28–35). Students can focus on questions raised by this painfully contemporary discussion between the most multicultural and multilingual figures in the novel.

> What kind of character is Hawk-eye? How much of a hero is he? If you've seen the 1992 film adaptation by Michael Mann, how is Hawk-eye in the novel different from the character played in the film by Daniel Day-Lewis? What does Cooper say about Hawk-eye in the introduction to the novel?
>
> What do Hawk-eye and Chingachgook each have to say about the reasons for, and the justice regarding, the loss of the Mohicans' land? What biblical parallels can you discern in their discussion? Does the narrator direct any irony toward either character?
>
> How does the discussion between Hawk-eye and Chingachgook foreshadow Heyward's decision to marry Alice? Why does Heyward say he wants to marry her (158)? What does it show about Heyward that he makes his choice before he even knows Cora is of mixed race?

The reader's introduction to Hawk-eye and Chingachgook is a debate that echoes Genesis to the point of parody. Chingachgook recounts how "we were happy" until his people mistook alcohol, Cooper's version of the forbidden fruit, as a means for obtaining spiritual experience; the Mohicans "drank until . . . they foolishly thought they had found the Great Spirit" then sold their land to the Dutch (33). Although Hawk-eye rationalizes this loss by saying that stronger cultures always displace weaker ones, he also concedes his friend's retort that Europeans' use of superior technology is less than honorable (31).

Yet on a more intimate level, each man is isolated by feelings of racial superiority. Chingachgook prides himself on being "an unmixed man" of "the blood of the Sagamores" and apparently believes that his blood cannot survive through intermarriage because it will die out when his son, "the last of the Mohicans," dies (33). Hawk-eye, despite saying "my people have many ways of which, as an honest man, I can't approve," views his white skin with "secret satisfaction" (31). Cooper's 1831 introduction to the novel describes Hawk-eye as less than a model of multiculturalism: "a man of native goodness, removed from the temptations of civilised life, though not entirely forgetful of its prejudices and lessons . . . betraying the weaknesses as well as the virtues both of his situation and of his birth" (7). In the central pun of the novel, Hawk-eye describes himself as a man "without a cross," as one whose ethnic background is not mixed, expressing the racism that prevents him from intermarrying, while figuratively suggesting that his actions fall short of Christian ideals (274). This pun implies that such ethnocentricity is the original sin, and gives new meaning to the modern term *cross-cultural*.

Playing God and Creating a Satan

Unlike the solitary Hawk-eye and Chingachgook, Cooper's Europeans are not otherwise innocent Adams fallen only in their unwillingness to mix intimately with other peoples. In the subsequent debate between Magua and Cora over the Native American fall brought about by the Europeans (102–10), Cooper emulates Coleridge, Lord Byron, and the Shelleys in depicting Magua as a satanic character who is more justified than Milton's Satan in rebelling, because Magua's fall has been caused not by Milton's deity but by imperfect human beings imposing their cultures' institutional practices.

> How is Magua's description of the Native American fall like, and unlike, Chingachgook's? What is Cooper's version of the forbidden fruit?
> What are Magua's accusations against Colonel Munro? What does Magua think would constitute justice for the wrongs he's suffered?
> How successfully does Cora answer Magua's Old Testament idea of justice with her appeal to Christian mercy?

Cooper, who not only read the works of such British Romantic writers as William Godwin and Coleridge but also met them in person, incorporates their revision of Milton's ideas in his novel to suggest he agrees that the human condition is more like that of Milton's Satan than that of Adam in *Paradise Lost*. Such diverse characters as Coleridge's mariner in "The Rime of the Ancient Mariner," Byron's *Manfred*, Godwin's antagonists in *Caleb Williams*, and the creature in Mary Shelley's *Frankenstein* accuse divine or secular authorities of creating an unjust universe in which the characters have acted on the best principles they could discover, fallen unwillingly into disaster and criminality, and then been condemned by those who created the rules in the first place. Frankenstein's creature sums up these experiences by accusing his imperfect creator of his own crimes: "I ought to be thy Adam; but rather I am thy fallen angel, whom thou drivest from joy for no misdeed" (Shelley 90). These characters, like Satan, are seldom entirely sympathetic; many of them, like Frankenstein and his creature, accuse others of being unjust gods while at the same time representing themselves in the language of disobeyed deities. While many of these writers reject Milton's theology in their works, they all reaffirm a Christian ethic in which renouncing self-idolatry and embracing humility and empathy are necessary to end vicious cycles of mutual accusation.

Magua's confrontation with Cora applies the logic of Frankenstein's creature to the representatives of European institutions and values. In biblical language more self-centered than Chingachgook's, Magua tells of being "happy" before the Europeans brought liquor, his abuse of which caused him to be ejected from the Eden of his tribe and driven to join the British army (Cooper, *Last* 102). Firewater is a forbidden fruit in which no God can be found but only the bitter knowledge of European injustice, although, as Chingachgook has learned, alcohol can also provide awareness of one's own responsibility.

But the Europeans did more than provide the temptation for Magua. Colonel Munro, like Milton's God, "made a law" against drunkenness, which Magua condemns because it is not "justice to make evil, and then punish for it." Cora initially defends Munro, her father, but after hearing Magua's argument admits to herself, if not to Magua, that this punishment was an "imprudent severity" that she does not know how to "palliate." Magua argues further that Munro didn't just punish him but flogged him on the back, not only imposing his European laws with unmerciful severity but also disrespecting the Native American warrior code (103).

Magua indicts a European form of justice so fallen that, although its wrongs do not excuse his Old Testament vengeance, no individual could be expected to achieve the Christlike self-sacrifice necessary to redeem it. For Magua, getting "what a Huron loves—good for good; bad for bad" means not only that Cora will be "within reach" to suffer physically when he feels the shame of his scars but also that the "heart of Munro" will realize Magua is doing the same thing to her that her father did to Magua—enacting his culture's justice while violating another's. Cora exhorts Magua to show "how an Indian can forgive an injury" (104), but she can't bring herself to prove that her Christianity is less hypocritical than European law by marrying Magua, as he demands, and in the process converting him while also saving her sister and Heyward. Cora's use of biblical language shows she understands but cannot bear the self-sacrifice her religion requires; she cannot "bow down this rebellious, stubborn pride of [hers], and consent" to, or even articulate, Magua's conditions, even though Alice's and Heyward's lives depend on her consent (109).

The Last Judgment at Fort William Henry: Tragic Responsibility for the Fall

Hawk-eye and the Mohicans may temporarily rescue Heyward's party from Magua and the Hurons, but the Europeans can't be rescued from the larger consequences of European colonial policy and ideology. The subsequent massacre at Fort William Henry is described in the language of the Last Judgment, and ironically, the most conscientious exponents of European ideals are most responsible for the massacre.

> What biblical references do Cooper's narrator, and Hawk-eye, use to describe the massacre? Who does Cooper describe as being judged?
> How, and to what degree, are Magua, the French commander Montcalm, and the British colonel Munro responsible for the massacre? What institutional values do the European leaders represent, and how are those values problematic?

Though the violence of the Hurons is a hellish "jubilee of the devils" (177), it is the Europeans at the fort who are facing their judgment day; they hear Magua's vengeful whoop with a "dread" similar to that "which may be expected to attend the blast of the final summons" (176). Those most responsible for the violence are the exemplary representatives of European policy, Munro and Montcalm. Montcalm most immediately provokes Magua's violence by disrespecting Huron customs regarding warfare and telling Magua that the French have achieved their own purpose by driving the "English squatters" off their land (170), a property-ownership perspective alien to Magua. Montcalm magisterially overrides Magua's objections by calling himself the Huron's "Canadian father" and telling Magua he should "prove" his authority with his people "by teaching his nation how to conduct towards our new friends" (169).

But Cooper's most tragic critique is to make Munro, the only European who sacrifices his personal ethnocentricity by intermarrying, also the proximate representative of self-righteous European law who inspires Magua's satanic anger. Unlike the accused authorities in works by Coleridge, Byron, Godwin, and the Shelleys, Munro is never confronted by his Satan; he never knows what he has done, and his ignorance represents how difficult it is to see one's actions as part of a collective process. The irony in Munro's less-than-divine exercise of authority echoes forth when Alice, in the midst of the massacre, cries out vainly, "Father—father! . . . Come to us, Father, or we die!" (176–77) while her father, though passing nearby, is too "bent on the high duty of his station" to hear her (177). Cooper indicates that even individuals who try to confront ethnocentrism, as Munro does through intermarriage, remain implicated in institutional injustices in ways they could never fully comprehend or control. To redeem this fallen state requires more than sacrificing one's ethnocentrism in personal relationships; it also requires respecting other societies' cultural and institutional practices.

The Trial of European Values

The second half of the novel suggests that there is one character who could metaphorically bear this cross. Ironically, though, it is not Cora, the European character who most closely adheres to Christian values. As Magua and others imply by calling her the "heart of Munro" (104), Cora is the heart of the best European principles her father represents, but her actions are figuratively held hostage because of the way Europeans have exercised those principles. To focus discussion about the trial scene in the second half of the novel (295–317), instructors can ask students the following:

> How are the Delaware portrayed differently from the Hurons? What makes the Delaware leader Tamenund an appropriate judge of whether the Europeans should remain Magua's captives?
> How does Magua characterize each tribe or race in his arguments during the trial scene (300–02)? How much justice is there in Magua's accusations? How do the behaviors of the European men before and during this trial confirm what Magua says?
> How does Cora invoke Christian mercy from Tamenund, and why does Tamenund reject her appeals? How are these appeals undermined by the Europeans' past and present actions, including Cora's?
> How does Uncas succeed in persuading his fellow Delaware first to let most of the captives go and then to help him rescue Cora? How does he address Magua's arguments and the Delawares' accusations? Why does he admit that Cora must remain Magua's captive? How is his behavior respectful of all the cultural values of the different parties?

Disguising themselves as Native Americans, the European rescuers desire only to extract those Huron captives with whose values they already identify. Heyward pretends to be an ally, a French healer—but when taken to help a dying Huron woman, he ignores her to search for Alice. Hawk-eye disguises himself in a shaman's bear suit, appearing as a creature of the forest but remaining a White man without a cross inside. David Gamut's motley disguises are superficial overlays for a character whose religious identity won't allow him to significantly appreciate other cultures. It is fitting that Heyward, Alice, David, and Hawk-eye are judged free to go, literally because they escaped, and figuratively because they are free of desire to interact significantly with another culture.

But it is more difficult to redeem what Cora represents from the legitimate grievances of the neutral Delawares, epitomized by the centenarian chief Tamenund. Like several of Cooper's Romantic influences, including Scott's *Ivanhoe*, Godwin's *Caleb Williams*, and Shelley's *Frankenstein*, Cooper's *The Last of the Mohicans* climaxes in a trial scene where a satanic character deploys his opponent's hypocrisies against what the opponent represents. When Magua comes to the neutral Delaware camp demanding the "justice" of reclaiming Cora as well as those who escaped him (302), the Delawares initially hearken to Magua's diabolical eloquence because his description of the "heart" of the White people confirms their experiences of European duplicity and "gluttony" for land (301). Influenced by Magua's arguments, Tamenund discounts Cora's pleas for Christian "mercy" and her reminder that her father was merciful to Tamenund, because all he can remember is the bigger picture, in which the Delaware have lost everything to the "thirst" of which even the "justest white men" are guilty (304). Tamenund doesn't heed Cora's further plea to identify with the paternal feelings of her father and to release Alice, because he sees himself as the father "of a nation," and from this perspective the Europeans seem a "proud and hungry race" who "claim, not only to have the earth, but that the meanest of their colour is better than the Sachems of the red man" (305). Ironically, Tamenund accuses the Whites of deserving no mercy because they are guilty of the ethnocentrism most immediately represented to him by Cora's rejection of Magua. Magua sneers at Cora for refusing him and denies any self-sacrifice on her part by saying she comes from a "race of traders" that has no principles other than bargaining (313). Cora's case is not improved by Hawkeye, who, after initially refusing to sacrifice his life for Cora's, bargains like an Old Testament Lot—or by Heyward, who insults Magua by trying to bribe him then yells after the departing Magua that he doesn't have to respect the laws of Delaware hospitality.

As Cora says to Tamenund, the only one who has a right to speak in favor of justice toward the captives is one who has honored both cultures—"one of thine own people," Uncas (305). When caught by the Hurons, Uncas wins their respect by displaying courage in the face of their torture. He later shows a different kind of courage when facing his cousins, the Delaware. His status as a Mohican sagamore is confirmed not merely by his tattoo but also by his courage in the face of false accusations against him and others. He also upholds the honor of the Delawares, and implicitly acknowledges the partial justice of Magua's accusations, by letting Magua take Cora, according to the "inviolable laws of Indian hospitality" (317). As soon as the demands of these laws are fulfilled, however, Uncas raises a war party and sacrifices his own life attempting to save Cora, implying that some European ideals are still worth emulating and dying to redeem.

The courage Uncas displays and his impartial dispensing of justice reveal the relative merits of Magua's, Cora's, and his own motives, so that his people support his attempt to free Cora. At the end of the novel his sacrifice, along with Cora's actions, reconciles the spirit of the Delaware, represented by the women of the tribe, to his and Cora's intermarriage in the afterlife, the only place where, as her "heart-broken" father says, "we may assemble around [God's] throne, without distinction of sex, or rank, or color!" (347).

Cooper's Significance Today

For our final in-class discussion, I offer the following questions to prompt students to consider the end of *The Last of the Mohicans* and the relevance of the novel to contemporary issues of cultural or ethnic conflict.

> How does Cooper portray the reaction of the Delaware women to Uncas's and Cora's deaths? What final judgments do Munro, Hawk-eye, and Chingachgook make about the meaning of these deaths? Does the end offer any hope that Cora's and Uncas's examples could be applied usefully to future ethnic conflicts?
>
> How do current debates about diversity echo issues raised by Cooper? Do well-meaning people — and public policies — still exhibit the same kinds of shortcomings Cooper attributes to Hawk-eye and Chingachgook, Heyward, Munro, and Montcalm? If so, what are some examples? Are Cora's calls to return mercy for injustice appropriate to twenty-first-century instances of ethnic injustice? Is Uncas's behavior an appropriate, or successful, way to respond to cultural injustices? Could either character be compared with, say, Martin Luther King, Jr.?

Having given the Romantic devil his due in Cooper's complex use of the biblical fall in *The Last of the Mohicans*, students may conclude that Cooper's political sensitivity to ethnic issues is not up to today's expectations. But more often they find relevant Cooper's effective pinpointing of ethnocentrism as an all-too-human weakness at the founding of America and the novel's portrayal of how that weakness was ironically aggravated in Europeans by the sense of superiority that they attributed to their laws and their religion. I urge students to employ both empathy and critical thinking in analyzing how a character such as Munro, who is conscious of his culture's failings and able to transcend them in his personal relationships, can still impose them on another people with disastrous results, and how this example may translate to understanding how, for example, government officials who imagined America could build democratic copies of itself in the Middle East fail to take the values and wishes of other cultures into account when imposing their ideas of lawfulness — or how police in America similarly fail when enforcing laws. On the other hand, I encourage students to apply to current examples the egocentric contradictions in Magua when he blames the White race for all Native ills (301–01), including his own lack of personal responsibility, returning the same evils in applying his Old Testament justice to relative innocents such as Cora. Students often learn to see the ethical virtues in Cora's application of her Christian values while also recognizing Cooper's point that Christians are actually called to the far harder role of acting like Christ than to the role of playing God. They can see as well Cooper's pointed observation in the novel that Christlike virtues are sometimes exhibited more successfully by someone such as Uncas, who isn't Christian. In the final discussion, I encourage my students to debate among themselves—mirroring Cooper's method in his dialogues—whether any contemporary figures could or should exhibit the willingness to embrace all sides in cultural disputes, even at their own personal expense, to the degree Uncas does. Students debate whether, as the Delaware women imply, Uncas and Cora can be a mitigating model for the future of their own culture.

NOTES

[1] For examples of such readings, see Haywood 172–74; "James Fenimore Cooper"; Flint 139; Tompkins 111, 118.

[2] Citations to *The Last of the Mohicans* refer to the edition published by the State University of New York Press and edited by Sappenfield and Feltskog.

[3] Lawson-Peebles lists scholars who have mentioned Milton in relation to *The Last of the Mohicans*, including John P. McWilliams, Joel Porte, and Robert Milder (136).

NATURAL ENVIRONMENTS

Collective Inquiry and Animal Studies in *The Pioneers*

Keat Murray

Elucidating the often subtle critique of American culture and history in Cooper's novels has been a mainstay of recent Cooper scholarship, but what happens when we look beyond the humans in Cooper's societies to include nonhuman animals who exist integrally and peripherally in those settings? What changes when we recognize the many animals whose interactions with humans contribute to the dynamic social milieus of Cooper's writings? It is true that class discussions and scholarship about *The Pioneers; or, The Sources of the Susquehanna* often do mention nonhuman animals, but important as these animals are, they are typically glossed over as nondescript characters who redirect critics to human social forms in Cooper's novel. A more complete view of the book, subtitled *A Descriptive Tale*, would plumb human-animal relations more deeply to account for the nonhuman animals Cooper depicts with subjectivity, agency, and an expressed stake in the events of the novel. Reading *The Pioneers* from the vantage of animal studies reveals the vital and consequential role of human-animal relations in the novel, underscoring a fundamental tenet of the field: "writing human history is always-already writing about animals" (Benson 5).

The paucity of critical commentary about Cooper's animals leaves room for instructors and students to embark together in a process of collective inquiry that lends learners agency in pursuing fresh questions about animals and humans. That animal studies is generally unfamiliar to students and new to Cooper studies helps instructors and students stimulate inquiry into new critical ground. Seeing how they can fill gaps in critical conversations motivates students to become more astute and creative than when they merely retread a path already worn by previous scholarship.

Collective Inquiry and The Pioneers

Collective inquiry is a teaching methodology and a model of cooperative investigation that can take many forms in group and organizational enterprises for decision-making, goal setting, and problem-solving. In this way, the shared inquiry and ownership that are requisite to successful cooperative activity in the classroom develop in students aptitudes and attitudes that they can transfer quite fluidly to professional and community settings.

In my classroom, collective inquiry typically involves students working in small groups to formulate and pursue researchable questions about a primary text and other texts that inform their efforts to make meaning from critical vantage points. In my early American literature survey course, collective inquiry works especially well, as undergraduates encounter texts, histories, and cultures to which they have had virtually no exposure beyond a middle school curriculum, popular culture, and political discourse. Literature students usually enter the course with a predisposition for a critical approach they have previously practiced, but few, if any, have had experience with animal studies. My approach to teaching the course is not bound to one or two critical perspectives but allows space for various critical strands to take the lead at different points in the course, similar to the way that runners shift positions during a long distance race. The suppleness of my approach accommodates students' preferences to privilege biographical, environmental, social, historical, and cultural contexts. Additionally, my approach cultivates a class culture where experimentation and provisional ideas are welcome and where the interdisciplinary breadth of animal studies across the liberal arts and sciences becomes less daunting and more inviting. And because the critical leanings of student groups vary along with the interdisciplinary directions they take, vigorous debate typically happens about the diverse—and often competing—questions and readings brought to the floor.

Collective inquiry is fostered early in the course when students break into small groups to complete various tasks, and by the time we reach Cooper's novel in the semester, group membership has undergone a few shuffles to keep things fresh. Because students have dabbled in animal studies and other critical approaches since our opening unit on creation and first contact narratives, they are perceptive of depictions of animals and human-animal interactions, alongside matters relevant to other critical perspectives. As we proceed through sets of chapters in *The Pioneers*, I provide manageable excerpts from selected resources—most of which are pre-Darwinian—in five threads: natural history, philosophy, zoology, British and American literatures, and recent scholarship in ethology and animal studies. These resources, which speak to constructs of animals that antedate Charles Darwin's assertions in *The Expression of the Emotions in Man and Animals* that many animal species have acute cognitive and emotional faculties, are shared with all members of the class and, thus, build interdisciplinary contexts for anchoring discussions about Cooper's animals.

To supplement our study of the first four chapters of *The Pioneers*, for example, I assign a few short texts, specifically Rene Descartes's February 1649 letter to Henry More ("Letter"), Philip Freneau's 1782 essay on horse abuse ("Pilgrim"), passages from Peter Edwards's "Nature Bridled: The Treatment and Training of Horses in Early Modern England" (155–58, 163–66), and a short overview of ethology from Margo DeMello's *Animals and Society* (349–53, 359–65). This sample of philosophy, social criticism, animal history, and exposition informs the questions and observations the student groups prepare during a ten-minute meeting at the beginning of class and then share in open discussion. The result is a meaningful, student-driven conversation about inquiries based on multiple texts, which, in turn, encourages close reading and more discussion. Inevitably, students cross-pollinate the conversation with connections they make between the readings, other critical approaches, and topics that spring from reading *The Pioneers*. By the end of the class meeting, not only have we identified substantial topics that register early in Cooper's novel (e.g., property rights, slavery, Native rights, natural conservation, and social class) but also we see how nonhuman animals figure prominently in how those issues unfold.

As the unit proceeds, I assign different readings from the five threads to inform the next series of chapters from *The Pioneers*. As we accumulate texts that bear on our study, groups develop multitiered questions about two or three threads they wish to pursue through additional research. It is satisfying to see how animal studies leads students to delve into academic areas they had previously not encountered. As their understanding of the interdisciplinarity of animal studies grows, they probe research databases, such as EBSCO's, designed for other fields to see how, for example, the biological and environmental sciences, philosophy, history, law, and criminal justice contribute to animal studies.[1] Thus, the structure of collective inquiry with instructor-selected resources prepares a foundation for more genuine student-driven research that often exceeds in quality and scope what students might do in teacher-centered discussions and typical essay assignments in literary studies. In time, the collective nature of the class grows as groups share their findings and broaden everyone's knowledge base, all toward making substantial connections between animal studies and the social, cultural, historical, and environmental aspects of Cooper's *The Pioneers*.

One caveat here is the volume of reading this approach entails. The readings from the five threads add to the demands placed on students, who are already expected to read Cooper's long novel and grapple with the challenges its style presents. To make this workload manageable, I dedicate just over three weeks to the unit and involve students integrally in each class. By the end of the unit, the payoff is manifold. Students become more invested in our work when they have autonomy, are accountable to each other, and become more conversant in their studies. Moreover, they benefit by entering the critical conversation about *The Pioneers*, seeing how collective inquiry in animal studies prompts them to reappraise literary texts and criticism. In the end, student projects, which need not focus on animal studies, take a variety of forms that can be shared in classrooms, at conferences, and on the Internet, all while requiring students to hone skills in collective inquiry that transfer to their personal, professional, and community lives.

Reading Cooper's Animals

A discussion of selected animal traces in *The Pioneers* alongside supplementary texts primes the pedagogical plan outlined above. While fiction by Cooper's American contemporaries generally perpetuated a Cartesian view that denied nonhuman animals subjectivity, reason, and agency, *The Pioneers* undermines Cartesian assumptions and other period discourse that rationalized the exploitation and suffering of animals in service to westward expansion of the United States, urban growth, and rapidly increasing agricultural and industrial commerce. The novel thus contributed to theriophilic writings and cultural practices that had affirmed the rational and emotional capacities of nonhuman animals, like those Erica Fudge and Nathaniel Wolloch have identified in their work about early modern theriophilic writings. In making this contribution, *The Pioneers* implicitly questions the Cartesian view, positioning readers to witness the Templeton settlers' dismissiveness—or obliviousness, as the case may be—to the cognitive, emotional, and moral qualities of nonhuman animals.

Unlike writings that are, as Susan McHugh says, "beholden to [the perspective that] animal-really-means-human" (8), Cooper's *Descriptive Tale* represents animals not as human substitutes or allegories but as species variously interacting with humans—as companions, competitors, adversaries, laborers, and game—and acting on their own interests in those capacities. In advance of the pigeon massacre in chapter 22, which is crucial to ecocritical readings of the novel, the book depicts some nonhuman animals as rational and emotional and as having a conscious stake in their relations with humans. By the time Natty laments the countless "victims" of "wicked" settlers (*Pioneers* 246, 247),[2] the novel has attributed sentience and agency to various animal species, thereby reinforcing its appraisal of humanity's arrogance. This is not to say that Cooper's animals are somehow free of anthropomorphic projections and anthropocentric biases; indeed, the extent to which they are begs interrogation. Still, Cooper's animals differ markedly from those in other literary works of the author's time. Frontier romances by Lydia Maria Child and Catharine Sedgwick, for instance, include many wild and domesticated animals, but none are ascribed subjectivity, cognition, or emotion. Child's animals in *Hobomok* lack thought and mindlessly react to stimuli, as the deer frozen by the "bewitching spell" of a hunter's torch (89). Moreover, in *Hobomok*, the sounds of indigenous animals have no identified purpose for the animals themselves, but for the English colonists, the "dismal" hoot of the owl and the "dismal" growl of the wolf are warnings of untold dangers in dark forests where Native peoples reside (89, 143). Some animals in Child's tale, such as the "clever" fox, reflect conventional anthropomorphic associations (145), and domesticated species are portrayed as one-dimensional instruments of labor and transportation. In Sedgwick's *Hope Leslie* many nonhuman animals live in borderlands between forest and settlement, where they are understood through the colonists' dualistic perception of the world. Tinged with romanticism, Sedgwick's gleeful birds are "worshippers of nature" (63), and other birds sound "ominous" warnings to their human neighbors (339). Elsewhere, references to nonhuman animals are packaged in anthropomorphisms that qualify human behaviors and propensities (51, 52, 197, 239, 279). Whereas Cooper's contemporary writers generally depict animals as Cartesian beings and anthropomorphic projections of humans, Cooper attributes thought, emotion, and will to many of the animals who populate his fiction.

Horses, for example, figure significantly in various sites in *The Pioneers*. Before encountering human characters and the deer shooting scene that sets the plot in motion in chapter 1, readers meet "the noble bay horses" who not only labor for Judge Temple but, as emblems of conspicuous consumption, also mark his wealth and status (15).[3] Later, in chapter 3, readers glimpse the horses' thinking as the equines approach a sharp declivity on the mountain path; knowing precisely what they face, the horses act accordingly: "The horses soon reached a point, where they seemed to know by instinct that the journey was nearly ended, and . . . they rapidly drew the sleigh . . . to the point where the road descended suddenly" (37). Worth examining here are phrases about the horses' consciousness of their location and of the peril of descent. That they "seemed to know by instinct" is remarkable for a couple reasons. In *The Pioneers*, the term "instinct" usually registers cognition and learned experience rather than innate compulsion, and Cooper uses the term more frequently for humans—at least six times—than for nonhuman animals—twice. When animals act instinctively, the narrator speculates on what seems to move them, and this speculation acknowledges the opacity of animal consciousness to humans, even while the narrator reaches tentative conclusions about animal memory and learning. What "instinct" means in *The Pioneers* can also be surmised by what humans do instinctively: one instinctive action is Le Quoi's act of desperation (50), another is a conclusion reached by a colonial community (32), and still others are Richard's prudence in an emergency (51), Ben Pump's return to consciousness after almost drowning (273), and Natty's preparations for a deer hunt (296).

In chapter 4, the human struggle to control the will of the horses becomes contentious. To repeated strikes of the whip, the horses respond as directed until they must step in high crusted snow, at which point "they positively refused to move an inch further" (48). Jones then applies the whip with "injudicious and . . . random blows," but the willful "refractory leaders" endure what they have many times suffered at the hands of Jones rather than submit to him (49).

The brutal treatment in this scene marks a common aspect of life for laboring horses in Cooper's time, to which writers and social critics, such as Freneau, objected. Given that Cooper had an interest in horses and made many sojourns to eastern cities where public discontent over their mistreatment was rising, his understanding of horse cognition likely heightened his sensitivity to their mistreatment as the demand for horse labor in commerce, transportation, and agriculture increased.[4] Human attitudes toward equines were changing: many people began to see horses "more as a technology than as . . . living being[s]" and as "machines . . . in terms of cost and efficiency" (McShane and Tarr 228).[5] Cooper's depictions of horses in *The Pioneers* and other novels counter these hardening attitudes and resist the transformation of the horse into machine technology.

Moreover, Cooper undercuts a deepening assumption in developing Western countries in the nineteenth century that the exploitation and suffering of animals is necessary for human progress (Wolloch 55–56). In the eighteenth century, objections to animal mistreatment came from Quakers who either took, as John Woolman did, a theocentric approach to abuse as a sinful act or objected, as William Bartram did, on empirical grounds that animals were rational, emotional beings with moral sensibility (Walters 165–66). When students consider Cooper's Quaker background and the Quaker voices in the writer's novels, as when Bob Betts in *The Crater* "imperiously demanded . . . we ought to feel for animal suffering" (80), it becomes clear that strands of Quaker thought weighed on Cooper's representations of human-animal relations. Chapter 4 in *The Pioneers*, for instance, follows the lead of Woolman and his fellow Quaker Benjamin Lay in splicing the issue of animal abuse to antislavery discourse by portraying the uncivil Jones using the same whip to threaten slave and horses alike.

In chapter 21, another scene involving horses is revealing. Jones, who repeatedly urges Temple to harvest more trees than would be prudent, rides his horse over deforested terrain that has become "not only difficult, but dangerous" because of the countless stumps and large roots exposed by rapid clear-cutting and accelerated erosion. Jones seems oblivious to the danger, but his horse "toiled [and] trotted with uncertain paces" and "stepped across the difficult passage with the sagacity of a man" (Cooper, *Pioneers* 232). The horse's quiet discernment, in effect, allows a human to remain unaware of the peril of his foolishness. To this point, young Elizabeth unwisely whips her filly to "bound . . . across the dangerous pass" (232), even as the horse, who usually "disdain[s] so humble a movement," decides to step with "unusual caution" (231). Thus, the filly wisely checks her own spirited impatience and that of her rider.[6]

So too does *The Pioneers* question suppositions of the French naturalist Comte de Buffon, who purports in *Natural History* that the American climate produces degenerate life forms (129). As Matt Sivils argues, Cooper repudiates Buffon's notions about American degeneracy in *The Prairie* (11).[7] It can be said that *The Pioneers* initiates Cooper's dispute with Buffon, first by casting environmental degradation as the result of human imprudence rather than a noxious climate, and second by countering what Janie Hinds calls Buffon's insistence that an "impermeable boundary" separates reasoning human beings and nonreasoning animals (658). Buffon resisted classifying humans as animals, while natural historians as diverse as Carolus Linnaeus, Georges Cuvier, and Charles Willson Peale accepted it. For Cooper, a boundary between humans and other animals is often difficult to see. A case in point in *The Pioneers* involves dog companions who exhibit keen awareness and morality. It is, for instance, through the consciousness of Natty's hunting dogs that readers first sense the unchecked brutality in the pigeon massacre: as "the attack commenced" (245), the hounds "crouch[ed] under the legs of their master, as if they participated in his feelings, at this wasteful and unsportsmanlike execution" (245–46). Similar is the moment when Elizabeth arrives home from a long absence and is greeted by the dog Old Brave, who immediately "seemed to know her" (62) and then "looked wistfully" when she leaves the room, "conscious that the house contained something of additional value to guard" (63).

We can also infer Cooper's knowledge of John Heckewelder's accounts of animals in Lenape culture in *History, Manners, and Customs of the Indian Nations*, which Cooper consulted to write about eastern woodland peoples in his novels. Cooper's well-documented reliance on the Moravian missionary Heckewelder's ethnography is evident in *The Pioneers*—in Chingachgook's name and description; in accounts of Native history, practices, and dispossession; and in Natty's proclamations about life and nature. *The Pioneers* is further tinged with Heckewelder's understanding of nonhuman animals in Lenape life: the Lenape hold an anti-Cartesian affinity with creatures, writes Heckewelder, "endowed by the Creator with the power of volition and self-motion." Heckewelder explains the Lenape belief that although humans claim "superior[ity] to all other animals," they are "only the first among equals" and must venerate their "intimate ties of connexion and relationship" with "all animated nature" (254). Several events in *The Pioneers* illuminate the profanation of these "intimate ties." Foremost are repeated references to the decimation of woodlands—landscapes scarred by countless "charred stumps," lumber piles growing faster than settlers can use wood, and maples "wound[ed]" by "careless" tapping (Cooper, *Pioneers* 242, 228, 224). Specific to animals in *The Pioneers* are the massacres of indigenous pigeons and lake fish by arrogant and wasteful settlers, whose behavior stands in stark contrast to indigenous practices (247). And as the caution of discerning horses and the virtue of dogs in the novel illustrate, the capacity for reason, emotion, and morality in Cooper's animals rivals that of their human counterparts, who are "only the first among equals" (Heckewelder 254). Cooper sketches Old Brave in this way, for he possesses "an intelligence but little inferior to [humans]" (*Pioneers* 290), and it is "courage" and "anger" (311)—not mechanical instinct—that move him to defend Elizabeth and Louisa from an aggressive panther protecting her cub. Readers are led to believe that if it weren't for Brave's "pampered laziness" (287), he could have triumphed over the mother panther without the intervention of Natty and his rifle.

Reading the Paratext of The Pioneers

Paratextual sites about animals in *The Pioneers* also work well for collective inquiry in the classroom. Cooper's 1823 preface, for instance, launches the book with a humorous analogy that compares the novelist caught between warring critics to a lock of hay between two asses (3). But perhaps more stimulating is the epigraph Cooper uses to introduce the pigeon shoot in chapter 22, a few lines from William Somerville's lengthy poem *The Chace*, a georgic that depicts animals with rational and emotional faculties.

Students tend to take special interest in the intertextual pairing of *The Pioneers* and *The Chace*. At first glance, the excerpt from Somerville's poem doesn't register animal traces, but reading the section in the poem about a rabbit hunt (bk. 2, lines 119–301), which parallels the pigeon shoot scene in *The Pioneers*, reaffirms the novel's reckoning of human obliviousness to animal suffering. The epigraph runs three lines: "Men, boys, and girls, / Desert th' unpeopled village; and wild crowds / Spread o'er the plain, by the sweet frenzy driven" (Somerville bk. 2, lines 197–99; Cooper, *Pioneers* 243).[8] Like the Templeton residents during the pigeon shoot, Somerville's "wild crowds" abandon their village to witness hounds and mounted huntsmen in pursuit of a female hare. That Somerville's village is "unpeopled" suggests a loss of moral civility that is redoubled in the image of "wild crowds" driven by a "sweet frenzy" to leave town to witness the sportive killing. The poem details the hare's maneuvers to elude her pursuers during the ritualistic hunt, until she becomes exhausted, she is caught, and her body is sliced open by the "impure" hands of the huntsman (bk. 2, line 282) who "dashes down / Her reeking entrails, and yet quivering heart" (282–83). Like the thousands of pigeons on the ground in *The Pioneers*, the hare's body yields little meat; her "puny," "mangled corse" (296, 286) only feeds "the Pomp, / Magnificence, and Grandeur of the Chace" (299–300). Somerville uses the personal pronouns "she" and "her" for the hare (272, 283)—as Cooper does for some animals in *The Pioneers*—and this practice might appear nominal until we consider the hare's rational and emotional sensibilities. Though in great "distress" (217), she remains "[i]ntent" to escape (213), but when "[p]ond'ring" her options (214), she becomes "doubtful what new course to take" (214). Thus, the hare refutes what human "cavillers deny" (207) to enhance their pleasure: "That brutes have reason" (208). Somerville makes plain "the short extent of human thought" that cannot comprehend the "strategems" of those killed by humans (209, 210). Ultimately, the hunter is proud of his kill, though he can only achieve the kill by the power of the horse he rides and the hounds he follows.

The Somerville epigraph invites students to examine how Cooper evokes sympathy for pigeons and other pursued animals in *The Pioneers*. Cooper's readers have ample reason to question the massive slaughter of pigeons that occurs merely as a sportive demonstration of human domination. Students note that their responses to the massacre are shaped by Cooper's characterization of the events as well as by Natty's repeated objections to the "wasty ways" of humans

(265). Moreover, they cite Natty's attempt to sympathize with the birds as an important moment. Here Cooper enlists the frontiersman to consult the victims themselves about the shameful tragedy, only to have Natty's efforts thwarted by their inability to communicate with humans: "looking up with their eyes on me, as if they only wanted tongues to say their thoughts" (248). In chapter 23, readers again witness unnecessary animal suffering, this time on the bank of the lake where a "whole shoal of victims" "were left to flutter away their brief existence" (259) as settlers pluck treasured bass from a bycatch that includes thousands of dying fish (261). And then four chapters later, readers are yet again positioned with a pursued animal, a "noble buck" (295) who in "fear" and "terror" flees his pursuers in one of the novel's most pivotal events.[9] Cooper heightens the buck's disadvantage by setting the chase in the lake, where the deer cannot outswim the hunters' swift canoes, despite his conscious "intention" to do so (296). He is briefly "sustain[ed] against the odds" but then, exhausted, succumbs to Natty's knife (298).

Had the pigeons in chapter 22, like the buck, been killed for their flesh, Natty and his dogs would not have objected to the shoot, but the massacre of the pigeons is not without its complications. Amid Natty's vehement objections to the massacre, Cooper exposes the frontiersman's self-righteousness as complicity when the frontiersman participates in the wrong he condemns. As Natty prepares to exit the field strewn with thousands of dead and dying pigeons, he claims moral superiority to those who needlessly slaughtered the birds, but then he himself adds to the wastefulness by shooting one more pigeon to boast that he only kills what he needs. While Natty's claim to have participated in the massacre on principle instantly becomes a matter of debate in the classroom, students see that Cooper softens objections a moment later when Natty looks into the eyes of the dying birds, who lack the means "to say their thoughts" about the shameful slaughter. That Natty kills one bird for himself, grants pigeons consciousness, and then cautiously avoids stepping on the wounded birds during his exit fails to make a positive impression on the Templeton settlers. Cooper is clear to note that Natty's display of "morality" is "utterly lost on Richard," who proceeds to command the assault with a cannon and countless muskets (250). In the meantime, students see the nuances of the situation more fully. They see, for instance, Natty's resistance to ventriloquizing for the birds as a way for Cooper to create sympathy for the pigeons while circumventing common tropes that cast animals in alterity to humans or that otherwise apply anthropomorphic terms to them.

Along with the Somerville epigraph, the massacres of pigeons and lake fish in *The Pioneers* prompt students to abstract the patterns they find in Cooper's depiction of domesticated and undomesticated species. They notice, for instance, that episodes in which humans kill undomesticated animals, who usually lack subjectivity, are often momentous and dramatically narrated, while domesticated species represented with subjectivity are often less conspicuous and sometimes seamlessly integrated into narration about the human social world. In turn, two notable exceptions—the killing of the noble buck in the lake and Brave's battle with the panthers—undercut the supposition but kindle new discussions about other constellations in Cooper's animal traces. Among the topics that students have pursued are forms of speciesism that show in the novel and the extent to which Cooper's depictions of human nature and animal nature are delineated. The latter topic has ignited much discussion that leads students back to passages in the novel as they seek vestigial notions about human and animal nature from our supplementary pre-Darwinian readings.

By the end of the unit, students grapple with several issues related to human-animal relations in *The Pioneers*. They speculate, for example, about Cooper's intentions in depicting nonhuman animals and are curious about animals in the writer's other novels. To address this question I provide passages from Cooper's oeuvre, which is peppered with significant animal traces.[10] Admittedly, while Cooper does attribute will and faculties of cognition and emotion to some animals in several of his books, *The Pioneers* stands as one of his most compelling ventures in presenting animal subjectivity as a matter of reckoning for readers. Cooper's representations of animals and their conscious lives attune readers to the critical function of animal subjectivities and interests in the novel.

Learning Outcomes

Students tend to respond positively when high expectations are set by the instructor, and collective inquiry is an effective vehicle for cultivating a working environment where the most challenging learning objectives in a course become achievable for all students. The plan outlined above scaffolds cognitive tasks perched atop Bloom's taxonomy of learning objectives, by having students analyze texts and their contexts, evaluate critical discourse, and create new readings of *The Pioneers*.

My approach to *The Pioneers* combines student-centered activities and cooperative learning to develop a community of scholars who share the trials and risks of formulating questions and constructing meaning from primary and secondary texts. Giving students opportunities to discuss ideas in small groups before they present them in a full class forum eases their misgivings about untried hypotheses and permits time to modify and refine them. Providing room for students to experiment with vantage points that defamiliarize human-animal relations by reframing them as constructs with interdisciplinary histories invigorates discussions about the texts students encounter in literature classes and, more broadly, about intersections in their university studies and cultural experience.

Students are generally intrigued by the working assumptions of animal studies. They want, for example, to evaluate the proposition that othering among humans stems from the way humans construct themselves as essentially different from nonhuman animals and, thus, can readily extend this distinction by attributing brute animality to human groups deemed as others. For some students, entrance into animal studies is guided by their familiarity with reading human identities in terms of race, class, gender, and other social differences that, in many ways, echo the logic of human-animal hierarchies. Readings of these identities and their complex intersections are transferrable to human-animal relations, especially the perception of animals as objects or subjects. Whether students adopt animal studies in their course projects is their choice, but pairing animal studies with other approaches during the course allows them to consider the implications of the anthropocentric perspectives that have likely dominated their classroom experience in English studies. In this way, reframing human-animal relations does the double work of unsettling critical perspectives students carry with them and pushing them to think about how they can reposition themselves to enter the critical conversation with a voice of their own.

NOTES

[1] V. Anderson is a useful historiographical resource I keep on hand to inform students' interdisciplinary research in early American animal history.

[2] Citations to Cooper's *The Pioneers* come from the edition published by the State University of New York Press and edited by Beard and colleagues.

[3] Wegener, "Marmaduke Temple," elaborates on Temple's conspicuous consumption.

[4] In 1815, Cooper bore a great loss when one of his horses was stolen (Franklin, *Early Years* 187–91). Cooper's interest in horse racing was, in part, sparked by the legalization of the sport in New York in 1802 and its growth in New York City, where Cooper attended events in 1821, prior to composing *The Pioneers*, and then in May 1823, when he was revising the first error-ridden printing of the novel (367, 385). At horse races held at the Union Course, Cooper was an interested spectator (not an owner or breeder) because of his reporting for *Literary and Scientific Repository* and *American Patriot* (Franklin, *Early Years* 383) and his involvement in the New York Association for the Improvement of the Breed of Horses, which sought to develop husbandry in the area, both culturally and economically (385–86).

[5] P. Armstrong argues "no animal was more central to the commerce of everyday European life than the horse, as a mode of transport, agricultural machine, agent of communication, weapon of war and tool of colonization" (8).

[6] In this way, Cooper's representations of sentient horses critique human imprudence, as does Jonathan Swift's *Gulliver's Travels*, a work Cooper knew well. P. Armstrong argues that Swift's Houyhnhnms and his anti-Cartesian position opened discursive space for other writers to create horses as characters (5–98).

[7] Cooper's critique of Buffon begins in *The Pioneers*, continues in *The Prairie*, and proceeds into *The Monikins*. Sivils closely reads Cooper's more complete critique of Buffon in the landscape of *The Prairie* and in the characterization of Doctor Obed Bat (125–40).

[8] Somerville's phrasing is "by the sweet frenzy seiz'd" (bk. 2, line 199), but Cooper's epigraph has "by the sweet frenzy driven" (*Pioneers* 243).

[9] This scene can be paired with Montaigne's essay "Of Cruelty" (306–18) and its "defenseless" stag who is chased until "out of breath and strength" and then, in tears, is killed (316).

[10] Cooper depicts animals in many of his novels, such as the "sagacious" dogs in *The Headsman* who, with their "inexplicable faculties" (102, 101), save drowning people and guide humans through snowy passes in the Alps (99–106, 323–30); a dog in *The Oak Openings* who is "conscious of the dignity and usefulness of the life he led" (189); bees in the same novel whose hive is "violently invaded" by a bee hunter and who "often know . . . more than a man" (43, 298); beavers in *Wyandotté* who are "cunninger 'an pale face—cunning as bear" (11); the "patient" donkey in *The Prairie* whose "voice" and "courage" save humans from being trampled by bison (Cooper, *Prairie* [Elliott] 172, 201, 202); deer in *The Wept of Wish-ton-Wish* who are "playful creature[s], when not pressed by hunger or by danger" (112); an ox in the same novel who is "not . . . willing" to be yoked (83); the whales in *The Sea Lions* who have become wise to human methods of pursuit and killing (155) and whose "character" and habits Cooper describes at length (157, 157–59); and the goat Kitty in *The Crater*, who is Mark Woolston's "glad" and "happy" "companion" (149, 165, 155).

Environmental Apocalypse and *The Crater*

Matthew Wynn Sivils

Humanity has a talent for disaster. From the great flood in the ancient Mesopotamian poem *The Epic of Gilgamesh*, to the threat of nuclear holocaust, to the quiet cataclysm of anthropogenic climate change, our species has crafted a panoply of literary and actual ends to our world. And many of these ends come in the form of large-scale environmental destruction. "Apocalypse," writes Lawrence Buell, "is the single most powerful master metaphor that the contemporary environmental imagination has at its disposal . . . for the rhetoric of apocalypticism implies that the fate of the world hinges on the arousal of the imagination to a sense of crisis" (285). Few early American authors are as adept at rousing this imagined sense of crisis as James Fenimore Cooper, and his 1847 adventure novel *The Crater; or, Vulcan's Peak: A Tale of the Pacific* is an especially pronounced example. In this maritime tale, Cooper's shipwrecked heroes—through a mixture of agricultural savvy, hard work, and dumb luck—ingeniously terraform a barren island into an earthly paradise. The prosperity and beauty they create draws others, and soon a burgeoning community forms, but with it comes devastation as the new settlers, lured by the prospect of individual gain, exact a heavy toll on the environment. The novel ends with the island and its community swallowed by the sea in what Cooper hints is akin to divine retribution for the sins of the settlers against each other and the land.

Over the following pages I discuss how I incorporate the final chapter of *The Crater* (445–59) into a graduate literature course called Imagining Apocalypse: Narratives of Environmental Catastrophe.[1] Approaching *The Crater* early in the semester, I spend the equivalent of one graduate seminar meeting presenting it as a key work in the American apocalyptic tradition.[2] I pair the class discussion of *The Crater* with a look at Thomas Cole's famed series of paintings, *The Course of Empire*. Also, to help students understand key elements of the genre, we read Buell's "Environmental Apocalypticism" (*Environmental Imagination* 280–308). Bringing these texts into conversation helps us to consider the origins of our present-day obsession with narratives of environmental disaster and to better understand the nuances of more contemporary apocalyptic texts.

Conceptualizing Ruin

Defining the concept of environmental disaster proves an instructive, if challenging, project that unfolds across the duration of the course. For convenience, I treat terms like *apocalypse, catastrophe, calamity,* and *disaster* mostly as synonyms, and I find it helpful to spend a few moments in class to note the linguistic origins of some of them. For example, I point out that, when divided into its constituent parts, the word *disaster* means "unfavorable star" and harkens back to the days when people believed they could read their future in the night sky, just as early seafarers would look to the stars to find their way. Thus, as Marie-Hélène Huet writes, the term *disaster* relates to "having been disowned by the stars that ensure a safe passage through life" (3).

This etymological understanding of disaster hints that such calamities often have at their core the human experience of environmental degradation. In modern apocalyptic narratives the cause of this degradation is usually not some irate divinity but rather blowback from humanity's arrogant tinkering with nature. And it is our ability as human beings to significantly alter our environment that complicates any conception of disasters as somehow divorced from human actions. "In seeking to bend nature to meet human needs," writes Theodore Steinberg, "we have blurred the boundary between the engineered and the natural. What is a natural disaster in a society that has so thoroughly tampered with nature?" (34). This question haunts the course, emerging from every reading and looming over every discussion; it becomes the springboard for more specific inquiries that help guide our understanding of the assigned texts. For example, if human beings are natural, then are disasters borne of human action also natural? If human beings now transcend the natural with our ability to so radically alter our environment that those alterations are visible from virtually any airplane window, then at what point do so-called natural disasters cease to be natural? Why do environmentally apocalyptic narratives remain so popular, especially now when they consistently populate our bestseller lists and appear in films, television shows, graphic novels, and video games? And why do these environmental horror stories—whether born of true events or of zombie-laden nightmares—so fascinate us while we, as a species, seem to all but ignore the actual environmental atrocities happening just outside our door? Cooper's *The Crater* functions as an illuminating point of departure for considering these and other questions about the character of the apocalyptic literary mode.

Readings for the Class on Cooper

I like to divide our in-class examination of *The Crater* into two sections, which might be taught either in succession over a single, longer class or over a couple of shorter meetings. In the first section we focus on how Cooper presents a window into early American environmental thought while also participating in a larger conversation that took place in the antebellum literary and art world, as evidenced in Cole's series of apocalyptically charged landscape paintings *The Course of Empire*. In the second section, we examine these same primary texts through Lawrence Buell's ideas about the five "ingredients" of environmentally apocalyptic literature (305).

While teaching the entire novel would be ideal, the difficulty in finding copies of the book and its length make doing so impractical within the parameters of this particular course, which aims to present students with a wide range of environmentally apocalyptic narratives. I find that I need not assign the entirety of *The Crater* to make use of Cooper's prescient critique of humanity's environmental practices. So instead, I provide students with a quick plot summary of the book and a copy of its cataclysmic final chapter. (I encourage students particularly interested in the novel to view their later seminar paper assignment as an opportunity to focus on the book in depth.) My plot summary makes it clear that Cooper punctuates his maritime adventure tale with a series of natural disasters.

The Crater follows the exploits of a young Pennsylvanian named Mark Woolston, and the narrative essentially begins with Mark joining the crew of a merchant ship, the *Rancocus*. The novel's first calamity occurs when the ship enters an uncharted Pacific reef just as it meets with a violent storm. The storm proves so powerful that in the morning only two crewmen, Mark and a man named Bob Betts, remain aboard—the rest of the crew having been swept overboard and lost. With the *Rancocus* hopelessly stuck in the reef, Mark and Bob decide to take shelter on a nearby small island that turns out to be the cone of a dormant volcano. Taking provisions and equipment from the ship, the two men begin the ambitious but crucial project of cultivating the crater floor of the volcano. Since the ship is carrying both livestock and agricultural supplies, they are well equipped for the task, and soon they are living off the land. This moment of success is short-lived, however, because a hurricane then hits the island and Bob, who is out on a small boat at the time, is swept away. On the heels of this tragedy yet another disaster strikes, this time in the form of an earthquake and the nearby eruption of a once dormant volcano. The earthquake turns out to be beneficial in that it further lifts the island out of the sea, greatly expanding its livable surface area while also giving rise to a thousand-foot-high volcanic spire that Mark calls Vulcan's Peak. In the fashion of a true romantic adventure tale, Bob, who miraculously survived the hurricane, sails back to the island fourteen months later at the helm of a ship called the *Neshamony*. Reunited, and in possession of this new ship, Mark and Bob set about creating a permanent colony, bringing over more settlers and supplies. The island settlement continues to grow and develop. Mark (now Governor Woolston) and his group must overcome several new challenges, including a pirate attack, hostile native people from neighboring islands, and—perhaps most difficult of all—squabbling between the settlers over property rights. Seeking a reprieve from the infighting, Mark, Bob, and their cohort of family and friends leave the island for a lengthy visit to the United States. But the two men eventually return to the island settlement, only to find it entirely gone. After searching the area, they find what they recognize as the tip of Vulcan's Peak breaking through the water. Cooper concludes the book as Mark and Bob realize in horror that a powerful earthquake has relowered the landmass, drowning the colony of five hundred settlers.

I ask students to come to class having read the plot summary, the novel's concluding chapter, and chapter 22 in Cooper's earlier novel *The Pioneers*—in which the villagers of Templeton revel in shooting at a flock of migrating passenger pigeons ([Beard et al.] 243–61). Additionally, students should have read the aforementioned chapter from Buell's *The Environmental Imagination*.

The Crater of Empire

We begin the class discussion by considering the chapter from *The Pioneers* and how its scenes reveal a fledgling strain of conservationist thought that rematerializes in *The Crater*, where Cooper presents an alternative vision of environmental apocalypse, one that includes the annihilation of humanity itself. In discussing the passages from *The Pioneers*, students tend to be surprised that Cooper, a writer so removed from our present-day environmental crises, writes in such a forward-thinking way about the natural world. We talk about how he criticizes the tendency for people to destroy the land they profess to love, even if that love seems reserved for those aspects of the land related to agriculture, hunting, mining, logging, and other forms of resource exploitation. In one of several conservationist vignettes scattered throughout *The Pioneers*, Cooper employs his most famous character, Natty Bumppo, to raise serious concerns about how the villagers of Templeton engage in the wasteful exploitation of nature. For example, when an enormous flock of migrating passenger pigeons flies over their settlement, the villagers begin shooting wildly upward, taking unabashed delight in killing as many birds as possible, even at one point shooting blindly into the sky with an old canon. Witnessing the scene of carnage, a disgusted Natty retorts:

> This comes of settling a country! . . . here have I known the pigeons to fly for forty long years, and, till you made your clearings, there was nobody to skear or to hurt them. I loved to see them come into the woods, for they were company to a body; hurting nothing; being as it was as harmless as a garter-snake. But now it gives me sore thoughts when I hear the frighty wings whizzing through the air, for I know it's only a motion to bring out all the brats in the village. ([Beard et al.] 246)

In class we examine how Cooper's conservationist message, here communicated through the voice of the hunter Natty, criticizes the wasteful and unsportsmanlike harvesting of animals. We likewise talk about Cooper's prescience in specifically warning against the overhunting of the passenger pigeon, which—because of overhunting and habitat loss—went from being the most numerous species of bird on the planet to, by 1914, being extinct.

While likewise concerned with the natural environment in *The Crater*, Cooper creates in that novel what might be termed an environmental morality tale, the conclusion of which draws together a different version of environmental disaster, one cast in almost biblical tones. When Mark and Bob return to the island, they find their thriving settlement replaced by the uncanny aftermath of apocalypse: "As Mr. Woolston approached this as yet strange spot, something in its outlines recurred to his memory. The boat moved a little further north, and he beheld a solitary tree. Then a cry escaped him, and the whole of the terrible truth flashed on his mind. He beheld the summit of the Peak, and the solitary tree was that which he had himself preserved as a signal. The remainder of his paradise had sunk beneath the ocean!" (455). Saving this reveal until the final pages of the book, Cooper presents the destruction of the island settlement and the hundreds of people who lived there as a horrific absence, an environmental erasure, which he hints might be a form of divine punishment for a people who had tainted the success of the settlement with greed and injustice. Still, Cooper emphasizes the geological sublimity of the disaster, which in one elegant stroke plunges the settlement to its doom below the sea: "It is scarcely possible to describe the sickening awe which came over the party, when they had assured themselves of the fatal facts by further observation. . . . These internal fires had wrought a new convulsion, and the labours and hopes of years had vanished in a moment. The crust of the earth had again been broken; and this time it was to destroy, instead of to create." With a lead-weighted line, the shocked protagonists sound the water, finding that what had once been a prosperous island community was now "a hundred fathoms deep in the ocean!" Cooper then writes:

> The lead gave fearful confirmation of the nature of the disaster, the soundings answering accurately to the known formation of the land in the neighborhood of the Peak. But, in the Peak itself, it was not possible to be mistaken: there it was in its familiar outline, just as it had stood in its more elevated position, when it crowned its charming mountain, and overlooked the whole of that enchanting plain which had so lately stretched beneath. It might be said to resemble, in this respect, that sublime rock, which is recognized as a part of the "everlasting hills," in Cole's series of noble landscapes that is called "the March of Empire;" ever the same amid the changes of time, and civilization, and decay, there it was the apex of the Peak; naked, storm-beaten, and familiar to the eye. (456)

Cooper thus ends his novel by citing—if getting the title slightly wrong—Cole's *The Course of Empire*. This highly influential series of five landscape paintings—which I share with my students through the New-York Historical Society Museum and Library website—follows a settlement's progression across the centuries, from a wilderness sparsely populated with hunters (in the painting *The Savage State*), to an agrarian paradise (in *The Arcadian or Pastoral State*), through its development into a magnificent classical city (in *The Consummation of Empire*), and then downward as the city falls prey to war (in *Destruction*), until the series concludes with a quiet scene of vegetation-adorned ruins entirely devoid of human life (in *Desolation*). In class we take time to discuss these paintings individually and then as a collective statement by Cole. Along the way I prime discussion by asking students to write down a sentence or two in response to various prompts such as, "How do Cole's landscape paintings align with Cooper's written portrayal of the landscape in *The Pioneers*?" and, "To what extent may we read these texts as cautionary tales directed to Americans when their nation was in the midst of the Industrial Revolution?" I then ask students to work together in small groups, sharing what they have written down. After they have engaged with one another, we come back together as a class to discuss their findings as a whole.

I find that discussing Cole's paintings in tandem with Cooper's novel helps contextualize the American environmental imagination of the time while also easing the class into a discussion of the nuanced environmental ethic of Cooper's similarly apocalyptic novel *The Crater*. When we turn to *The Crater*, I ask students to again form small groups and to consider questions such as, "To what degree is the disaster that concludes *The Crater* one of human as well as of nonhuman origin, and how might these origins complicate Cooper's message?" and, "Cooper writes that the final view of Vulcan's Peak recalls one of the hills in Cole's *The Course of Empire*, but do you see other similarities between these texts by Cooper and by Cole, especially in how they portray the role of human actions in exacerbating disastrous changes in the natural environment?" I find it useful to remind students that Cooper was writing years before the publication of such game-changing works of environmental thought as Charles Darwin's *On the Origin of Species* and George Perkins Marsh's *Man and Nature*. I provide further context by briefly mentioning some key texts contemporaneous to Cooper's later writing, such as landmark works of environmental science and philosophy like Charles Lyell's *Principles of Geology* and Ralph Waldo Emerson's *Nature*.

A Recipe for Disaster

Having placed Cooper's environmental thought within this larger transatlantic antebellum period, I move to the second part of our class discussion, in which we consider *The Crater* and Cole's paintings in association with Buell's chapter "Environmental Apocalypticism." While Buell only briefly mentions *The Crater* (instead taking as his touchstone Leslie Marmon Silko's *Ceremony* and Rachel Carson's *Silent Spring*), his chapter nevertheless works well to contextualize apocalyptic thinking within the larger American environmental literary tradition. Buell rightly positions *The Crater* in the first wave of American works of fiction to reflect a concern with humanity's interaction with the environment, writing, "Apocalypticism is an old American tradition. . . . Among nineteenth century fiction, the vision of the world or microcosm thereof coming to a cataclysmic end governs Cooper's *Crater*, Poe's *Eureka*, Melville's *Moby-Dick*, Twain's *Connecticut Yankee*, and Donnelley's *Caesar's Column*, to name but a few examples" (296).

One of the main values of having students consider Cooper's *The Crater* in association with Buell's chapter is that each text contributes to an understanding of the development of American environmental apocalypticism as a literary tradition with deep roots in religious thought that has nevertheless undergone a secular ideological shift linked to the rise of a fledgling conservationist ethic. This shift can be traced back to seventeenth-century advances in cosmological thought (by Isaac Newton and others), which had gained considerable momentum in America by the eighteenth and nineteenth centuries through the Enlightenment and its attendant scientific and industrial impact on the human relation with the land. In discussing where this change in apocalyptic thinking began to emerge in America's nineteenth-century literary discourse, Buell writes, "For the first two centuries of settlement, American environmental thought remained millennial rather than apocalyptic, driven by the vision of wilderness as an inexhaustible resource waiting to be transformed into productive farms, towns, and cities, in the spirit of the biblical promise that the desert shall blossom as the rose" (301). By the mid-nineteenth century, however, America's environmental thinking began to demonstrate a change, one presaged by books like *The Crater*.

In class we discuss this change: the emergence of the idea, indeed the fear, that the products of the natural world were finite, that the exploitation of natural resources resulted not only in their depletion but also in the degradation of the environment, that the wholesale hunting and harvesting of various species drove those species to extinction (a concept virtually unknown in previous centuries), and that all of these disastrous eventualities could be traced back to the human exploitation of the land. Buell lists what he terms five literary "ingredients" or "modes of perception" that, as he puts it, "subserve environmental apocalyptic ends" and that are therefore necessary for the birth of an American conservationist ideology. These ingredients include "interrelatedness, biotic egalitarianism, magnification, conflation [and] the sense of immanent environmental peril" (305). My students and I consider Buell's ingredients (which we refer back to in the remainder of the course) as tools for reading both *The Crater* and the environmental apocalyptic tradition in general. I point out how the first four of these ingredients serve to decenter humanity's place in the natural order, to remind us that we are not at the top of some imaginary, Neoplatonic great chain of being, but rather a species with a literal connection to a complex and almost inconceivably large biological network. I explain that despite their conservationist leanings, Cooper's *The Pioneers* and *The Crater* maintain a firm belief in humanity's supremacy over the land and its creatures. So while I address Buell's first four ingredients and their uneven acceptance in the nineteenth century, it is his fifth ingredient—the recognition of an approaching environmental doom—that becomes an especially instructive entry point for considering how environmental apocalypticism emerged in Cooper's *The Crater* years before it became codified in nonfiction antebellum texts. As our class time draws to a close, I ask, "In what ways do *The Crater* and *The Course of Empire* convey Buell's fifth ingredient of an apocalyptic narrative, that is, a 'sense of immanent environmental peril'"? Once we have made some inroads into answering this question,

I conclude by reminding students that while twenty-first-century readers may be disappointed by the limitations of Cooper's conservationist leanings, Cooper was in fact well ahead of his time in proposing a human responsibility to the environment. Ultimately, Cooper's fictionalized landscapes portray an America awaiting the romantic ruin of society.

My goal is that by the end of the lesson students will have made progress toward an appreciation of the American apocalyptic tradition, one that will help them shed light on other texts stretching from Cooper's day to our apocalypse-obsessed present. Our subsequent discussions lean toward the idea that apocalyptic narratives are inherently environmental and that our culture has developed this genre to convey a shared environmental anxiety. As the pieces begin to come together, my students often recognize that a paradox resides at the heart of this tendency toward the dire: that while humanity faces a growing collection of self-inflicted environmental problems, we nevertheless increasingly thirst for stories (as conveyed in our bestselling books, television shows, movies, and video games) about alien attacks, wayward meteors, and, of course, legions of hungry zombies. As we attempt to make sense of this trend, I ask my students if our love of imagined apocalypses amounts to a convenient cultural distraction, one that allows us to engage in benign fantasies while helping us to avoid our actual environmental reality. In some ways then, *The Crater* serves as one of the first in what is now a rich tradition of environmentally infused horror tales, simultaneously leveraging our love of the sensational and our fear of a coming environmental comeuppance. At the end of the course, my students and I consider the idea that humanity mirrors the environmentally myopic settlers of *The Crater* and that Cooper's novel cautions us that if we fail to act for the communal good then humanity risks a dire reckoning.

NOTES

[1] Designed for graduate and advanced undergraduate students, my Imagining Apocalypse course is, as its name suggests, devoted to works of fiction concerned with environmental collapse. Over the semester, I assign texts such as Silko; Le Guin; Vonnegut; Atwood; and McCarthy. I also assign extracts from nonfiction primary texts such as "The Land Ethic" from Leopold (201–26); the chapters "A Fable for Tomorrow" and "Nature Fights Back" from Carson (1–3, 245–61); and the chapter "Down the River" from Abbey (151–95). Along with these primary texts, I incorporate a handful of secondary sources including Steinberg; Garforth; Horner; and Kauth.

[2] At Iowa State University I teach graduate courses that meet once a week for three hours, so my lesson is meant for a class meeting of that duration. It should, however, prove simple enough to modify this module to fit other types of class meetings.

Indigenous American Poetics in *The Prairie*

Betty Booth Donohue (Cherokee Nation)

⊘ James Fenimore Cooper's Leather-Stocking novels are filled with Indigenous American characters who bring into sharp focus the Native presence running through these volumes. Cooper's long-familiar characters—Chingachgook, Hist, Uncas, Rivenoak, Arrowhead, Magua, and the Squaw Hags—do more than enhance the romance of the Leather-Stocking saga with their stereotypical depictions as good or bad Indians. These personae are much more than Native stock characters. They are signifiers of an American Indian literary influence in Cooper's works. The argument that Indigenous Americans have influenced American writers is a proposition that is steadily gaining ground among literary scholars in the United States. Beginning with the Spanish-language writings of Inca Garcilaso de la Vega, a Peruvian of Spanish and Inca descent, there has been an obvious Indigenous element in the literatures of Latin America that critics have found impossible to discount.[1]

From the time of the first European settlements in the Americas, Native and colonial lives were closely intertwined. Each group learned from each other. European Americans today readily acknowledge that Indigenous foods, languages, tools, agricultural practices, roads, political systems, military techniques, and medicines were quickly embraced and put to use by early immigrants. These various artifacts and systems facilitated colonial life and eventually became permanent features of American society. Corn, coffee, cocoa, and potatoes were turned into culinary staples, while words like *puma*, *skunk*, *moose*, and *raccoon* supplemented seventeenth-century English. In the Revolutionary War, the colonists chose to forsake European military formations and adapt Native guerilla warfare tactics, which contributed to their victory (Russell). Benjamin Franklin studied the governing principles of the Iroquois League before helping to draft the Constitution (Grinde and Johansen 20). Later, old Indian trails became major interstates. For example, most of what is now US Route 69, an interstate highway running from Minnesota to Texas, was once the Osage Trace. Doctors continue to use quinine and ipecac to treat malaria and amoebic dysentery, respectively. Whether Americans realize it or not, every time they reach for a bowl of popcorn, sip a Coca-Cola, light a cigarette, or travel Sunset Boulevard from Beverly Hills to Santa Monica, they are dipping into Indigenous material culture.

Indigenous lifeways migrated to all aspects of colonial life, including European literary imaginings. A substantial number of early American writers were touched by Native literary traditions and cultural praxes so that their works exhibit Indigenous influence just as our foods, political systems, and roads do. Many of these Native rhetorical practices have made subtle inroads into Ameri-

Betty Booth Donohue 101

can thought and letters and arguably can be found in the works of a significant number of writers running from William Bradford to Philip Roth.

At the time of first contact with Europeans, Indigenous Americans had a well-developed, highly complex literary tradition that had been verbally passed down for centuries. Indigenous Americans, who were often literate, had developed several different writing systems and mnemonic devices. Examples of some of their early books, such as the Aztec and Maya codices, are presently housed in museums scattered across Europe. Before contact, Native peoples created poetic and prose narratives and devised powerful texts to effect change in people and events. Some of these narratives were written while others were passed on verbally in a body of compositions now referred to as the oral tradition and some of these compositions have since been published.[2]

Cooper wrote during a tumultuous period in the history of American Indian affairs. In the early nineteenth century, Native Americans were being displaced by land takeovers and adverse congressional actions, and they also faced the loss of tribal members due to disease. Cooper was aware of the United States government's various designs to dispossess Native Americans of their land and eradicate Indian life. By 1826, President Thomas Jefferson's assimilation policies had been in place for decades, Indian peoples had been displaced innumerable times, an official relocation policy had been drafted by President James Monroe's administration, and many Native populations had been decimated by war and disease. Cooper anticipated that the government would continue to devise measures to eliminate Native cultures and populations from the continent. Given these circumstances, Cooper believed, as did countless other American writers, that Indians would eventually vanish, and thus his title *The Last of the Mohicans* refers to this anticipated outcome. Happily, however, Indians have not vanished and are still in the Western Hemisphere although in fewer numbers. What is more, Cooper, along with other writers, was able to ventriloquize or subconsciously transmit many Indigenous literary traditions to us through his writing.

To recognize the Native poetics working through Cooper's novel *The Prairie* scholars must first set aside a Western, rational mindset and become receptive to a Native *Weltansicht*. Learning to read like an Indian will not present undue difficulties because Native attitudes and writings often display metaphysical attributes like those of some of today's popular fantasy novels such as *The Lord of the Rings* or *A Game of Thrones*. Second, scholars must recognize Native rhetorical protocols. Third, they must track these protocols through the twists and turns of plot in *The Prairie* and assemble them into a comprehensive, symmetrical Native narrative. In short, readers must learn to approach a text from the margins and read from the outside in. Because feinting is an old Indian trick, it is imperative that readers pay close attention to the text and not be misled by the apparently obvious. For instance, when analyzing a passage like the prairie fire episode in which Hover lifts a bison hide and finds a warrior, consider the bison skin more than the young chief under it (1168–69).[3]

A brief overview of Native literature, such as my volume on the subject (Donohue, *Bradford's Indian Book*), will get readers started. To summarize, traditional Indigenous American works are not mimetic: the representation of reality, however conceived, is not their intent; nonetheless, such Native works are generative and do have a definite purpose. As the Kiowa writer N. Scott Momaday explains, "By means of words one can bring about physical change in the universe" (7). Central to this logos theory is the understanding that the spoken word has power and that certain words, particularly the names of places and individuals, have inordinate power. Speaking such words, or adding breath to them, intensifies their power and allows them to cause other things to move or change. Over the centuries, these inspired words have been integrated into sacred ceremonies that also include ritual protocols and actions such as music, dance, and art. Certain forms of these ritual protocols are now known as medicine.

Analyzing how Native words empower a text is part of reading like an Indian. For instance, *The Prairie* alludes to Cherokees and to several Plains nations: the Konzas (Kaws), Omahaws (Omahas), Osages, Pawnees, several divisions of Sioux, the Dacotahs (Dakotas), and the Tetons, Cooper's name for Lakotas. These names transfer power to the text, as do the names of Native characters like Hard-Heart, Mahtoree, and Weucha. According to E. Soteris Muszynska-Wallace (194–95), the Sioux designations Weucha (Shake Hand) and Mahtoree (White Crane) were taken from Meriwether Lewis and William Clarke's 1814 *History of the Expedition*, while the name of the Pawnee chief Wang-e-wa-ha, or Hard-Heart, derives from Stephen Long's 1823 *Expedition . . . to the Rocky Mountains*. Granted, these names are likely transliterations or approximations of the names of the Native individuals encountered by Lewis and Clarke and by Long, but they represent a genuine attempt by Cooper to replicate actual Sioux and Pawnee verbal utterances in *The Prairie*. Cooper's use of other Native appellations like *Mississippi, Missouri, hominy*, and *moccasin* adds culture, history, religion, tradition, and geographic space to his text. The sounds of these words amplify their power.

Another vital component to Native literature is the creation account. Similar to histories, these accounts call up the prelapsarian past, set the thematic trajectory of an oral literary work, and center the listeners in terms of the geographic locations essential to the narrative. Creation accounts also spell out the listeners' proper and expected relation to human and other life-forms, and they acknowledge the power of ancient deities. Cooper begins *The Prairie* with a creation account describing particulars of the Louisiana Purchase so that immediately the reader is oriented to a specific place and time that will mold and contain the narrative. Cooper rounds out his text with creation accounts for most of his major characters, and all of the characters are given at least a context or history that partially defines them. They are part of a larger text, often a text set in a place designated by Native power words such as Kentucky or Tennessee, earlier Native homelands. Cooper thus perhaps unintentionally adheres to Native rhetorical protocols with his nexus of characters, landforms, and Native names.

In addition to insisting on the power of the spoken word and the importance of history and place, works in the sacred oral tradition always contain land and animal narratives. Native literature asserts that the earth, animals, and human beings should be viewed on one metaphysical continuum: they are one and the same thing. For example, in Cooper's text, Hover, a Kentuckian, and his state, Kentucky, are metaphorically joined. Hover is also closely allied to bees (913), so that we find in the novel a metaphysical continuum of Hover, Kentucky, and bees that represents people, places, and animals. Critical also is the Native belief that the land is the residing place of narrative. When the old gods finished creating the earth, they departed but left their essences in the earth so that now the landscape contains the narratives of the gods, tribal histories, and sacred, primal knowledge necessary for living a life of harmony and balance, the end goal of these narratives. Because the earth is animated by spirits, it can think and act. In tribal sacred literature, the land narrative of an ancient oral composition is considered to be the interpretative center of the work, and the animal narratives in the same composition echo the land narrative's truth. Both land and animals demonstrate agency. They generate plot, and their actions are as important as the activities of human characters, who, unlike human characters in Western literature, are never the prime movers. The animal-like characters are not quadrupeds as we understand them. They are entities who are more than human and who have taken the forms of familiar animals, and they impart wisdom and necessary information to people. They frequently provide a salvific function.

Additionally integral to Native oral literature are a bifurcation of texts into masculine and feminine thematic parts and a reverence for medicine and its creative capabilities. In traditional Native works, respect is paid to the old gods, and readers are exhorted to keep the traditional ways the ancients taught them. These oral compositions are sprinkled with references to tobacco, corn, and wampum. Tobacco is used to lift one's prayers to heaven; corn is an essential food, while corn and corn pollen are Native sacramentals. Wampum refers to Native writing, agreement making, and promises to adhere to agreements made.

Tricksters and contraries appear in these compositions for comic relief and for imparting moral or intellectual lessons. Tricksters help human beings understand life's complexities, perplexities, deceptions, and betrayals even though their methods are sometimes painful. For example, in one oral composition, the Cherokee trickster Rabbit demonstrates that no matter how clever one thinks he is, it is ill-advised to attack a tar wolf (Mooney 271–72). Contraries (called *heyokas* among the Lakotas) are tribal members who do things backward, perhaps in an effort to give others a different perspective on whatever is considered normal. Often they display supernatural powers. As John Plant notes, both Lakotas and Pawnees have their own versions of contraries (16–21).

In addition to old gods, creation accounts, compassionate animals, sheltering landforms, and other rhetorical devices, traditional Native literature also includes a system of constant transformation signaling the belief that nothing ever goes away but continues to exist in different forms. One example of such transformations is Hector, who, over the course of the Leather-Stocking saga, transforms from a pup to an old dog to a preserved dog and presumably to a spirit dog when he accompanies Trapper to the next world. Another example is Inez, who transforms from a beloved daughter to an unfortunate bride to a caged beast to a wife.

Closely allied to the precept of constant transformation is the Indigenous American concept of time as not linear but fixed. What Western civilization categorizes as past, present, and future is only one experience in most Indigenous American worldviews. Everything is always present, but not always visible, just as the stars are always in the sky but are visible only when and where it is dark. As the world turns from night to day, stars seem to go away only to return, as does Hector, whose transformations in *The Prairie* stay true to his essence.

Readers can see how these stylistic devices play out by examining *The Prairie*'s land and animal narratives. A land narrative, in Indigenous American literary theory, is composed of references to features of the landscape: mountains, valleys, vegetation, bodies of water, winds, directions, and the heavenly bodies. The land narrative controls the plot, establishes the themes, and demonstrates a conscious agency (Donohue, *Bradford's Indian Book* 5–6). In *The Prairie*, the land, not Trapper, is the primary character. A passage from the first page of the creation account opening this novel declares that the land narrative is in control of the text: "[The] fertile country [*gives*] . . . command of the great thoroughfare of the interior, and *plac[es]* the countless tribes . . . within our controul; it *reconcile[s]* conflicting rights; . . . it *open[s]* a thousand avenues to the inland trade; . . . [and] it *assures* us a neighbour that will possess our language, our religion, our institutions, and . . . our sense of political justice" (Cooper, *Prairie* 887; emphases mine).

Throughout the novel, the land provides succor, including water and shelter, to all the travelers. Swales, runs, and prairie grasses, either green or blazing, save the major characters from death on more than one occasion. Tall grasses hide Ellen, Bumppo, and Hover from the Sioux until Hector gives them away (920); the grass and fog cover Mahtoree's men in their successful capture of Ellen, Trapper, and Hover (933); and the land's "ragged rock," resembling a human being, a "Pharos" (973, 1014), and the water nearby provide safety for the marooned squatters. The land narrative points out the place where Asa was murdered. At the novel's end, the land receives the bodies of Hector and Trapper and absorbs them into its narrative.

In *The Prairie*, animals, or the more-than-human beings who take animal form, work together with the earth to create a Native text. Numerous reptiles, animals, and insects materialize in Cooper's novel, but Hector and Asinus are perhaps the most essential animals to the plot's development, to reinforcing the novel's themes, and to establishing the Indigenous narrative. They function in the novel much like the more-than-human beings do in primordial times in traditional Native literature. Hector has certain godlike or superhuman characteristics. The progenitor of a noble race of dogs—"truer breed[s] in nose and foot" than other hounds—Hector is a human-like friend, traveling companion, lookout, and issuer of warnings (1007). Prudent and exemplary, he has an affinity with the divine. He has "used and not abused the gifts of his Maker" (987). Hector frequently warns Trapper of impending danger, and he mirrors Trapper in that he "will number his days when his work amongst the game is over" (963). Like a human being, the hound has a command of language and is able to talk to his owner. "[W]hat is it, dog? tell it all to [your] master" (915). Dependable and trustworthy, Hector will "never strike a false trail," and he can sense evil (916). He points out the violated thicket where Abiram killed Asa (1028). After death, Hector's essence remains with Trapper until the bodies of both characters are interred (1310–17).

Obed Battius's little donkey, Asinus, is perhaps the novel's most complicated character. His first introduction to readers suggests that the ass could be a shape-shifter, a being that appears in many Native traditions. The naturalist Battius, after having seen and heard the ass from a distance on the open prairie, declares him to be a monstrous, bat-like beast or a *"Vespertilio; Horribilis, Americanus."* This monster is approximately eleven feet long and eight feet tall with serrated teeth and horns (957). As the "beast" draws nearer, however, Battius's fellow traveler, Ellen, points out that the monster is actually the physician's own ass (958). Here the undulating, shimmering, mirage-creating prairie and the ass work together to advance both character delineation and theme: Battius lives in scholarly isolation separate from the reality of his fellow travelers, and the prairie is a place of mystery and terror as well as peace and beauty.

Second only to Trapper, the ass is a hero. When Middleton, Inez, Ellen, Hover, Battius, and Trapper are caught in a bison stampede, the ass brays, and his "alarming and unknown cry" startles the bison (1007). The beasts divide their route and avoid trampling the principal characters. His timely act thus allows the plot to continue. Although the ass's voice delivers the main characters from certain death, Trapper wants to kill him so that his brays will not reveal their hiding place to enemy Sioux who are hunting nearby. Distraught, Battius pleads that he will "answer for the discretion of Asinus, who seldom speaks without a reason" (1110). Seeing how much Battius loves his animal and recognizing that Asinus has human attributes, Trapper does not kill the ass but orders him tied down and muzzled (1111). Asinus recovers from this indignity and carries his master away from the marauding Sioux in order not to impede the movement of the others of his party. During this episode, Asinus displays human language comprehension and free will. When told to separate from the larger party, Asinus "willingly obey[s]" (1134). He executes Trapper's command to move quickly, but when Battius rides him too hard, Asinus bucks him off. Later the ass lovingly allows Battius to remount, and he continues at a pace that is natural for him (1135).

When necessary, Asinus can move with the speed of a horse. In this particular episode, however, his speed produces unhappy results. After racing across the prairie and becoming too exhausted to continue moving, Asinus requires rest and causes the party to stop. This break results in the group's being caught in a prairie fire, and the group is forced to leave him behind as they escape the blaze (1143–66). Later, the wily Weucha discovers Asinus tethered on the burnt prairie and rides him into Mahtoree's camp, where the Sioux hold the principal characters captive (1178). The Sioux, perhaps as a parody of an ancient Plains ritual, tie a strangely decorated Battius to the ass's back in an effort to deride the naturalist and thus encourage the Sioux women to kill him. In order to keep Battius safe from murderous Sioux women, Trapper keeps Battius tied to Asinus to frighten them with "Evil Spirits" (1224), thus allowing the ass, whose species has never before been seen by the Sioux, to protect his owner. Not only does the strange animal's presence convince the women of Battius's supposed powerful medicine, power typical of a contrary according to Native traditions, but at Trapper's prayerful injunction, Asinus lifts his voice and brays at a critical moment. The unfamiliar sound terrifies the Sioux women, who believe that the voice has loosened Middleton's and Hover's cords, and they scatter, thus giving Middleton and Hover an opportunity to revive themselves (1250–51). At this narrative juncture, Ishmael Bush reappears and takes the travelers into captivity once more, and Asinus is again forcefully relocated (1251–1307). This relocation perhaps anticipates the removal of the Cherokees, Chickasaws, Choctaws, Creeks, and Seminoles from the southeastern United States to Indian Territory, in what is now Oklahoma, which began about seven years after Cooper published *The Prairie*. Like them, Asinus too is eventually relocated to an Indian territory when he is set free from Bush captivity. He is sent to live among the Pawnees, where he spends the remainder of his days on land reserved for Native Americans. There he enjoys his transformation into an Indian pony (1307).

Notwithstanding the Indigenous literary protocols operating in *The Prairie*, language is the subject of the novel. Under the novel's overarching preoccupation with language—human, animal, and unvoiced—runs a thematic tension between orality and literacy, perhaps replicating the tension between Native and European American cultures as they struggle for national ascendancy; however, Native literary theory will argue that here orality and literacy should not be regarded as oppositional binaries (Allen xiv) but rather as different manifestations of the earth's major communication systems. Orality and literacy, with their various adumbrations, dimensions, expressions, and personifications, explore that notion. In many Indigenous American ontologies, thought precedes language, and language creates the earth as well as the animate and inanimate objects found on it. Just as important, in these ontologies both animate and inanimate objects are sentient beings. They have a spirit and possess a language. It is the business of human beings to understand and respond to these complex languages whether they are human, animal, mineral, or vibratory. For example, it is said that Tȟašúŋke Witkó, or Crazy Horse, carried a sacred rock under his arm that protected him from non-Native people (Bray 67). The two were always interfacing, and the warrior was not killed by a White person. In much the same way, Trapper interacts with or listens to the prairie. He responds to its warnings, understands its future travails, and finds comfort in its sights, smells, and sounds. For him, the prairie, like Witkó's rock, is a living entity that gives him peace.

When teaching *The Prairie* in the context of its Indigenous American poetics, instructors may encourage any Native students taking the class to express their insights into the novel. Engaging with Native students gives other students cultural insights that are sometimes difficult to access through print material alone. Instructors might also suggest that students attend Native gatherings such as church services, powwows, or events at various tribal headquarters. Most cities of any size have Native groups that welcome visitors. Crucial to a successful Indigenous reading of *The Prairie* is a visual, geographic understanding of the novel's setting. Students unfamiliar with Nebraska could look online for images of the Platte River and its surrounds. Encouraging students to trace the characters' journeys through the area will cement the geography and the plot in their minds. The Hallmark film adaptation of Willa Cather's *O Pioneers!* would serve as an interesting thematic contrast to *The Prairie*, and it also provides accurate representations of Nebraska's grasslands. For those students quite unfamiliar with nineteenth-century Plains Indigenous peoples, watching films like *Dances with Wolves*, *A Man Called Horse*, or *Little Big Man* can provide helpful images. These films will acquaint viewers with various western Native American nations, their homes, and their animals and with western landscapes. That being said, the anthropological information in the films is occasionally problematic.[4]

Playing into the tension between literacy and orality in *The Prairie* may inspire students to go hear a storyteller perform or to attend a class without taking notes. Then at a later date, from memory they could recite to other class members the points covered in the performance or class. This task would enable students to learn firsthand the importance of mnemonic devices and how the interaction between speaker and listeners—when tone, vocalizations, or pauses are considered—can possibly reveal additional or deeper meanings. Students could also memorize and recite a personally meaningful passage from the novel or a poem that evokes *The Prairie*'s sentiments. The film *Dreamkeeper* accurately supplies interesting Lakota legends and reinforces notions of orality. For a research project, students could learn about White Buffalo Calf Woman and compare her to Cooper's character Inez in *The Prairie*.

Teaching a Native interpretation of Cooper's novel will accomplish several things: it will expose students to Native thought and attitudes; it will attach human faces like Hard-Heart's to the United States government's Indian Removal policy and the harm it caused; it will help students understand through a red lens current issues of race, White privilege, misogyny, land misuse, and the resulting climate change. An Indigenous interpretation of Cooper's texts will open up American literature more generally for students. Seen anew through Native interpretations, the plethora of animals and the obsession with land in other American novels will make a different kind of sense. Ahab's whale in Herman

Melville's *Moby-Dick*, Grey Beaver's wolf dog in Jack London's *White Fang*, Alec's stallion in Walter Farley's *Black Stallion* series, and Alexandra's prairies in Cather's *O Pioneers!* can take on a new and deeper significance.

NOTES

[1] For detailed delineations of such critical evaluations, see Dibble and Anderson; Bigelow; and Herrero.

[2] See Haile; Wyman.

[3] Citations to *The Prairie* refer to volume 2 of *The Leatherstocking Tales*, edited by Nevius and published by the Library of America.

[4] Instructors who wish to teach the Indigenous American poetics in *The Prairie* may consult or assign supplemental readings like Donohue, "Remembering"; Dooling and Jordan-Smith; Fire and Erdoes; Lacey; and Weltfish. These sources contain background information on subjects mentioned but not covered in depth by this essay. *Red Readings*, a 2018 special issue of *Transmotion* edited by Scott Andrews (vol. 4, no. 1), demonstrates additional approaches to Indigenous interpretations of canonical works of American literature. The volumes by Kovach and by Younging are critical for teaching Native persons and grading or editing their writings.

LANGUAGE AND FORM

Interactive Identities: *The Last of the Mohicans* in English Literature Courses for Nonmajors

Elaina Anne Frulla

In the contemporary college curriculum, English instructors often teach required general education literature courses in which most students are largely not English majors. In this situation, I find one common obstacle is student resistance to literary ambiguity. Nonmajors unaccustomed to literary ambiguity are frustrated when they cannot find a definitive meaning for a symbol, character, action, or text as a whole. Students want to force ambiguous elements into tidy categories. They often want characters, for example, to be heroes or villains, leaders or followers, or strong or weak. However, such efforts to categorize run up against the contradictions and inconsistencies endemic to literature.

To help students grapple with literary ambiguity, I teach a unit on James Fenimore Cooper's *The Last of the Mohicans: A Narrative of 1757*, focusing on its exploration of the flexible theme of identity. While exploring the ambiguous identities of Cooper's characters and the world they navigate, students likewise reflect on their own complex identities. Understanding the novel's success in the general education classroom begins with Jane Tompkins's revitalizing chapter on *The Last of the Mohicans* in *Sensational Designs* (94–121) in which Tompkins argues that Cooper attempts to "make sense of how men live in groups" by analyzing character types, categorical transgressions, and the conflicts within and between characters (99). Tompkins describes Cooper as a writer with "an obsessive preoccupation with systems of classification—the insignia by which race is distinguished from race, nation from nation, tribe from tribe, human from animal, male from female" (105). Readings of Cooper's characters as allegorical representatives of a particular theme are compatible with Tompkins's commentary. James Franklin Beard notes that Cooper "deploy[s] characters with greater attention to thematic logic and less to strict probability" and that Cooper's poetic freedom is most visible "in the ruthlessly consistent manner in which characters, conceived in terms of implicit or explicit norms, are employed to serve thematic purposes" (xxxii). Paul C. Gutjahr states that Cooper's characters operate as "allegorical figures who represent the novel's most important themes: civilization, nobility, religion, family, violence, and justice" (Introduction 21).

However, Cooper's seemingly rigid "systems of classification" are not devoid of ambiguity since main characters are seldom able to maintain or represent a singular identity for the novel's duration (Tompkins 105). Students discover that what appear to be easily classifiable surface identities are actually more complicated than initially presumed. To use Nina Baym's phrasing in reference to Cooper's female characters, organizing Cooper's characters "according to types or stereotypes" can be "more confusing than clarifying" (699). Dana D. Nelson notes that while "Cooper's contrasting characters ask more questions than they answer," they offer "a window into changing models of identity and interrelation in the early United States" (125). Yet students find Cooper's ambiguous characters manageable because the novel first establishes a foundation of readily recognizable "systems of classification" for the characters before challenging that foundation (Tompkins 105).

Tompkins claims that *The Last of the Mohicans* serves as a "meditation on kinds," and through repeated contact between "starkly opposed cultural types," it attempts to "calculate exactly how much violation or mixing of its fundamental categories a society can bear" (106). Building on Tompkins's commentary, Nelson explains that Cooper groups characters in the novel "across lines of class, habitude, and race" to "provide readers a series of contrasts that foreground the problems of creating new [American] identities" (125). Such commentary illuminates the unique learning opportunity general education courses present—the diverse groupings of various student majors from the humanities, the sciences, and business transform the space of the classroom into a contact zone that mirrors the contact zones presented in *The Last of the Mohicans*. Since, as Tompkins notes, the novel's "various combinations and confrontations of characters, groupings, and regroupings test the possibilities of coexistence" (113), students can also "test" these possibilities by reflecting on their own experiences of contact and conflict with people of different identities in various social settings. What's more, through analysis of the characters in the novel, students grow to appreciate literary ambiguity as they explore how their own identities defy generic categorization.

One of the most obvious advantages to teaching English majors is that they have willingly chosen to study literature and, therefore, do not need to be convinced of its value. The nonmajors who predominantly fill general education courses, on the contrary, often openly admit they are fulfilling a graduation requirement. The fact that their presence is largely involuntary generates a range of concerns and anxieties for them, especially when they are presented with a novel as intimidatingly big and old as *The Last of the Mohicans*. Below I address common questions students raise prior to beginning the novel: Will I be able to keep up with the reading schedule? Will I understand what I read? Do I need to know a lot about the 1800s to understand what I read? I devote five to six weeks to *The Last of the Mohicans* to keep the reading load for each class session manageable. Of course, the novel's length is not the only impediment students might face in reading it. Students are concerned about their ability to follow the novel's unfamiliar or old-fashioned language, and, undoubtedly, the dense, descriptive, and sometimes convoluted nature of Cooper's writing style slows the reading pace and potentially causes problems in comprehension.

To tackle concerns about reading comprehension, approximately two hours of class time are dedicated to introducing the novel, in which I provide two preliminary handouts to help students feel more comfortable and confident as they begin reading. The first handout succinctly covers historical context, including information on Cooper, the status of the American historical novel in the early nineteenth century, and the political climate of the era. It also highlights some key quotations from Cooper's 1826 preface and 1831 introduction to the novel. The second handout introduces preliminary information on the novel itself, including notes on the writing style (the use of long sentences and highly descriptive language, etc.), pace (initially slow, but rapid in moments of intense action), setting (rural colonial New York during the French and Indian War), characters (their names and occupations and the chapters in which they are introduced), and plot (the basic chronology of events); plot points are summarized by chapter.

Students find particularly useful the background on the novel's characters and plot. The way Cooper presents characters but withholds their names in the novel's early chapters can prove confusing and frustrating for some students. Prior to creating the second prereading handout, I noticed that students had difficulty keeping track of who characters were and when they were speaking, often mixing up characters in discussion. While students were capable of eventually figuring out who was who, their initial confusion not only wasted a lot of time but also deflated their morale, so the second prereading handout identifies the names of key characters and where they are introduced in the novel. Additionally, the multitude of Native tribes introduced in the novel proved overwhelming for students, so the handout also presents the commentary by Gutjahr from his introduction to the Broadview edition of the novel. He writes, "Although the historical reality of the Native American alliances was considerably more complex, Cooper builds his novel around two competing Native American groups: Lenni-Lenape (Delaware), Mohicans vs. Mengwe (Iroquois, Maquas or Mingoes), Mohawks, Oneidas, Senecas, Cayaugas, Onondagas, Tuscarora, Former Hurons" (24). The British-Mohawk alliance and the French preference for the Hurons are established in the handout's brief chapter plot summaries, which are adapted from Warren Walker's *Plots and Characters in the Fiction of James Fenimore Cooper* (86–92). When students have a basic understanding of what's happening in the novel before they start reading, they read with more confidence and devote more energy to elements of the text they might otherwise gloss over. As students grow more accustomed to Cooper's writing style, they rely less heavily on the summaries.

Students are often concerned about how they'll know what to focus on as they read and about whether they'll have to take notes. *The Last of the Mohicans*, of course, presents dozens of avenues for exploration, but the thought of following so many different leads can be overwhelming for nonmajors. Designating a theme to pursue, such as character identity, focuses class discussion and guarantees that students' notes will be relevant to the writing assignments. I recommend that students keep a running list of physical descriptions as well as personality and behavioral traits for each character identified in the novel, including page numbers for reference. Students should also note any descriptions or behaviors that appear to be out of character. Some of my students have even organized this information using Microsoft *Excel* spreadsheets.

Nonmajors in my class often wish to know if they'll be held to the same standards as students majoring in English. I usually train English majors to write thesis-driven literary analyses that are evidence-based and sometimes also research-based, that exhibit originality in critical thinking, and that range in length anywhere from three to fifteen pages. While my nonmajors still write a lot and must support their commentary with textual evidence, I do not require them to write unified multipage essays, develop debatable thesis claims, or engage in extensive research. My nonmajors instead write paragraph-length responses to two writing prompts per week spent with *The Last of the Mohicans*. The course has a participation component, so students must share their responses during class to generate discussion. Sharing responses also helps nonmajors recognize the value of hearing out and responding to their peers' diverse perspectives, which emerge from studying ambiguous elements surrounding identity in the novel.

The writing prompts are of two types. The first type of prompt is informal, and students may format their responses as a bulleted list. Students compose their response commentaries during class in under fifteen minutes. For the prompt, I select three to five passages or scenes and assign students numbers based on the number of passages. Students respond to the passage corresponding with their number. This type of prompt asks students to reflect on language related to identity in a specific passage from the novel. For example, one prompt asks students to compare character reactions to a key event that takes place in the assigned passage. Although these responses are not graded, I do check them for completion.

The second type of writing prompt is formal (responses cannot be formatted as a list) and graded. Students receive a handout with one to three questions, each question requiring a three-to-six-sentence response. These prompts allow students more freedom to select passages of their choice. For example, one prompt asks students to select a passage describing the natural landscape and to consider how the imagery might metaphorically relate to human identity. Students have one week to complete their responses, which are graded according to their ability to respond to the prompt questions directly and to support all commentary with valid textual evidence.

The general education course in which I teach *The Last of the Mohicans* fulfills a graduation requirement that students learn about challenges in the twenty-first century, including cultural diversity, social interaction, and global citizenship. In literature courses fulfilling this requirement, instructors are not limited to teaching twenty-first-century texts and are encouraged to use texts from earlier eras to explore challenges that are still relevant today. Therefore, both types of writing prompts ask students to describe their personal identifications with the novel, unlike the types of literary analysis I train English majors to compose. For example, one prompt asks students to select a character relationship (friendly, familial, romantic, and so forth) and compare it to a personal relationship of their own. Comprehension of the novel's contemporary social relevance is essential to prove the value of literary study to nonmajors. More specifically, throughout their study of the ambiguities surrounding character identity in the novel, students begin to recognize the inherently ambiguous nature of their own identities. Below I outline some of the insightful student commentaries that emerge from several of the formal, graded writing prompts.

Before students can feel comfortable exploring the ambiguities of identity, they need a not-so-ambiguous foundation. The first graded writing prompt covers the first five to seven chapters of Cooper's *The Last of the Mohicans* and asks students to use their notes to establish baseline identities for three of the following characters: Hawk-eye, Chingachgook, Magua, Duncan Heyward, Uncas, David Gamut, Alice Munro, and Cora Munro. Students describe their perceptions of each character and predict the role each character might play later in the novel. Students must consider how the characters are introduced; the terms the narrator uses to describe their appearance, personalities, and behaviors; and the words the characters use to describe one another. Students tend to place characters in familiar generic categories like hero, villain, sidekick, love interest, damsel in distress, voice of reason, comic relief, and so forth.

By drawing on descriptive language, student predictions usually highlight Cooper's use of seemingly obvious character types. Hawk-eye's "muscular" build (*Last* 29), "natural turn with a rifle" (31), and "practiced senses" (48) and Chingachgook's "full-formed limbs" (29), "composed" demeanor (33), and "warrior" status suggest these characters will be the novel's heroic leaders.[1] The fact that Hawk-eye's identity is clearly mixed—the character is a "white man" but socially Indian (29)—poses no problem to establishing his identity. For students, his designation as a hero categorically overrides his mixed affiliations. The same logic applies to other mixed identities of characters. Magua's "sullen fierceness" (17), "fierce countenance" (18), and "cunning" behavior in deceiving Heyward suggest Magua's status as a villain (40). Though Major Heyward is a "soldier in knowledge" (38), Hawk-eye's assessment of him as "over young . . . to hold such rank" suggests he is too inexperienced to lead, making him a sidekick to the heroes (38). Additionally, Heyward's "handsome" and "manly figure" suggest his potential as a romantic lead (23, 27). Descriptions of Uncas, like those of Heyward, emphasize his youth, his "noiseless step" (33), "flexible figure," and "fearless eyes" (52), and they suggest he will be important to the group's safety. But interestingly, students often do not see Uncas as a potential hero but, like Heyward, as another helper to the heroes and usually cite Uncas's deference to Chingachgook's and Hawk-eye's experience and wisdom. David Gamut's "ungainly" physical appearance and "awkwardness" (16), as presented in one of the novel's lengthiest physical descriptions, suggest Gamut could be the novel's comic relief. However, students also note that his sensitivity and "natural taste and true ear" for religious music suggest his potential to provide emotional support for other characters (59), particularly the Munro sisters. While Hawk-eye describes both Munro sisters as "flowers" who were "never meant for the wilderness" (46), students note the physical differences between the "dark" Cora (19) and the "fair" Alice as well as their personality differences (and some students immediately ascertain that Cora is biracial). Alice's "most juvenile" demeanor (18), "timid" nature (60), and dependency on other characters lead students to identify her as the damsel in distress, while they identify the "more mature" (19) Cora as the stronger and more intelligent sister based on her "rich, speaking countenance" (56), "steadiness" (60), and "noble-minded" nature (61). Students frequently label Cora as the voice of reason. Despite the physical contrasts, the beauty of both sisters, who have "light and graceful forms" (27), grants them potential as romantic interests.

During class, students discuss key points from their written responses and work together to develop a mutually agreed on master list of baseline identities for the characters. They discuss the similarities and differences in their predictions, accepting some and dismissing others. This work usually goes smoothly since many students find satisfaction in the process of definitively classifying characters in the familiar generic categories listed earlier.

Later prompts ask students to actively engage with the ambiguities of character identity by considering ways in which the novel challenges or complicates the agreed-on baseline identities of its characters. Instead of allowing students to slip into the convenient tendency to ignore, dismiss, or gloss over moments that interfere with these established baseline identities, prompt questions ask students to examine those moments carefully. Likewise, students reflect on and critically question their own perceptions regarding, for example, why forcing characters into singular categories like good and bad is such a pervasive way of thinking about identity.

Ambiguity itself is an ambiguous concept, so it is important for me to present students with a clear definition to work with. The first informal writing prompt presents students with William Empson's sixth category of literary ambiguity (out of seven), which entails interpreting an element of a literary work that seems to hold a "contradiction" within it (176). In preselected passages, students identify ambiguous elements and explain what makes them ambiguous. A corresponding graded prompt asks students to locate on their own additional passages suggesting character ambiguity. The following examples represent some of the most frequent points students raise in the graded prompt.

One of the first identity contradictions that students notice occurs when Gamut's singing reduces Hawk-eye to "scalding tears" as "he felt his iron nature subdued, while his recollection was carried back to boyhood" (59). Students seldom miss this emotional display, even though it reveals a weakness in Hawk-eye's character, because it only serves to humanize him and does not actually interfere with his status as good.

Producing evidence that could complicate Hawk-eye's status as purely good proves more difficult, not because such evidence is lacking, but because students naturally want Hawk-eye's goodness to remain intact and thus tend to overlook anything that would compromise it. Students are also initially prone to see character inconsistencies as flaws on the part of the author and as damning to the merit of a work because they have been led to believe that a well-crafted fictional character should be consistent. To combat this tendency, I present students with excerpts from chapter 33 of Herman Melville's novel *The Confidence-Man: His Masquerade* (74–77). In this chapter, the narrator steps outside the narrative and directly speaks to readers who may be confused by a character's behavior in the previous chapter: "To some, it may raise a degree of surprise that one so full of confidence, as the merchant has throughout shown himself, up to the moment of his late sudden impulsiveness, should, in that instance, have betrayed such a depth of discontent" (74–75). The narrator continues, "[The merchant] may be thought inconsistent, and even so he is." While "it may be urged that there is nothing a writer of fiction should more carefully see to" and "nothing a sensible reader will more carefully look for, than that, in the depiction of any character, its consistency should be preserved," the narrator rebuts this argument for consistency by citing another common demand of fiction: trueness to life. He explains, "[I]s it not a fact, that, in real life, a consistent character is a *rara avis?*" (75). This commentary helps students begin to understand contradictions as potentially realistic character traits, not as flaws.

When prompted to find evidence of identity contradictions after having discussed the realism of ambiguous characters, students do not come up empty-handed. First, students identify Hawk-eye's repeated and, at times, unnecessarily drawn out dismissal of David's occupation as a psalmist. Hawk-eye, though claiming no "offense," recommends David "part with the little tooting instrument in [his] jacket to the first fool [he] meet[s] with, and buy some useful weapon with the money" (115). Whether or not Hawk-eye truly means no "offense," students find his comments needlessly cruel. They also note that Heyward's shortcomings in navigating the forest are treated more briefly and respectfully by Hawk-eye. Second, students find Hawk-eye's periodic arrogance and concern for his reputation off-putting. During the shooting match with Heyward, Hawk-eye is overconfident in his skill and forgets about his responsibility to protect his companions as he "stubbornly bent on maintaining his identity" (298). Heroes are supposed to be humble and to prioritize protecting the defenseless. However, it is important for students to understand that such elements complicating Hawk-eye's heroic identity do not necessarily make Hawk-eye bad. The problem is the generic nature of ideas like good and bad and the ways readers are prone to insist on conformity to such ideas. Most students easily identify with this point by considering their own behaviors and interactions. We all have moments when we are concerned about our reputations and how others perceive us. We all have moments when we say or do something hurtful or offensive to those closest to us. Such moments reveal the complexity of our identities.

Additionally, students do not deny Chingachgook's wisdom, bravery, and loyalty, but there are aspects of the character that they find unsettling. For example, Chingachgook is described as a "spectre" (45), as a "spectral looking figure" (54), and even as "death-like looking" (113). These ghostlike descriptions make sense in terms of how, as Hawk-eye explains, Chingachgook "strikes his enemies when they least expect him" (57), but students still sense sinister connotations behind such descriptors. Their suspicions are confirmed when Chingachgook kills and claims the "reeking scalp" of a French soldier whom Hawk-eye recently assessed as not a threat. Hawk-eye attempts to justify Chingachgook's behavior, explaining that it "would have been a cruel and an unhuman act for a white-skin; but 'tis the gift and nature of an Indian, and I suppose it should not be denied!" (138). Students are not ready to accept Hawk-eye's justification for Chingachgook's not-so-heroic act. They expect Chingachgook to commit deeds of "apparent cruelty" when there is "real necessity" (47), such as when he kills David's colt, but they fail to see the "real necessity" of killing and scalping a harmless soldier. They also note that the nonthreatening David, though presumed crazy, is never harmed as he meanders throughout the Huron village.

Magua has a complicated identity that brings out the most passionate commentary from students. Though his actions in the present cannot be justified, students empathize with his past as he recalls how the Hurons had "done him wrong" by stripping him of his title of chief, giving his wife to another chief, and exiling him from the tribe (95). Students are particularly moved by Magua's oration in which he describes how he "was born a chief and warrior among the red Hurons of the lakes; he saw the suns of twenty summers make the snows of twenty winters run off in the streams, before he saw a pale face; and he was happy!" until "his Canada fathers," the French, "came into the woods, and taught him to drink the fire-water, and he became a rascal." Students claim there is no substantial evidence proving he was villainous in his years of happiness before the French arrived and "made him a villain" (102). Students also note Magua's "earnest attitude" as he recalls Munro's mistreatment: "Magua was not himself; it was the fire-water that spoke and acted for him! but Munro did not believe it!" Magua's punishment, to be "tied up before all the pale-faced warriors and whipped like a dog," some students argue, is unfit for a transgression in which no one was harmed. They recognize the shame Magua feels for the "marks left on the back of the Huron chief, that he must hide, like a squaw, under this painted cloth of the whites." Even Cora is rendered "silent" and unable to account for the "imprudent severity" of her father, Munro (103).

Randall C. Davis writes that "despite Magua's pointed attack on Euro-Americans for providing liquor to his people ... [Magua's] own description (as well as his own example) of an excited, unpredictable force spurred on by 'fire-water' is hardly calculated to elicit unmitigated sympathy for the 'drunken Indian'" (222). But "unmitigated sympathy" is what many students express for Magua's circumstances. Despite the novel's setting of 1757, students inevitably read the novel's characters and events with a contemporary understanding (e.g., students refuse to see Munro calling his daughters "prattling hussies" as amusing or endearing [Cooper, *Last* 156]). In American society today, alcoholism is understood as a prevalent and debilitating disease that results in consequences for those afflicted by it that are similar to what Magua faces in the novel, such as the loss of a job (for Magua, the loss of his title as "chief" [102]) and the alienation of family and friends (for Magua, exile from the Huron nation and the loss of his wife, who is given away) — consequences that inevitably entail grief and can provoke anger. Students are not surprised that Magua, without resources or support, finds his anger evolving to the extent of murderous revenge. Some students reject labeling Magua as a villain upon examining his past.

Even Alice has a moment in which she contradicts her identity as a damsel in distress. When Cora relays Magua's proposal to take Cora as a wife in exchange for the safe return of Alice to her father, Alice rejects that option, preferring to sacrifice her safety. Cora asks, "What says my Alice? for her will I submit without another murmur," to which Alice replies, "No, no, no; better that we die, as we have lived, together!" (109). Students are surprised not only by Alice's capacity for bravery but also by the fact that the wise and maternally protective Cora would task her sister with the difficult decision.

As students examine evidence of contradictions in the identities of the novel's characters, they also juxtapose those identities. For example, one graded prompt asks students to compare and contrast two characters (comparing Chingachgook and Munro as fathers and leaders is a popular choice) and to analyze what emerges from moments of contact between those characters (e.g., when Munro and Chingachgook interact at their children's funeral). Several students even point out an intriguing similarity between Magua and his seeming opposite, Hawk-eye: an underlying insecurity manifested in their consistent repetition of declarative statements. Just as Magua repeatedly insists, "Magua is a great chief!" (169), Hawk-eye over and over asserts he is "a man without a cross!" (70).

I am always excited to watch students who are not majoring in English become genuinely invested in *The Last of the Mohicans*. During the reading experience, students grow to understand that ambiguity is not a concept limited to the realm of art but also is pervasive in the realities of their lives. Students realize that, like Cooper's fictional characters, they cannot narrowly be defined. They also understand the consequences of forcing identities into generic categories for the sake of convenience. Moving forward with readings in the semester, students more readily embrace ambiguity instead of resisting it.

NOTE

[1] These and subsequent quotations from Cooper's *The Last of the Mohicans* are from the 1983 State University of New York Press edition edited by Sappenfield and Feltskog.

Applying Pedagogies of Recovery to *The Pioneers*

Lisa West

I have found James Fenimore Cooper's novel *The Pioneers* challenging to teach for several reasons: students find Cooper's sentence structure and descriptive expansiveness off-putting; they find the novel's length and the pace of reading overwhelming; they turn to easily accessible supplemental reading guides (published by SparkNotes, SuperSummary, GradeSaver, etc.) as a substitute for their own engagement with the text; and they feel less confident in their reading and thinking because they see those guides as authoritative. These challenges mutually reinforce each other in an unfortunate cycle that continually erodes student agency in approaching the text: students don't like the novel, they don't read it, they turn to supplemental materials, and they feel they cannot write about it in a meaningful way.

As a regular participant in the Just Teach One project and a proponent of the recovery of the works of early American women writers, I am familiar with pedagogical techniques for bringing the recovery of literary works into the classroom. The website *Just Teach One*, directed by Duncan Faherty and Ed White, makes freely available each semester a different out-of-print text written before 1830 so that teachers of early American literature can introduce it to their classrooms. The website asks teachers to blog about their experiences using these new texts to help foster a wider conversation about textual recovery from this period. The website *Sedgwick Stories: The Periodical Writings of Catharine Maria Sedgwick*, directed by Deborah Gussman and supported by other Sedgwick scholars, involves students in transcribing, editing, and annotating out-of-print material. The Wide, Wide World *Digital Edition*, a website directed by Jessica DeSpain, also incorporates undergraduate research and classroom exercises.[1] Conferences of the Society for the Study of American Women Writers and the Society of Early Americanists, as well as smaller author society symposia, increasingly sponsor sessions on innovative pedagogical work relating to lesser-known texts, including assignments that ask students to write notes or annotations for those texts, research historical background or publication history, or engage in other forms of scholarship that are part of the recovery process. I have had success assigning edition or anthology projects that ask students to position a lesser-known or out-of-print text within a constellation of more familiar material. From these experiences, I know that such involvement empowers students and frames their reading, thinking, and writing as both meaningful and part of a collaborative venture.

It is possible to apply some of these pedagogies of recovery to a canonical text like *The Pioneers*. By canonical, I am referring less to notions of literary greatness than I am gesturing toward what Faherty and White refer to as an "operative canon," the limited selection of texts that are made available for the classroom and that are deemed financially sustainable for publishers (107); this canon is perhaps best identified by the presence in the marketplace of "multiple editions of the same set of texts" (106), which tend to be the same texts that generate reading guides by SparkNotes and other publishers. I have used the following questions to consider how I can apply pedagogies of recovery to *The Pioneers*: What adjustments in terms of how I teach would be necessary? Would applying these pedagogies change students' approach to *The Pioneers*? Would students actually read it—and like it—and be motivated to write about it in a thoughtful manner? Would students feel that the work they do on *The Pioneers* is as useful as the work they do on, for example, Susanna Rowson's *Sincerity* or another text without a sizeable digital or critical footprint? The rest of this essay explains the assignment that I most recently used as a midterm assignment for a lower-level undergraduate class, Approaches to American Literature before 1900, and that is the result of several semesters of experimentation. I do not claim that the assignment itself is of primary value; the underlying pedagogical strategies and goals are more important. Consequently, the assignment does not need to be used in its entirety; depending on the class and the students, a single component of the assignment might be sufficient to change the experience of students when they read *The Pioneers*.

The assignment, which I outline in the following handout, asks students to form groups and to collaboratively produce (or build, to use a term from the digital humanities)[2] a critical edition of *The Pioneers*.

> Your group will compile an edition of *The Pioneers* that focuses on your group's chosen research topic and that includes the following:
>> An introduction outlining your goals for the edition and providing both an overall summary of the novel and an introduction to your research topic. Each group member may write a different section of the introduction.
>>
>> Annotations to the novel that range from historical context to comments about literary technique (such as narrative structure) and interpretive comments linking the text to your topic. Think about directing the annotations to future students of this class.
>>
>> A series of related texts at the back of your edition. Each group member should write a headnote and annotations for a related text. You can choose texts from a narrow time frame centered on the publication of Cooper's *The Pioneers*, such as the 1820s, or from a broader time frame, such as 1787 to 1899.
>>
>> A bibliography that includes sources for your annotations and at least three academic peer-reviewed articles or book chapters on your topic. Dictionary or *Wikipedia* entries will not count toward the minimum of three academic sources.

In addition to your critical edition, each group member will write a one-to-two-page reflective essay about the edition, the research process, and related ideas.

I recognized that, since this project was asking students to rely less on the authority of existing editions of *The Pioneers* and more on their own constellation of ideas and chosen texts, we needed to discuss the novel and make consistent efforts at defamiliarizing both it and its critical footprint. Therefore, I focused on that process of defamiliarization for three class sessions before asking students to break into groups. My first intervention in students' reading was to give away the ending of the novel. In earlier iterations of the course, I had pointed out key passages in the novel that drop hints about Oliver Edwards's identity and had alerted students to other essential passages (such as the backstory in chapter 2) that would make more sense after they finished the novel. In current iterations of the course, I tell them about Oliver's identity, the significance of the character's family background, and the resolution of the story before we read the opening sentences. My students never seemed interested in the mystery attached to Oliver's identity anyway. Or, to be more precise, I find they are more interested in tracking the clues from a position of foreknowledge than by simply reading from start to finish. They are fascinated by other characters' assumptions about Oliver and enjoy discussing the likely responses of nineteenth-century readers to the novel's treatment of Oliver.

Once I give away the ending, it is easy to make other interventions to encourage students to read *The Pioneers* in a nonlinear fashion. I try to look at the excerpts I select as isolated passages, not as representative moments in a novel, and to talk less about character as a consistent trait and more about how character works in particular scenes. For instance, I ask students whether "Indian John" is the same character as Chingachgook (Cooper, *Pioneers* [Penguin] 28), and, if he does seem different, whether that difference is because we encounter him in other situations or through the eyes of other characters. I also conduct in-class group exercises in mapping places in the novel (such as the layout of the town or what we know of the inside of the mansion), illustrating passages, creating time lines, and tracking the conversations and relationships that are featured in different public places, such as the inn and the church. These short activities break the hold that reading guides have on my students because they engage students in thinking about writing about place, community building, and social identity. Likewise, I encourage students to question the nation-building paradigms and the celebratory focus on Natty Bumppo that have become the most common elements in the text's critical history and to be open to new ways of reading the text. These preassignment strategies share much in common with what Ryan Cordell, Benjamin J. Doyle, and Elizabeth Hopwood call a "kaleidoscopic pedagogy," one that, like a kaleidoscope, "fractures an otherwise singular entity into an array of seemingly disparate parts that remain in intimate relation" (4).

While our preliminary activities avoid using the novel's chapters as hermeneutic units and challenge the students' sense of the text as a novel, I do provide students with chapter summaries, but I write those chapter summaries to suggest how noncontiguous chapters work together and refer to earlier and later material. While I encourage students to use the summaries I prepare, I also encourage them to use alternative reading guides as long as they are upfront about what they are using and how it informs their reading. When students know *I* know they rely on other materials, those paratexts can become more productive parts of our class discussion. Instead of fighting against all the output dedicated to summarizing or interpreting the novel, we work with it—or challenge it, as the case might be.

After three sessions in which I apply the "kaleidoscopic pedagogy" (Cordell et al. 4), the students form groups to discuss the focus of their critical edition, its intended audience, and other issues. In spring 2019, groups selected Templeton as a republic, race, the intersection of race and religion, and environmental issues as the foci of their respective editions, although I can imagine many other possible areas of focus. We also specified a common audience for all the critical editions: a future section of the course Approaches to American Literature before 1900; I told the class that I will include the most provocative or coherent projects on the course's *Blackboard* website the next time I teach the course. In other years, groups have chosen different primary audiences, ranging from high school readers to the general public to participants in a particular academic program, such as on law, politics, and society or on women's and gender studies.

Guidance and interim deadlines are important. For each class meeting I specify a certain work product (with minimum page length) that needs to be completed, so that each component of the assignment can be drafted with enough time for revision before being assembled into a critical edition. Not only do the interim deadlines allow me to give feedback (and prevent students from procrastinating), they also ensure that each class period we have student work we can review together. The process is iterative; consequently, the students have time to think about the assignment's overall goals as well as to appreciate the varied approaches to each task. In spring 2019, we spent two days in the library, working directly with a librarian on using primary source archives and secondary source databases. While students reported that we could have spent less time overall on the assignment, for this particular semester I designed it less as homework done outside class and more as studio work completed in class. Without careful guidance, on the writing process as well as on the research, I don't think the assignment works as well.

Annotations Component of the Assignment

The annotations component of the assignment surprises me the most because students enjoy doing the historical research for their explanatory notes on *The*

Pioneers. And this component levels the experience of the different student populations who tend to make up a lower-level class; students not majoring in English report feeling more competent since their annotations do not rely on what they perceive as disciplinary expertise, while majors have to do different kinds of research than what they usually do for thesis-driven literary papers. In addition, the annotations component reminds me that the language and historical references in *The Pioneers* are just as new to students as those in, for example, Leonora Sansay's *Secret History; or, The Horrors of St. Domingo*; Salic law, the Haitian Revolution, and the cultural significance of maple sugar are equally foreign to students whether they encounter references to these topics in a canonical or lesser-known text. For me, the biggest payoff of this component of the assignment is the way it shifts the student role significantly from that of a novice reader abiding by materials provided by experts to that of an expert addressing readers who have less experience with the text. Requiring citations for the annotations ensures that even if students find information from another edition of *The Pioneers*, they still have to do additional research to meet the requirements for the assignment. I also encourage students to use *ThingStor*, a new material culture database run by the University of Delaware's Center for Material Culture Studies, even though its interactive list of objects only dates back to 1830. Topics researched by one or more students in spring 2019 include Salic law, passenger pigeons, county court systems, Delaware Indians in New York, girls' boarding schools, Moravian missionaries, and Anglican religion. Originally, I had worried that this component might feel like busywork, but instead students find it engaging, and they clearly connect this kind of research to the other demands of the critical edition assignment.

In addition to short factual or historical annotations, I also ask for interpretive annotations, such as close readings of selected passages from *The Pioneers*. Here is where students in spring 2019 shone. In particular, the two groups focusing on race produced the most thoughtful and nuanced writing about race I have seen from students studying *The Pioneers*. For example, one student constructed a series of readings on the novel's Black characters, focusing on descriptions of affect. In the series, she traced how signs of emotion were connected not to a character's sense of interiority but to external forces: the cold brings tears to Agamemnon's eyes (Cooper, *Pioneers* [Penguin] 18); the social ritual of the turkey shoot makes Brom laugh (193). The series of readings, placed one after another, provides a commentary on how the novel's Black characters are marginalized by being given not only childlike reactions but an incapacity to react to their condition of slavery or racial otherness. Another spring 2019 student provided close readings of Western European and Irish immigrants in the novel, focusing on details of how, for example, Mrs. Hollister's Irishness is a rejection of traditional standards of female virtue. Being freed from a thesis or sustained argument lets students focus on the details of each passage they choose to write interpretive annotations about. Interestingly, in spring 2019, many chose not to arrange their interpretive annotations in chronological order in their critical editions, based on a reading of the novel from start to finish, but instead to provide an order that significantly altered how classmates (and future students) read their material.

Through these writing exercises, students become experts in small moments in *The Pioneers*. Not only do they feel satisfaction in their chosen areas of expertise, but they also have shown me a new way to approach close reading. In the past, either because students were not reading or because they were intimidated by all the critical material on the novel, I felt that students shied away from complex or provocative readings. With this assignment, I feel they are confident in getting past the general comments most often found in reading guides. Without a doubt, writing interpretive annotations results in more nuanced, complex thinking than other writing I have assigned on this text.

Related-Texts Component of the Assignment

If the annotations component requires students to do more historical work, the component on related texts requires investigation into primary sources and material from the 1820s. I ask that students take seriously the notion of a hard copy critical edition if they are submitting the assignment as a hard copy—and to take seriously the notion of a digital edition if they are submitting their project as such. They cannot, for example, just include the entirety of *The Federalist Papers* in a hard copy project but instead have to make decisions about what passages to include, whereas in a digital edition they can embed links in their work. I also ask students to write a headnote or introduction that summarizes the entire related text, explains or glosses the selections that have been included, and connects the selections to *The Pioneers*. This component thus combines research, selection, excerpting, and summary writing. In spring 2019, before turning to Cooper's *The Pioneers*, we used the Hackett edition of *Wieland*, by Charles Brockden Brown, so students had already been exposed to a critical edition before they were asked to create a critical edition of Cooper's novel; I also placed Norton, Bedford, and Broadview critical editions of nineteenth-century novels on library reserve as additional models for ways related texts could be incorporated into editions.[3]

I find this component particularly useful in discussing the relevancy principle of the recovery of texts through the creation of new critical editions. In their critical edition projects, students choose to write about topics that speak to them and that seem current; *The Pioneers*' resurgence as a novel that anticipated later environmental concerns is one of many examples of how a historically distant text can be framed in a way that makes it relevant to students. This component, however, asks that students find relevance in connections not to the present but to contemporaneous documents, debates, conversations, and writings. They engage in what I call horizontal reading, or reading across texts, rather than vertical reading, or reading for depth. Because I read drafts of each component before final revisions, I can ask specific questions directing students to link their related texts more closely to their annotations and to their overall sense of their project. In turn, their work on annotations often influences their research direction and the related texts they want to include in their critical editions. While many of the related texts chosen in my spring 2019 class were those I expected—Thomas Cole's "Essay on American Scenery," chosen by the group focusing on the environment, and Abigail Adams's "Remember the Ladies" letter to John Adams, written on 31 March 1776, chosen by the group focusing on Templeton as a republic—others were not. I was surprised by the selection of the eighteenth-century writings of Moravian missionaries, Susan Fenimore Cooper's letters to her father regarding religion that were written in the 1830s, early-nineteenth-century newspaper articles on immigration, and excerpts from the writings of W. E. B. Du Bois (I gave the relevant group permission to include Du Bois's work, which falls outside the time range I typically allow for related texts). While summary writing may be low on Bloom's taxonomy of learning objectives, in this context summarizing is challenging and rewarding for students. And this component also addresses Bloom's highest level of learning: creating. The related texts component differentiates each group's critical edition from other editions and is a major factor in students having a sense of creating something new rather than responding to something well-worn.

Introduction and Plot Summary Components of the Assignment

The introduction and the plot summary are the first components students draft but the last to undergo revision. I am writing about them last because of their central role in pulling the project together. The first drafts, as expected of initial work, tend to be tentative and generic. I have to encourage students to conduct secondary research to elaborate on key terms or concepts, such as *race*, which was understood differently in 1793, when the novel is set, from how the word was understood in 1823, when the novel was published, and from how it is understood now. My input on this aspect of research is tailored to each group's focus, and I think that makes it more meaningful for students, many of whom use their research for later papers in the semester. In upper-level courses, I would expect a higher standard for the introduction by, for instance, treating it as a kind of literature review related to the group's focus, whereas here I only require three sources to guide the group's work.

The plot summaries can be almost identical from group to group in the first draft. However, students who in the past likely turned to plot summaries as neutral, authoritative supplements to (or substitutes for) reading, soon recognize that the plot summary is, like other forms of writing, interpretive, selective, and not necessarily neutral. Because we spend class time sharing works in progress, students can see the potential for each project and suggest to peer groups how to make their introductory material more distinctive and connected to their project. Word choice, which characters in the novel to name, and which plot points to stress cumulatively make a difference in the shape of each critical edition, and attending to these details in class shows students that their work can be a viable alternative to those reading guides that seem to be factual and authoritative. As Kristina Straub comments in her response to the notion of surface reading, "We are always and never getting it right, and it is this open-endedness and ability to turn corners onto as-yet unimagined questions and answers that I value about my profession" (141); in the case of students, this sentiment might apply to the process of learning from a canonical text.

Does this assignment, as it has developed over several semesters, meet the challenges I set? Responses from spring 2019 suggest that it does. Students' reflective papers report that while students do not really like the novel, they find the assignment a powerful learning experience, and they write with appreciation for the text as well as for their broadened sense of the role fiction plays in larger cultural unfolding. Perhaps more important than actually liking the book is getting past liking as a prerequisite for reading—which this assignment helps students do.[4] But do students read *The Pioneers* when taught this way? Several students from my spring 2019 class admitted they did not read the book cover to cover; indeed, this project did not require them to do so. But, if I can acknowledge different ways of reading, then I can argue that they did read it. Furthermore, as this assignment unfolds, there are numerous opportunities for discussions on reading, interpretation, and the goals of literary studies; such discussions are arguably more useful than reading any given text cover to cover. Do students write about *The Pioneers* in a more engaged way? I can report that the writing for this assignment is unequivocally more engaged, less dependent on underacknowledged sources, more varied, more accepting of ambivalence in the novel, and more focused than writing I have previously seen on *The Pioneers*. So yes, the assignment meets my goals, while also making me rethink the value of those goals.

Using this assignment as a midterm project rather than as a final one is vital because students can return to their research repeatedly in the second half of the course and because I can assign some of the related texts from students' critical editions when we read later novels; the critical editions become class archives for future work, which makes them that much more meaningful products. The assignment is flexible and variable, with options to cut or expand different components. We can even more openly discuss external reading guides and pedagogy about reading. I learned from this assignment that instructors can adapt the pedagogies for recovery to a canonical novel—in part because recovery is not merely about reprinting material so it is available. Recovering a work can also involve resituating it, reconnecting with it, rethinking one's ideas about it, and revising one's writing about it. *The Pioneers* needed to be recovered in my classes precisely because I was teaching it in a way that made it feel stagnant—no doubt largely because of the challenges I identify at the start of this essay but also because of the way I was tacitly responding to those challenges. This assignment successfully recovers *The Pioneers* for me as well as for my students.

I see the payoff in a variety of ways not having to do with the novel itself. Students gain firsthand experience with the process of compiling an edition that makes them, their peers, and future students read a canonical novel differently from the way they feel it is commonly presented. They track the process whereby their editions diverge from each other, and they witness the class producing multiple versions of the novel rather than a singular, definitive one. Even though there are numerous published editions of this novel, none of them are quite like the edition each group produces; despite the canonical status of *The Pioneers*, there are many ways students can resituate it and realign it with contemporaneous texts through secondary research. I am confident that no one who takes the class will ever read introductions, notes, or other editorial material the same way after this experience.

NOTES

I would like to thank the students in the fall 2015, spring 2017, and spring 2019 iterations of my course Approaches to American Literature before 1900 for helping me develop and reflect on the assignment described in this essay.

[1] *Just Teach One* has a sister website, *Just Teach One: Early African American Print*. Both sites include teaching reflections. The website *Sedgwick Stories* "aims to be a comprehensive, searchable digital collection of the stories, tales, and sketches written by Catharine Maria Sedgwick (1789–1867) between 1822 and 1864" ("About"). The website The Wide, Wide World *Digital Edition* addresses transatlantic reading and publication, exploring the "textual and visual variants from 174 reprints" of the nineteenth-century bestseller *The Wide Wide World*, by Susan Warner ("Home").

[2] For more on the concept of building an edition from the perspective of the digital humanities, see Woidat 137–38.

[3] Such works could include Hawthorne; Chopin; and Sansay, *Secret History* and *Laura*.

[4] Here I am reminded of a comment made by Best and Marcus: "many readers might find that to refuse to celebrate or condemn their object of study is, in practice, both difficult and discomfiting" (18).

Narrative and Survival Strategies in *Satanstoe*

Robert Daly

By using a particular mode of attention, instructors and students can learn from James Fenimore Cooper's novel *Satanstoe* both how to read literature and how to grow up and live in the United States and the world. They shall, however, need to take some time to do so. Cooper's genre of choice was not the haiku but the episodic romance, part epic and part bildungsroman. In her "Historical Introduction," Kay Seymour House notes, "In addition to the English-language editions . . . *Satanstoe* was published in French by Baudry in Paris in 1845, and commencing 4 August 1845 it was also published as *feuilletons* by the *Bibliotheque choisie* of the *Constitutionnel*" (xxxiii). This form of publication affords us an excellent way of reading the novel. Feuilletons, leaflets folded into a periodical, enabled readers to engage works intermittently, in small sections. In Cooper's time, even long works were read this way, since family members read aloud to each other. Trying to read a long novel in one sitting would be more like binge-watching a television show, the opposite of feuilleton reading and a far more difficult and less rewarding way of reading Cooper's novel. Feuilleton publication ensured, moreover, that readers could not skip ahead to see how things turned out in the novel. They had to dwell, for a time, in uncertainty.

The teaching method I outline here works well for many long works, but it can best be explained through a discussion of *Satanstoe*, a novel that illuminates the lives of the narrator and other characters as they live them and try to make sense of them in order to live them better. The novel makes explicit, in the developing mind and character of its narrator, many of the techniques implicit in Cooper's better-known works, and it serves similar individual and cultural processes. Though published late in the writer's career, it is, I think, the best place to begin one's study of Cooper's works. Accessible, intelligible, and focused on the transition from youth to adulthood, it is told by a dramatized narrator who grows up before our eyes in the act of living, interpreting, and narrating his story and who always links past, present, and future.

I teach *Satanstoe*, in its entirety, accord it two to three weeks, put its page count on the syllabus so students can see in advance how long it is, assign a short work for the class sessions before and after the novel, and urge students to read Cooper's novel carefully in small but frequent bits, starting as soon as possible. If, as Erica Weaver argues, "we have grown dissatisfied with a practice of critique founded purely on disbelief," then students may benefit from "an influx of critique motivated by belief in the powers of texts to transform the minds and lives of their readers" (60). She notes that earlier readers both "approached nature as a massive tome open to interpretation" and "sought books themselves as guiding frameworks for lived experience, deriving principles for ethical life from their textual encounters" (59). Cooper made quite explicit his own linking of literature and life. In 1823 he wrote to Richard Henry Dana Sr., "If I am able to create an excitement that may rouse the sleeping talents of the nation . . . I shall not have labored entirely in vain" (*Letters* 1: 94). In 1831 he wrote to his fellow sailor-turned-author Eugène Sue to express that, by writing about his experiences, "you will do a real service to your country" (*Letters* 2: 56). In class we consider how *Satanstoe* informs our lives and life in the United States more generally.

Our strategy of patient and informed attention, of reading as fellow interpreters, makes it easier for us to follow the many interpretations and revisions that Cooper's characters and narrators undergo, to increase both the overall range and serial focus of our attention, and to recognize, as Jennifer Ratner-Rosenhagen puts it, that "historical actors do not just think in their moment and in their tiny spot on planet Earth. They also live in an ideational realm where they are communing with thinkers or moral worlds from elsewhere." Ideas function similarly: "Ideas are never frozen in their time and place, nor are they vapors that float in some otherworldly transcendent realm" (5). They remain "so fluid, so multivalent, and so prone to redefinition when they come into new conditions" (5–6) that we readers need to "achieve a little epistemic humility" (6), as do the characters we read. We need to read both past and future, even as they do.

In "Rereading the Future," Cynthia Port argues for a double and complementary view of time: "While it's true . . . that we can't speak to our younger selves, I think it's worth attending to the ways our reading selves seek to peer ahead into the future as well as to reach back to the past" (642). Readers "might consider how their own contexts and perspectives have changed and perhaps become more self-aware about the ways in which they also peer forward as they read" (644). One way readers can do so is to consider young characters in an old book, who peer ahead into their future from out of our past. Rachel Trocchio argues that memory affects affect. Though it may not make us young again, it can remind us of our continuing immaturity. We have more to learn, and with luck, we shall always have more to learn. As she puts it: "Memory launches . . . possibility" (697), and "[a]s recollection . . . memorial style gathers these truths into a glaring moment of testimony that irradiates our hearts. We may walk again (and again) the line from one stage of preparation to another" (714). Deidre Shauna Lynch and Evelyne Ender offer a similar observation and admonition: "in another sense of *reading*, reading never stops," and "[t]his observation serves, too, as your advance notice: reading lies before as well as behind you," so always quite soon, "it will again be time for reading" (1081) and rereading.

Cornelius would agree. As the narrator of Cooper's *Satanstoe*, he argues that without narratives such as his, there can be no communication between generations: "It is easy to foresee that this country is destined to undergo great and rapid changes" and that, "without light literature," with only "a life passed within our own limits," there will be "little hope that any traces of American society, in its more familiar aspects, will be preserved among us" (7). Such traces are needed since Corny and his friends are young, so it is not entirely surprising to find them puzzled in love and looking forward to future clarifications. The country itself is in its adolescence: "This period in the history of a country, may be likened to the hobbledehoy condition in ourselves, when we have lost the graces of childhood, without having attained the finished forms of men" (383). Corny grows up during the last part of the French and Indian War. At its end, in the Treaty of Paris in 1763, France ceded to England all its possessions along the St. Lawrence Valley and its land claims east of the Mississippi. After that, the language and culture of what would become the United States gradually narrowed in the direction of England and then New England. Cooper knew that the dream he gave to the repellent character Jason Newcome in *Satanstoe*, of America as merely a larger version of Jason's hometown in Connecticut, was in danger of coming true.

In the novel, Cooper takes his readers back to the liminality of American culture in its adolescence, when various tribal Native American cultures and French, Dutch, English, African, Irish, German, and other cultures mixed in what Wayne Franklin terms a "loose cross-fertilization" of cultures (*James Fenimore Cooper: Later Years* 77). No longer children, not yet adults, the multicultural youngsters in and around Albany at this time are rather like the rest of us, even now. Cooper preserves the cultural multiplicity and concomitant sophistication of this era. The many characters have different perspectives, and to survive and thrive in this world, they need to see and interpret from perspectives other than their own.

Early in his narrative Corny announces, "I shall not attempt the historical mood at all" or "make a silly attempt to write a more silly fiction" (Cooper, *Satanstoe* 8). His narrative is, in effect, a bildungsroman, a novel on the development of character through the acquisition of knowledge. I explain to students that Johann Karl Simon Morgenstern had, in 1819, coined the term *der Bildungsroman* (a formation novel), in which we see the character "develop before our eyes" (Boes 651). Johann Wolfgang von Goethe had published an early example of the genre, *Wilhelm Meister's Apprenticeship*, in 1795 and 1796. Thomas Carlyle translated that book and published it in English in 1824. The idea of the bildungsroman was, then, in general use. As the dramatized narrator of Cooper's *Satanstoe*, Cornelius is not omniscient and not always reliable, but we can see his growth as the book continues.

The technique of having a major character narrate the tale is unusual in Cooper's novels, and it has the effect of plunging us into the interpretive action and depriving us of the safe aesthetic distance of a spectator who watches the characters' struggles with empathy but without direct involvement. In his translator's introduction to Hans Blumenberg's *Shipwreck with Spectator*, Steven Rendall notes that the spectator who sits safely on dry land and watches a shipwreck "embodies theory (the Greek word *theoria* derives from *theoros*, 'spectator')" (Blumenberg 2). Readers of a tale told by an omniscient third-person narrator have much of the interpretive work done for them and may seem far better informed and far safer than they are. In life there are few safe havens, and instructors may wish to quote to students the epigraph from Blumenberg's book, "Vous êtes embarqué." You are embarked, as are we all. We are all and always, already and forever at sea, and the best way to get beyond our puzzlements is less to rely on the *obiter dicta* of questionable authorities than to get better at navigation.

Corny frequently acknowledges and ponders over his puzzlement, writing that Anneke Mordaunt "was regarding me with an expression of countenance that I did not then know how to interpret" and later that she turned "her face toward me with an indescribable character of fun and feeling in it, as fairly to puzzle me" (Cooper, *Satanstoe* 191, 192). Much later he makes a clear distinction between the young man who lived the events and the older one who now preserves their traces in his narrative: "These were the notions and sentiments of a very young man, it must be confessed, but I do not know that I ought to feel ashamed of them" (257). Ingenuous hero and dramatized narrator, he is also one of us, and we get better at envisioning and interpreting America even as he does.

We all go through this process of learning to navigate society as we grow up. Cooper acknowledged his own progress in this regard when he wrote from Paris in 1831 that "Albany... was the only outlet we had, in my childhood, to the world" and "a place of excellent social feelings and friendly connexions" (*Letters* 2: 155). He knew radical Romantic subjectivity, as found in bildungsromans like Goethe's *Wilhelm Meister's Apprenticeship*, might be necessary but would not be sufficient for him. George Sand read *Satanstoe* in French as it came out in feuilletons, starting in August 1845. In 1856 she judged it "one of Cooper's best novels... all the more thrilling because, thanks to the confidence and clarity of the observations, it is one of the most intelligible" (265). She praises Cooper as an "instinctive enemy of what we call 'fine style,' and of the kind of Byronism which he frankly makes fun of," and she praises Corny's "calm objectivity" as an "important property [that] we perhaps underestimate" (265) but that can both "touch the heart" and "satisfy the mind" (269). In one of his "most intelligible" novels, filled with young readers, Cooper takes us back to the adolescence of American culture, so that we may read it better, and to our own adolescence, so that we may continue to grow up and make a better job of it.

This circumspect epistemology leads Corny, his friends, and us to enact the process Ratner-Rosenhagen delineates, to connect different times and places from which they and we can learn. In defense of his narration, Corny argues that without stories like his "there is little hope that any traces of American society, in its more familiar aspects, will be preserved among us." Without "literature, to give us simulated pictures of our manners and the opinions of the day, I see scarcely a mode by which the next generation can preserve any memorials of the distinctive usages and thoughts of this" generation (Cooper, *Satanstoe* 7).

Michaela Bronstein argues for "a model of literature that is less concerned with drawing out complex meanings and more invested in delivering messages" in "an attempt not merely to represent history but to interact with it" (127).

For her and the rest of us, the "world's script is always both written and still being written," and "the most clearly received message is the starting point for readerly activity, not its end." Readers of literature and life are always "choosing whether to call into life the literary seeds of the past in order to decide what future they wish to make" (134).

This process really is a matter of life and death. It is, according to Nancy Easterlin and others, biologically adaptive. In *A Biocultural Approach to Literary Theory and Interpretation*, Easterlin argues for an "adaptationist literary criticism" (219) based on the theory that narrative is universal among human beings and therefore likely to be biologically adaptive: "literary representation rests on biogenetic foundations," and "certain features" of "human nature have a biologically defined character and are not subject to choice or cultural construction" (218). Narration, she argues, helps us to survive and thrive in the larger world outside literature. In a later journal article, she extends this survival value to literary interpretation, which she describes as "meaning construction . . . a fundamental life process that we . . . make special or elaborate in literary texts" ("Functions" 678). "One *use* of literary studies, as opposed to literature itself, is to increase the efficacy of meaning-making processes and the conscious awareness of human beings as interpreters of their reality by teaching a rich tradition of literary works and engaging in communal interpretation" (679), as instructors and students do, both in and out of class.

Cooper emphasizes throughout *Satanstoe* that interpretation is communal, that we need each other, present and past, "for the old to draw on their experience . . . and the young to live in hope" (440). The desire to get beyond their own limited perspectives, ambiguity, and communal interpretation leads a group of knowledge seekers in the novel to go to Mother Doortje, a fortuneteller in Albany, to learn the future while sparing themselves the effort of attending to the past and present.

The comic aspects of the scene are highlighted by Cooper, who enters his narrative with a splendidly deadpan footnote: "*Doortje—pronounced Doortyay—means Dorothea. Mr. Littlepage uses a sort of corruption of the pronunciation. I well remember a fortune-teller of that name, in Albany, though it could not have been the Doortje of 1758.—EDITOR" (*Satanstoe* 258). That the fortune-teller of Cooper's day could not actually be the character in the novel goes without saying, but Cooper is being playful. We do not know how Corny pronounces the fortune-teller's name, only that he is mistaken, a minor error that becomes important since he recognizes that he has much to learn and therefore undergoes metanoia in order to correct himself, thereby avoiding more major and consequential errors, some of which overcome his confident friends and other contemporaries like Jason. Corny learns; Jason thinks he already knows. Jason is quite certain that the culture of his little town in Connecticut is the best, indeed the only necessary, culture. Others need not be learned but only quickly dismissed in the drive to make all culture a copy of his New England hometown culture.

Unlike Jason, Cooper is trying to preserve in his novel a culture that values diversity. The Albany culture in *Satanstoe* is not based on uniformity or even likeness. It is based on interpretation, knowledge, and choice. Susquesus, a reliable and skilled messenger, interpreter, and hunter, was born into the Onondaga tribe, went to live with Mohawks, and now scouts for the English. In his early naivete, Corny is troubled by this cultural multiplicity and doubts the scout's loyalty. But again, he is mistaken. His very modesty and epistemological circumspection cause him to reinterpret and to realize that what he thought was a weakness in Susquesus is, in fact, a source of strength in the scout's character and ability.

Aware that there is much he does not know, Corny keeps trying to learn, and we learn with him. His companions know too soon and leap to conclusions. Convinced that they are somehow superior to Mother Doortje, sure of their own abilities, and inattentive, they are easily taken in. Corny pays attention. He notices that Doortje does what is commonly called a cold read by paying close attention to the people before her: "Doortje's eyes were by no means fixed, but I remarked that they wandered from person to person, like those of one who is gathering information" (263). But if she is only a grifter, why make so much of her? Cooper acknowledges in a parabasis, a direct address to the reader that serves to lessen aesthetic distance, that "the reader may be disposed to smile" (262) at a trust in fortune-tellers and to feel smugly superior. The book repeatedly warns against precisely this attitude, the refusal to acknowledge ambiguity and one's own limited knowledge, by showing how it inhibits learning.

Satanstoe is named for a peninsula said to have been formed by the imprint of Satan's toe, and the novel was occasioned by the Anti-Rent War in upstate New York from 1839 to 1845, but the book spends comparatively little time on either the legend of the peninsula's formation or the history of the war. Instead it focuses on the regenerative power of what Wayne Franklin calls "the innocent memories that give such buoyancy to the Albany section of *Satanstoe*" (*James Fenimore Cooper: The Later Years* 360) and on the dangers of smugness, solipsism, and especially cultural narrowness. The novel shows how both the desire to escape ambiguity and the illusion that one has escaped it might allow Satan to get a toe in, but Cooper is not writing a tragedy, and he undercuts even Corny's small pretense of worldly wisdom with a quick footnote: "It is quite evident that Mr. Cornelius Littlepage was, to a degree at least, a believer in the Fortune-Teller's art. This was, however, no more than common a century since." Cooper adds that, even in his own time, people in Albany consulted "a celebrated dealer in the Black art," as did the Dutch, the Germans, the English, and even the sophisticated French. In the mixed culture of the time, customs and monies mixed: "Each of us laid a French crown on the table" (*Satanstoe* 263). Cooper notes that even in more recent and supposedly more sophisticated times, human beings have remained somewhat credulous: "Mademoiselle Normand existed in the present [nineteenth] century, even in the skeptical capital of France." In a final irony, Cooper concludes the footnote with, "But, the somnambulist is taking [the] place of the ancient soothsayer, in our own times" (*Satanstoe* 264)

The subtext of the fortune-teller scene takes some reading. Before meeting Doortje, Corny is more predisposed to learn from the encounter than are Dirck, Guert, and the Reverend Thomas Worden. Corny pays closer attention to details and becomes more accurate in his interpretations as the scene goes on, even as his companions become less so. His skeptical companions think they already know the truth about fortune-tellers and will not be tempted, so they pay less attention and are easily taken in. Corny is less confident, more aware that he could be wrong, and so more inclined to self-correction. He begins the encounter with what Coleridge called "that willing suspension of disbelief for the moment, which constitutes poetic faith" (6), and he ends it with a much more informed and accurate view than that of his companions: a view of Mother Doortje's considerable natural abilities and a conviction that she has no supernatural abilities.

Though brighter than his companions, Corny is like Dogberry, the night watchman in Shakespeare's *Much Ado about Nothing*, whom Cooper quotes as his epigraph to chapter 13 of *Satanstoe* (181; Shakespeare, *Much Ado* 4.2.20–22). The title is a multilayered pun, one layer of which means much ado about noting, about paying attention. Where the nobles in the play are used to being right, or at least to not being corrected, and are therefore more certain of themselves and more than a little slow on the uptake, the night watchmen, Dogberry and Verges among them, are known to be comic idiots, compelled by circumstances and other characters to keep learning all the time. They penetrate the slander that has suckered the nobles into believing evil and unlikely things about the tellingly named young woman Hero. As early as act 4, scene 2, in the lines that Cooper quotes, Dogberry reacts to Conrade's announcement that Conrade is a gentleman by saying, "Masters, it is proved already that you are little better than false knaves: and it will go near to being thought so shortly" (4.2.22–25). Dogberry is correct in his assessment of Conrade and Borachio but too optimistic about its being "thought so shortly" by the other principal characters. Instead, it takes a long while and a lot of explanation for the "false knaves" to be recognized as such. Finally, late in act 5, scene 1, Borachio, that most accommodating of villains and most patient of teachers, has to explain the con to Don Pedro and Claudio before concluding with words that should haunt us all, "What your wisdoms could not discover, these shallow fools have brought to light" (5.1.238–40).

Like *Much Ado about Nothing*, *Satanstoe* foregrounds our need to interpret. It offers readers a case study in how Cornelius grows up and learns to make sense of his world as well as of other times and places. By indicating that America was, at this time, in its adolescence and still needed to grow up, the novel implies that its readers have much to learn from Cornelius's example (Cooper, *Satanstoe* 383). We still do, and in my classes we make both our uncertainties about the novel and our interpretations of it as explicit as we can, in order to watch ourselves learning as we go along.

Rodolphe Gasché argues that a focus on circumspection, uncertainty, and probability is what we need now: "All necessity, as it enters into public argumentation, thwarts as well the participation of the audience in the making of the argument, without which there cannot be any deliberation worthy of the name" (43). Corny is young and does not even pretend to know it all. In Gasché's worldview, this focus on probability and community makes him more, rather than less, persuasive: "Without applying in advance known concepts or standards to particular actions, judgment singularly discriminates between those actions that cement the public space, thus reanimating it, and those that put it in jeopardy" (222). Like Corny, we remain young as long as we go on learning and developing our judgment. Since we interpret Cooper in his time but for the purposes of our own, that interpretation is aided by some recent ideas, as we have seen.

The marriage in *Satanstoe* of Cornelius and Anneke (Anna Cornelia) Mordaunt, whose middle name literarily links her to Cornelius, will produce multicultural children who will grow up in a richly diverse country. Kay Seymour House focuses on the uncertainty and flexibility of youth in arguing that "*Satanstoe* is a young book, and the Albany Dutch are the liveliest group in Cooper's novels" (*Cooper's Americans* 103), that the book focuses on "the rites of passage from boyhood to manhood" (104), and that "Cooper's narrative, beginning with the boyish escapades of the two heroes, Cornelius Littlepage and Dirck Van Valkenberg, in Albany, ends with the triumphant return of Cornelius and his marriage to Anneke Mordaunt" (107). Cooper's story links English, Dutch, African, French, and Native American cultures and past, present, and future. Corny hopes that his narrative will leave "the old to draw on their experience for its pictures, and the young to live in hope" (Cooper, *Satanstoe* 440). The detailed knowledge that the present is not merely a repetition of the past affords us hope that the future need not be merely a repetition of the present.

Cooper is, I think, America's first cultural comparatist. Though he is less relativist than Herman Melville, he favors a cultural mixing that is sometimes also racial and sometimes not. Like Susquesus, Corny joins other cultures with his own and benefits from that cultural complexity and knowledge, as may we, when we join Cooper's cultural communities with our own.

Mary Monson, Girl Detective: Cooper as a Mystery Writer

Barbara Alice Mann

In 1850, James Fenimore Cooper published his last novel, *The Ways of the Hour*, an ambitious mystery, or detective, novel. Despite its intricate plot, literary critics and teachers of the detective genre have been unaware of its existence, probably because the novel challenges Victorian tenets on womanhood and would have left unhappy Victorian critics to sink it from literary view. For those critics, the high crime in *The Ways of the Hour* would have been its two unlikely main characters: the cautious criminal Sarah Burton, and the woman she framed for her crime, the unlikeable antiheroine Mary Monson. Monson is both the detective in the novel and its unreliable narrator, and she is not only arrested for arson, theft, and murder most foul but also takes over as her own aggressive lawyer at her trial's end, having fired her expensive New York lawyer, Thomas Dunscomb, the male protagonist, whose blind bumbling gets her convicted. Besides ferreting out the true culprit, Monson also exposes an embarrassing paternity scandal around the excruciatingly decorous Dunscomb, who turns out to be Monson's sometime grandfather (Mann, *Cooper Connection*, 151–54). This was all too much for Victorian readers to bear, but today, *The Ways of the Hour* deserves a place in the modern canon of detective mysteries.

In seminars on nineteenth-century English-language genre literature with a focus on detective mysteries, I have students read multiple pieces, simultaneously, to notice various aspects of the genre at hand. The primary text for the seminar is *The Ways of the Hour*, and students will ideally read the entire book within the first two weeks of the course, although there are always those who stretch it out. For them, I list by week those pages that are vital to the week's discussion. Then, as the semester progresses, other shorter texts and excerpts are assigned week by week to bring out processes and progressions in the genre. Together, these works display the features of mysteries that developed as the genre was being worked out.

In teaching *The Ways of the Hour* in the past, I have made a point of noting that in Cooper's day there were few rubrics, genres, or terms to help readers assess such a plot and such characters as are met with in the novel. Notwithstanding, there is one female detective who stands out as Cooper's model. She appeared in the first known detective novella, *Das Fräulein von Scuderi: Erzählung aus dem Zeitalter Ludwig des Vierzehnten*, by Ernst Theodor Amadeus Hoffmann. The tales of Hoffmann quickly became quite popular in many languages. *Das Fräulein von Scuderi*, renowned as Hoffmann's masterpiece, features the real-life Madeleine de Scudéri, the witty, detective-like author of tell-all novels about people at the court of the French king Louis XIV (Röder 39–56). Here was a model of a female detective, twenty-two years before Edgar

Allan Poe's male detective hit the scene in Poe's short story "Murders in the Rue Morgue." I have students read the English translation of Hoffmann's story, *Mademoiselle de Scudéri: A Tale from the Age of Louis XIV* (*Tales* 17–84), alongside the first week's readings in *The Ways of the Hour*, and I use group discussions in class to go over similarities in character and concept between the two works. This approach helps students track Cooper's development of Mary Monson, and the discussions let students see how to come at Cooper's models and inspirations.

Cooper was also personally acquainted with Elizabeth Fries Lummis Ellet, a well-known writer who frequently worked from German texts. Her knockoff of Hoffmann's *Mademoiselle de Scudéri*, a short story entitled "Cardillac the Jeweler," appeared in 1843 in the *United States Magazine and Democratic Review*. Beginning in 1842, Cooper corresponded with Ellet on literary issues, and he visited her in 1848, recording that she was "a very nice little woman" (*Correspondence* 1: 356–57). Not only is the detective in Ellet's short story a woman, but her villainous "Cardillac" seems so normal as to run under the radar, like Cooper's low-key Sarah Burton, not to mention the coprosecutor in *The Ways of the Hour*, the shrewdly competent Frank Williams. Thus, in week 2, I have students read "Cardillac the Jeweler" for comparison with concepts and structures in Cooper's novel, and in class we discuss the similarities in concept and structure among the three pieces read so far. This helps students grasp Cooper's advancements in envisioning the settings of mysteries and analyze narrative structure.

Starting in this second week with "Cardillac the Jeweler," I assign students to compose a five-hundred-word comparison of *The Ways of the Hour*, *Mademoiselle de Scudéri*, and "Cardillac the Jeweler," with their insights concerning mutual story developments, and to post the essay on the *Blackboard* forum, or discussion board, for the class. Thereafter, in weeks 3 through 7, students post essays on the materials covered in class, in the readings, or in both, depending on which source pinged their radar that week. For each essay assignment, students are required to read and substantively comment on two of their classmates' essays.

In week 3, I have students read Richard Alewyn's "Origin of the Detective Novel." Alewyn argues that Hoffmann's *Mademoiselle de Scudéri* anticipated all the elements of detective fiction commonly attributed as firsts to the works of Poe. Here is another significant connection: Poe and Cooper corresponded in 1836, and Poe frequently reviewed Cooper's novels. In an 1845 review, Poe even placed Cooper "at the head" of "the more popular" contemporary novelists, ahead of Nathaniel Hawthorne and Charles Brockden Brown (Poe 390). Cooper was certainly aware of Poe's work and no doubt read the adventures of Poe's detective, C. Auguste Dupin, who debuted in "Murders in the Rue Morgue." Importantly, in *The Ways of the Hour*, Cooper follows Poe's format involving multiple clues, the grisly twist of double murders, and a falsely accused suspect. Cooper's unbalanced Monson also follows the format used by Poe, who tended to make his perpetrators sensational, and sometimes insane—or even, as in "Murders in the Rue Morgue," simian. Thus, for the third week's coreadings with the assignments in *The Ways of the Hour*, I have students read "Murders in the Rue Morgue," with an eye to its themes of sanity and insanity, with group and class discussion to follow.

In weeks 4 through 7, I divide students into three groups, each of which is assigned to read and evaluate a novel—Wilkie Collins's *The Woman in White*, Seeley Register's *Dead Letter*, or Collins's *The Moonstone*—against *The Ways of the Hour* using the rubrics of Alewyn and Franco Moretti as touchstones of analysis. Each group presents its findings to the class, leading class discussions in weeks 4, 5, and 6. In week 7, a summary analysis and comparison of all four novels forms the basis of class discussion. This discussion includes the whiteboard construction of several Venn diagrams illustrating the interactive parts of the novels' plots.

In composing his crime novel, Cooper pioneered several firsts now attributed to the subsequent novelists Register and Collins (Harrington 13). In its extended legal proceedings, *The Ways of the Hour* provided the first procedural fiction, sixteen years before the publication of Register's *Dead Letter*, usually considered the first fiction to spotlight legal proceedings. In *The Ways of the Hour*, Cooper also offered the first full-length detective novel (since *Mademoiselle de Scudéri* was a novella), for Cooper's novel was published in 1850, Collins's *The Woman in White* in 1860, Register's *Dead Letter* in 1866, and Collins's *The Moonstone* in 1868. Again ahead of Collins, Cooper first offered female characters, particularly his pheromonal antiheroine and his unrepentant criminal, who did not confine themselves to Victorian norms for women. With the sedate thief Burton set against the seemingly imperturbable yet defective detective Monson, Cooper also cleared the path for all the misleadingly unflappable perpetrators and deceptive detectives that would appear in later detective fiction, firsts typically awarded to Collins. These pioneering elements of Cooper's novel are important for instructors to mention to students, especially women's studies students, when they present the promise of Cooper's models and his story development in the mid-nineteenth century.

In week 8, we look at *The Ways of the Hour* and women's rights in terms of the New York Married Women's Property Acts, and I assign students to read two short pieces, Judith E. Harper's "New York Married Women's Property Acts" and Jane Johnson Lewis's "1848: Married Women Win Property Rights," for historical background. The "cup and saucer" laws about which Dunscomb complains so bitterly through two-thirds of the novel (e.g., Cooper, *Ways* 479), and class discussion of their historical contexts, bring into focus important motives of both Monson, in claiming her wealth, and Burton, in stealing hers. (Dunscomb's turnaround on the law on behalf of Monson at the end of the novel is an interesting sidelight.)

As their first half-semester project, students are assigned to read one of the Register or Collins novels that their group didn't read, comparing and contrasting it with *The Ways of the Hour* in terms of either the female characters or the setting. Students may prepare either a paper or a project. Papers should be three pages long, double-spaced, and should cite three vetted outside sources not treated in class. Projects derive from students' majors (or research interests) and may take whatever form that students' imaginations suggest but should cite three vetted outside sources. In the past, a student in psychology created mind maps of characters for comparison, while a student in computer animation created memes of pertinent scenes. Whether students do papers or projects, they share their work with fellow students in twenty-minute oral presentations during class in the second half of the semester (weeks 9 through 15). Students may use limited talking points, and their presentations should be accompanied by appropriate electronic images. I usually assign one presentation per class meeting, but the frequency of presentations can be adjusted depending on class size. A class discussion led by the student presenter follows each presentation.

As an extra credit assignment worth one week's forum participation grade and due by the end of the first half-semester, students may write a five-hundred-word essay about *The Big Bang Theory* episodes that spoof the orangutan killer in Poe's "Murders in the Rue Morgue": in these episodes the character Penny has a recurring B movie role as an oversexed killer gorilla in *Serial Ape-ist* and its sequel, *Serial Ape-ist II: Monkey See, Monkey Kill* ("Hofstadter Insufficiency"; "Friendship Turbulence"). Students' essays, posted on the *Blackboard* forum, must explain and analyze the sexist, racist, and classist cultural dog whistles that the faux movies satirize and must connect them with treatments of women in the pieces that they have read so far.

From weeks 9 through 15, in addition to classroom work for each week, every student prepares a five-hundred-word essay for posting on the *Blackboard* forum, and students must substantively comment on two of their classmates' essays. Starting in week 9, the focus shifts to formal analysis of mystery tales. Students are assigned to read a chapter from Franco Moretti's *Signs Taken for Wonders* (130–56) by week 10. In his important study of nineteenth-century detective novels, Moretti delineates their recurring and necessary elements. Although Moretti looks to Arthur Conan Doyle's Sherlock Holmes stories for his base texts, the elements of detective novels that he discusses are easily identifiable in *The Ways of the Hour* and other early mystery tales. Week 9 is devoted to a class discussion of genre elements identified by Moretti and to consideration of how Cooper's novel and one of the other novels mentioned earlier, by Register or Collins, conforms with these elements. Starting in week 9, students write on the *Blackboard* forum, examining the elements set forth by Moretti, including the character types of the criminal (week 9), the detective (week 10), and the sidekick (week 11) and the structural features of the story's stasis (week 12), the trial scene (week 13), the crime (week 14), and the solution (week 15).

Of course, all these elements are carefully considered in class discussions, as suit the instructor's style, to prepare students for their weekly assignments. Throughout seminar discussion of these elements, students are to draw on all the works they have read so far as evidence in testing, analyzing, and critiquing these elements for how they fit with *The Ways of the Hour* and their other selected novels. Students are free to offer amendments to or refinements of Alewyn's and Moretti's prototypes.

In his characters and in the structure of *The Ways of the Hour*, Cooper anticipates all of Moretti's rubrics. For the reader, I list how Cooper accomplishes this feat, point by point, below, but in teaching the novel, through in-class discussions and the prodding of my questions in the weekly forum, I allow students to have their own aha moments. This bread-crumb approach to the novel allows students to own the discovery of Cooper's prescience, which fixes Moretti's rubric in their heads in a way that lecture simply cannot.

According to Moretti, the criminal is never a member of the bourgeoisie, but always a "noble" (139) trying to regain a fortune or an "upstart" who "aspires to a sudden social jump" (140). Interestingly, throughout Cooper's *Ways of the Hour*, Monson is denigrated as a larcenous "aristocrat" (134), whereas the actual criminal, Burton, is a farmer's wife looking to improve her social status with the stolen five thousand dollars (worth roughly $150,000 today [149–50]). Additionally, the criminal "always acts consciously," a trait Cooper gives Burton (and, by the way, Monson [Moretti 248]). Under questioning, Burton is meticulous with her words, speaking with "taciturnity and gravity," carefully reflecting on every syllable before uttering it (Cooper, *Ways* 435). An offshoot of the conscious criminal, according to Moretti, is the "stepfather" motif, in which a parent attempts to seize the child's fortune (140). Monson has two putative stepfathers in her middle-aged, larcenous husband, le vicomte de Larochefort, who lusts after her inheritance (Cooper, *Ways* 492), and in her lawyer and secret grandfather, Dunscomb, who has denied her access to her paternal heritage. Dunscomb also meets Moretti's stepfather description in projecting his erotic frustrations onto Monson. Dunscomb is so physically attracted to Monson that his obvious arousal excites town gossip (216).

According to Moretti, the detective neither pities the criminal's victims nor is repulsed morally by the crime but is enticed by the piquancy of events (135). Clearly suffering from what is probably bipolarism (a disease not yet diagnosed but identifiably characterized by Cooper), Monson seems to thrive on risk and danger while in her manic state. However, absent immediate peril, she collapses into an obsessive inability to function rationally. As such, she is completely self-serving; the victims and the crime play but little into her calculations. The detective, says Moretti, is also a dilettante who does not care about the law for its own sake (142–43). Monson certainly does not care, but she is just as certainly a well-heeled dilettante. Moretti adds that, psychologically, the detective is able to "understand" the competing motives of the criminal, using knowledge of those motives to unmask the criminal, precisely as Monson does during her crafty cross-examination of Burton, during which she tricks Burton, Perry Mason–style, into a dramatic confession on the witness stand (Moretti, 140; Cooper, *Ways* 470–73).

With Holmes in mind, Moretti puts forensics squarely in the purview of the detective, noting that the science and technology of the detective novel should "always live up to expectations" in revealing the truth (143). Here, Cooper inserts Dr. Edward McBrain into his novel, transferring the forensics from Monson to her erstwhile champion, the good doctor (who is somewhat prescient of Dr. John Watson in the Sherlock Holmes stories). McBrain clinches the vital skeletal evidence, showing that, instead of being husband and wife, both of the victims were female, mistress and maid (*Ways* 42, 102, 440). Moreover, the murders are shown to have been accidental deaths. Monson correctly demonstrates for the court that during a fire, the heavy plowshares stored in the attic fell through the burning floor, which was also the bedroom ceiling, delivering the death blows to the heads of those sleeping below. No human hand was lifted against either victim (472). Finally, Monson figures out and shows that Burton had planted the evidence implicating Monson (451).

In requiring a slower sidekick to act as a "puppet" of the detective, Moretti was obviously thinking of Holmes's sidekick, Dr. Watson (146), but in *The Ways of the Hour*, Monson has multiple slower sidekicks, whom she shamelessly exploits. Her steadiest sidekick is Anna Updyke, whom Monson connives into aiding her in her jailbreaking jaunts, even while Monson steals her boyfriend on the side (Cooper, *Ways* 267). Monson's other major sidekick is Dunscomb, who, as Moretti requires of the sidekick, ultimately plays "into the criminal's hands" while amassing "useless details," thus to reach false conclusions (Moretti 146, 147). Incorrectly assessed details lead Dunscomb to believe Monson guilty on all counts, to the aid of Burton, who plants evidence and withholds information (Cooper, *Ways* 150).

As for stasis, Moretti observes that the detective plot moves in retrograde, its whole point being to travel from the present back to the beginning of the story: "that is, it abolishes narration" (148). It is quite true that, for all the frantic activity in Cooper's novel, the story is remarkably static. All that happens is that a badly wound skein of yarn is unraveled and reballed correctly; what was wrong is put back to rights, as Burton, not Monson, takes the fall; Dunscomb recognizes his desertion of family and takes in Monson; Anna Updyke swipes her beau back from Monson; McBrain recovers his medical reputation as his forensics are vindicated; and Monson regains her independence and fortune through divorce from Larocheforte. All things have rewound to the beginning for a satisfying do-over.

In the mid-nineteenth century, Moretti notes, the focus of detective novels moved "from execution to the trial," that is, from the religious preoccupation with the culprit's spiritual salvation through confession, to mundane courtroom procedures (138). *The Ways of the Hour* is nothing if not a courtroom drama, in which Monson is actually convicted and sentenced to death before she takes her legal appeal into her own hands (Cooper, *Ways* 461–62). Salvation is nowhere in sight as a goal in the novel.

Next, says Moretti, the crime itself typically involves a theft as a "violent redistribution" of wealth and status (139). Without question, this happens in *The*

Ways of the Hour, as Burton helps herself to the loot of the deceased, even as a relative of the deceased, in corrupt league with the coprosecutor Williams, attempts to squeeze Monson for the same money. Moretti also claims that beneath the "obvious" action of the plot, there is a more subtle sociological action, "deep and hidden" just like the crime (151). Cooper's social commentary throughout the novel reflects on little-seen aspects of the characters: Cooper comments on current social prejudices and the misadventures they precipitate. Equally deep is the moral drama occurring subliminally between Monson and Dunscomb in the novel, but further commentary on this complexity of the novel is so profound that it requires its own article to elucidate (Mann, "Maria Monk" 156, 160–62).

Finally, Moretti lists the solution to the mystery, whose function is to replace the "fable's 'moral.'" By presenting scientific authority as unimpeachable, the detective novel "satisfies the aspiration to certainty" (149). In *The Ways of the Hour*, McBrain's forensics are entirely exonerated, while Monson's insightful hypotheses are irrefutably supported by fact and logic. At the same time, Moretti says, nothing outside of the detective novel's bubble is allowed to disturb the proffered "science" of the solution as final (149). No thorny issues redound on anyone to puncture the social order reinstated by science. Thus, no legal consequences ensue either for Monson's evidence tampering, which the protagonist commits in laundering away some of the supposedly stolen currency, or for Williams's attempt to extort five thousand dollars from Monson in exchange for dropping the criminal proceedings against her (Cooper, *Ways* 227, 300, 304–05). Instead, Cooper ends his novel as if it were a classic comedy with two weddings: with Monson's family, fortune, and freedom restored and with the happy retirement of Dunscomb, now in the role of fond grandfather to Monson. Cooper does quite a bit of glossing in the denouement but thereby keeps the world of the novel spinning properly on its axis.

For their final project, students again have their choice of a traditional paper (three pages long, double-spaced, with three vetted outside sources not treated in class) or a project combining the subjects they are majoring in with classroom material (and requiring three vetted outside sources). Students who choose to write a paper use the Moretti genre elements to evaluate *The Ways of the Hour* in terms of whichever of the following works they have not yet read: Collins's *The Woman in White*, Register's *Dead Letter*, or Collins's *The Moonstone*. In the past, I have had students with majors in women's studies, social work, history, anthropology, and other subjects examine the elements of women's budding empowerment as displayed in *The Ways of the Hour*, particularly in how Victorian norms of women's behavior get upended by Monson, the accused; Dorothy (Dolly) Goodwin, the thief; and Updyke, the sidekick, who talks like a Victorian but acts like a rebel. Students in medical fields can look at the forensics of the day in Dr. McBrain's and the other physicians' expert opinions, while students in psychology can look at Monson's mental health. The options are as wide as the students' imaginations allow.

Second half-semester projects are presented to the class during weeks 15 and 16, and they can be a lot of fun. I had an engineering major, for instance, who created a board game based on Chutes and Ladders, using class work as the benchmarks. She 3D printed the pieces and, after a brief explication of how the game worked, had students play it in class. Students eagerly lined up to try their hands at the game, and they only reluctantly left the classroom at the end of class. A social work major created a role-playing session and had class volunteers assume various personae discussed in class to work through conflicts, while another student in computer science created a computer game with multiple outcomes, based on decisions made at each of the game's conundrums, and had the class play the game together. Students enthusiastically shouted out their choices, greatly enjoying the new predicaments that presented themselves.

Using the sources and explications detailed in this chapter, literature instructors can easily create a Cooper component for any course that has a unit focusing on detective fiction.

Language Diversity in Cooper's Novels
Anna Scannavini

The portrayal of language difference in novels by James Fenimore Cooper set in America and in Italy offers specific affordances for teaching his novels in an Italian classroom. Challenges and opportunities can be derived not only from the Italian characters that populate his Italian novels but also from the multilingual settings represented in those novels and in his American frontier novels. Here I discuss how I investigate such uses of the novels with a class of Italian students working toward a master of arts degree in modern foreign languages. When asking these students to investigate Cooper's multilingualism, I expect them to work from their roots in the Italian language and through all the attending dislocations and relocations of character and subject matter that reading fiction in a foreign language entails. In the process, we bring to the surface the complexities of Cooper's writing, while stretching the field of study to include more diversified actors, languages, and countries than would a largely intralingual approach to reading Cooper's works that focuses on the United States in relation to England.

Bibliomigrancy

A nice paradigm for bringing out the complexity in Cooper's novels is the open process B. Venkat Mani defines as "bibliomigrancy" (145). According to Mani, books belonging to a given tradition are read differently when migrants from that same tradition carry them to new countries. Because of the migration progress, books are confronted by constituencies in the new country, producing in the case of novels new interpretations of characters and their adventures. The paradigm responds, it seems to me, to the entire project of questioning Cooper's multilingual settings, as it imbricates two levels of circulation: extrinsic circulation of books in Europe, especially Italy, and intrinsic circulation of transnational characters inside those same books.

The intrinsic migrancy in Cooper's novels can be quite complex. In *The Last of the Mohicans*, Cooper brings to bear not only his knowledge of colonial powers but also what he learned about Native Americans from the writings of the Moravian missionary John Heckewelder (472), as well as the memories of his neighbors in New York State. When, on the other hand, he writes about Europe, his view goes well beyond England, looking at the European mainland, with a special preoccupation with France, whose politics he came to understand better, and became involved with, during his European stay, especially thanks to the agency of the Marquis de Lafayette (Franklin, *Cooper: Later Years* 16–22). In Italy, his novels were translated and entered the national market by way of the cosmopolitan Italian intelligentsia that, in the 1820s, was beginning to struggle for national independence. To these intellectuals everything American was interesting. They looked for information on the new American republic, and they also looked for information on Native American peoples (Sullam Calimani 12; Scannavini 24–25). Cooper's Native Americans in particular became inextricably linked to early Italian understanding of the Americas and cultural consolidation within them. The circulation of Cooper's books offers students a chance to reflect on early-nineteenth-century American literature as a space suspended between hopes and betrayed possibilities, not only for Cooper but also for Italy.

Such suspension has a counterpart in the representation of multilingual encounters in Cooper's works: looking for such encounters should teach students to cope with their positioning in front of cultural difference, when there is a need for intercultural communication. Like them, Cooper's characters can be confronted by a diversity of languages, they can be forced to use a language that is not their native one, or they can be mocked because of their accented English, as sometimes happens in Cooper's dialogues. Observations of local Italian accents depicted in Cooper's works, and the puns made on the pronunciation of English in such accents, prompt reactions in the classroom, and I welcome students' objections, frustration, or anger, as long as these reactions offer a chance to discuss how efforts to speak other languages are inevitably the object of observation by others and require a bit of humility in the speakers as they struggle to find a place in cross-cultural representation.

Scholars have responded to the transnational turn currently obtaining in American studies in Europe by plunging into the field of cultural migrancy. In 2008 *RSA Journal*, the journal of the Italian Association of American Studies, devoted space to a forum titled "Teaching American Studies in Europe: Challenges and New Directions for the Twenty-First Century." The forum gathers the ideas of a number of scholars teaching in European universities and can well be taken to represent the future of American studies in Europe. Given the inherently transatlantic interest of the journal, it should come as no surprise that the dominant discourse in the forum is more or less openly indebted to the transnational turn in the field. As Lorenzo Costaguta and Virginia Pignagnoli observe in the forum's introduction, all the contributors claim that transnationalism and interdisciplinarity are key factors in their work, as they are in the work of Donald Pease and Robyn Wiegman in their 2002 book *The Futures of American Studies* (Costaguta and Pignagnoli 163).

According to Costaguta and Pignagnoli, Pease and Wiegman's anti-exceptionalist view of American studies reconfigures the history of the United States as an arena of ruptures more than of continuities, of undecidability more than of fixedness. The editors' double call to open up to the possibilities of ruptures as a way to "[abandon] well-established narratives and [focus] on less debated aspects of U.S. history" (163) sounds to me like an invitation to return to Cooper's novels to investigate the tension they enact between social closure and "the romantic sympathies which [Cooper] embodied in loners and outcasts" (Baym

709). Close reading and discussion in class often highlight such tensions and ruptures, echoing in a revealing way Geoffrey Rans's claim that, in *The Pioneers*, "Cooper may have preferred to say something else, but what he actually writes is pessimistic in the highest degree" and involves radical criticism "of America and its values" (69).[1] When read by students, in other words, Cooper's novels yield easily "the richer, more subtle readings" that they deserve (Franklin, *James Fenimore Cooper: The Later Years* xviii). Classwork, moreover, also shows that Cooper's representation of language as a multifaceted affair can be used in teaching.

Profiling a Classroom

The Italian master's degree (*laurea magistrale*) in modern foreign languages comprises two years of coursework in two, or more, foreign languages and literatures and in history, geography, and anthropology. An objective of the degree is for students to reflect on the many aspects of language contact: contrastive analysis, language fractures and realignments, the possibilities of translation, and intergroup communication. In other words, they must learn to open up to cultures different from their own.

The class I write about comprises fifteen or twenty students with a B2+ or C1 level of language competence (according to European standards) and a basic knowledge of nineteenth-century American literature. Students' control of English should be enough to read texts of some complexity, but probably not enough to disentangle autonomously the variant spellings, such as the idioms employed by Leather-Stocking, that suggest local variants of English.

Course of Study

Besides requiring information on the expected learning outcomes of a course, European syllabi must include a list of the texts to be studied. I always divide in advance the list of study texts into primary and secondary sources.[2]

Primary Sources

I usually select primary sources from two sets of works by Cooper: the Leather-Stocking novels and the books about or set in Italy (*Gleanings in Europe: Italy*, *The Bravo*, and *The Wing-and-Wing*). I select *The Last of the Mohicans* from the Leather-Stocking saga for the pragmatic reason that the book is Cooper's best-known novel in Italy, thanks to Italian adaptations for young readers as well as renditions of the story in films and graphic novels. I generally teach the novel along with *The Pioneers*, as the two novels offer a good sample of the strategies Cooper uses in his fiction to represent language diversity.[3] I begin with *The Pioneers*, focusing on its representation of first-generation French and German immigrants in the United States. I teach these characters as representative of the multilingualism that was present early in the country's history, putting them over the course of the semester in a triangular relation with characters in *The Last of the Mohicans* and *The Wing-and-Wing*.

Step by step, the triangle formed by the three books is meant to involve students in a process of cross-reading. When we eventually come to *The Wing-and-Wing*, the misunderstandings and puns that emerge in the novel from the use of French, English, and Italian work as a looking glass for the class. At that point, I return to *The Pioneers* and *The Last of the Mohicans* so students can reset their points of view in an act of external migrancy that should reinstate Native peoples (Italian *and* American) as actors and question the means of their portrayal. If time permits, we go back to tap what students know of the Italian risorgimento in order to sample its mutual connections with American national formations.

Secondary Sources

As the course focuses on language, students should have some notions of early America's linguistic context—including the notion that Cooper had at his disposal early descriptions of Native languages. A handout can provide this context, glossing Cooper's reference to Heckewelder in the 1826 preface to *The Last of the Mohicans* (472). Given Cooper's sometimes confusing descriptions of indigenous nations, moreover, the students will need a modern reference handbook, and I use *The Columbia Guide to American Indians of the Northeast*, edited by Kathleen J. Bragdon. I also supplement *The Columbia Guide* with James Axtell's "Babel of Tongues," used as an introduction to the arena and mechanisms of language contact. Because there has been much work done recently on communication (both spoken and printed) between cultural and linguistic groups in early America, we do have multiple possible references on the encounters and negotiations happening in the Northeast in the period when Cooper's novels were set.

A new addition to the course is the essay collection *The Language Encounter in the Americas, 1492–1800*, edited by Edward G. Gray and Norman Fiering. What is particularly attractive about *The Language Encounter in the Americas* is its variety of angles on the interaction of language and communication in various North and South American sites. As Gray observes in the introduction to the book, a variety of vantage points is necessary because language and communication are not always "necessarily related." Language is "a medium of communication," but it is also possible to "communicate without language," while the opposite is also true: language can be used "without communicating, as one might in prayer or song," or, in the case of language encounters when an unintended or unrelated meaning is transmitted, "between two resilient objects," the result being a "meshing, mingling, or interface of like minds" (1).

All these possibilities are represented in the conversations, assemblies, meetings, and deliberations that are so vital to many of Cooper's plots and that prompt the reader to consider issues such as deliberative democracy (see Gustafson, *Imagining*; and Begg). Although providing a good methodological background, *The Columbia Guide to American Indians of the Northeast* and *The Language Encounter in the Americas* do not engage Cooper's work. Aspects of Cooper's work with language are the object of essays that can be assigned to students as they begin to contemplate their own final papers (see, for example, Ganter; Goddard; or Schachterle). None of them, however, focus on multilingualism. When working on multilingualism in Cooper's work, I use Lawrence Rosenwald as a source. Rosenwald, who acknowledges his debt to the groundbreaking work of Marc Shell (Rosenwald, *"Last"* 9; Shell, "Babel" and *American Babel*), further develops Shell's paradigm in his *Multilingual America*, a book that devotes a whole chapter to *The Last of the Mohicans* (20–47).[4] The chapter acknowledges that, while *The Last of the Mohicans* does not explicitly oppose the United States government policy of Indian Removal, the novel also does not endorse "savagism," or cruelty, in that policy (45). Rosenwald's conclusion provokes discussion on the situation of Native peoples in *The Last of the Mohicans*, and in class we analyze a number of the novel's multilingual events, assessing their relevance and meaning in the narration. I point out that although English is required by the intended readers of the novel, inside the novel the use of English is not a given and does not supersede the languages of the Native characters.

I continue by asking students to find places of reciprocity in the novel. I suggest that reciprocity is already fully asserted in the third chapter of the book, when Natty and Chingachgook hold a sustained conversation about the mutual rights of the Delaware people and the Europeans (Cooper, *Last* 499–508). Speaking "the tongue which was known to all the natives . . . between the Hudson and the Potomack," they set off a series of metaphors of the two peoples' progress throughout America as a reciprocity progress that generates war from two opposite directions: west and east (501). Astutely hidden from the ears of White characters, the conversation shows that the middle ground is full of discourse, private and public (see, of course, Magua's rhetoric [419–21]). Natty's insistent exchanges with other characters are even more to the point: the stubborn defense of Natty's friends in the character's exchange with Heyward in *The Last of the Mohicans* (at Glens Falls [525–26]) and Natty's memories of Glimmerglass Lake, recounted in conversation with Oliver Edwards, in Cooper's *The Pioneers* (293–98). Natty's loquacity is sometimes laughable, as when the character starts prating in front of attacking enemies, but cannot be dismissed. It shows that even if Natty flees the sound of axes, he does not necessarily flee the sound of words—countering Natty's enshrinement as the first in a line of antisocial frontier heroes.

Later in the course we will see that long stretches of dialogue also occupy *The Pioneers* and *The Wing-and-Wing*. Here, however, dialogue serves to create distance between the narrator and some of the characters. *The Last of the Mohicans* creates a bridge between English and other languages by staging and taking seriously the linguistic and social complexities implied by the act of speaking.

Learning Outcomes

To go back to the *RSA Journal*, and more specifically to the question of "the theoretical frameworks that are best suited to teach the multiple histories and the multiple contradictions of American Culture" (Costaguta and Pignagnoli 162), it should be clear that in my approach the theoretical framework depends fully on the study of language in action and of the self as linguistic actor. I aim to provoke reflection by students on the potentialities of linguistic actors in a transnational environment (where they may act as cultural mediators, translators, or interpreters). Consequently, the syllabus asks students to focus on a few basic issues in the novels of study: the representation of dialogues between first-generation European immigrants in a recently established settlement and the positions of Natty and John Mohegan (Chingachgook) with regard to that specific multicultural situation in *The Pioneers*, the representation of language negotiations in *The Last of the Mohicans*, and the transatlantic importance of European languages in *The Wing-and-Wing*.

As already mentioned, I wager that moving from the multilingual domestic scene of *The Pioneers* to the international Mediterranean scene in *Gleanings in Europe: Italy* and in *The Wing-and-Wing* will motivate students to reflect more deeply on their experience as second language speakers under scrutiny by others. Can they recognize themselves in Cooper's characters? Can they recognize themselves in the distress of Mohegan or Natty in front of *The Pioneers'* foreign invaders? What mistakes and errors, if any, in their use of English do students have in common with Cooper's Italian characters? I intend that students learn something about the inner and outer workings of othering and, above all, that they learn that the prevalence of a language—including American English—is not natural but the result of social and cultural drifts and choices. The most attentive of the students will have learned to reflect on the mental and emotional contact zones they inhabit any time they use their second languages of study.

In Cooper's books such contact zones range from linguistic encounters between European invaders and Native societies (with the attending circulation of languages and lingua francas, such as those represented in *The Last of the Mohicans*), to contact between different European constituents in the occupation of the North American continent (in *The Pioneers*), to lexical insertions used to remind the readers that characters speak a foreign language the narrator has translated into English. Discussion on Cooper's attitude to English, and to the role of American English as an imperial language, can follow from a discussion of these contact zones.

Teaching Cooper's Works

After I introduce the general rationale of the syllabus, we begin the course with Cooper's *the Pioneers*. The already mentioned multilingual community of

European immigrants in Templeton has its correlative in the "composite order" of Richard Jones and Hiram Dolittle's architectural plan for the settlement (41), an aggregate system that foregrounds Templeton as a diversified cultural scene. The scene immediately puts forward the question of whether national languages are natural elements that define a unitary nation, producing symbolic identification.

Students will compare their experiences as nonnative speakers of English with the experiences of *The Pioneer*'s characters who migrate inside the novel and perform as bilinguals in their own turn, though they sometimes speak broken English. Although perfunctory, this fundamental act of migrancy will raise questions on the many (equally perfunctory) stories in American culture that construct the United States as a monolingual unit (Cowell 64). Such questions will open the way to introduce two divergent notions: first, that the English-language mainstream in American culture is supposedly a means of symbolic identification (B. Anderson), and second, that, notwithstanding this symbolic identification, literatures in foreign languages—Native languages included—continued to be produced in the United States, as widely evidenced by Marc Shell in his *American Babel*.

I always allow students the first two classes of the course to make their acquaintance with the universe of *The Pioneers* and its characters. As a much needed complement, I lecture on the historical and geographic setting of the Leather-Stocking saga, which students further familiarize themselves with through brainstorming, reading maps, mapping the Northeast of the United States as it was during the period in which the saga is set, and individual presentations on salient issues—generally by volunteers. During this time, the students have two full weeks to read up to chapter 15, and then we are able to plunge into the novel. Here a first problem arises, one that must be understood and addressed for the course to be effective. As opposed to American students, Italian students are generally trained to avoid naïf readings. This could be positive, except that Italian students translate their training into a habit of memorizing received explanations and lessons (obtained from sources that can range, a bit uncannily, from literary histories, to introductory materials, to other students' notes from previous courses, to the Internet, to whatever they can put their hands on). As a consequence, they tend to keep on the safe side by accepting received authority and eschewing personal opinions. Their presentations are often mechanical and unoriginal.

To counter this inclination and encourage students to produce original work and avoid received explanations or analyses, I insist on the secondary sources as a required theoretical basis that students should question and discuss. Discussion should prompt them to produce their own cognitive maps and to reflect on how to present them in public. I ask students to work in small groups, and when we meet again in class, they must have written maps, notes, or both on the chapters they have read. I then ask them to divide among themselves the burden of giving brief oral presentations; discussion with the other groups is supposed to follow each presentation.

The pace of the class changes when we focus on variant spellings in *The Pioneers*. I stop lecturing altogether and leave students to their own resources (both at home and in class). Individual home assignments are to translate the voice of at least one character (two if they wish) into Standard English. Variant spellings in the novel are rarely written about, and it will be difficult for students to find ready-made explanations. At the same time, at least some of them find the problem-solving aspect of the assignment an attractive proposition, a stimulus for them to carry on. When they begin to formulate original ideas, we work out guidelines on how to proceed to the task of more abstract interpretation. We retrieve some of the English phonetics students have already learned in previous courses and talk about how spoken language can be conveyed in writing. We look into the mispronunciations by the characters Hartmann and Le Quoi, as French and German accents should be familiar to students. They might share small stories of their own linguistic blunders when speaking another language or of a foreigner speaking Italian. That is the moment when their stereotypes must be questioned and when we discuss how Cooper's more or less stereotypical misspellings serve characterization.

At the end of this unit, I assign passages from Benedict Anderson's *Imagined Communities* (1–7, 37–46) and from Bragdon's *The Columbia Guide to American Indians of the Northeast* (37–61). Class discussion follows, as students draw from what they have read and discuss the meaning of *identification*, investigating whether the word is as simple as it seems to be. At that point the silence of Mohegan in *The Pioneers* comes to the fore in our discussion and leads students to view Templeton as a metaphor of the waste resulting from European colonization and transformation of the American landscape. Before the end of this unit, students must return to the subject of language, and I assign excerpts from texts dealing with the sociology of language. Group presentations in class are intended as a passage to the following unit, on *The Last of the Mohicans*. The third unit is devoted to *The Wing-and-Wing* and to the thickly populated contact zone of the Mediterranean. My expectation is that students will build on the work they have done in earlier units.

I always conclude the course by spending one or two classes on the risorgimento, including on Paola Gemme's groundbreaking reinstatement of Italy's subjectivity in the discussion of American travelers to the country. I contend that all of Cooper's Italian writings—from *The Bravo*, to *Gleanings in Europe: Italy*, to *The Wing-and-Wing*—inscribe, although mutely, the risorgimento. *The Wing-and-Wing* in particular forebodes the failed insurgencies that, in the 1820s, just a few years before Cooper's arrival in Italy, started the Italian fight for independence. In view of this history, and after students have read *The Wing-and-Wing*, we return to Admiral Caracciolo, the Neapolitan republican who is dishonorably hanged by Nelson in the novel; I read in class passages from letter 33 of *Gleanings in Europe: Italy* (295–300), starting from "I have told you little in these letters of the Italians themselves" (295), and compare them to the portrayal of Ghita and Caracciolo in *The Wing-and-Wing*. Then we discuss how Cooper, in *Gleanings in Europe: Italy*, shuns the Italian predicament and the

Italian intelligentsia, especially in Florence, that befriended him. I ask if Cooper's shunning actually amounts to a disavowal, as John Conron and Constance Ayers Denne claim (xl–xli). I wager that the passages in *Gleanings in Europe: Italy* bring to the fore once more a hesitancy in Cooper that is inherent in the political question of the difficult passage from eighteenth-century illuministic cosmopolitism to nineteenth-century sentimental proclivity in American fiction, a question that certainly concerns Cooper but that can also be usefully extended even to contemporary fiction.

NOTES

[1] That Cooper's "terms of American dreaming" were "full of concern for the fate of the leveled continent and the scattered native populations" is also made very clear by Franklin (*James Fenimore Cooper: The Early Years* xxviii).

[2] Italian universities don't have university bookstores as US universities do. Students find the required readings in the university library or by buying them from independent bookstores.

[3] Citations to Cooper's *The Last of the Mohicans* and *The Prairie* refer to volume 2 of *The Leatherstocking Tales*, edited by Nevius and published by the Library of America. Citations to *The Pioneers* refer to the edition published by the Library of America.

[4] I don't assign Boggs as required reading because her chapter on Cooper and translation has sometimes proved too intricate for my students to work out (61–89).

VISUALITY AND CINEMA

Wyandotté and American Scenery
Michael Demson

If there were ever a novel that begged a stage adaptation, it would be James Fenimore Cooper's late historical novel, *Wyandotté; or, The Hutted Knoll: A Tale*. Not only is the novel structured in easily discernable acts, much of the dialogue and action is overtly histrionic, and the novel is everywhere preoccupied with scenery. Even the alternative title, *The Hutted Knoll*, suggests a stage, referring to the promontory on which the novel's pioneers settle and the action unfolds. With the overtly theatrical dimensions of *Wyandotté* in mind, I require my undergraduate students to plan a stage adaptation of the novel, taking into consideration the various felicities and difficulties that such a project inevitably must embrace or overcome.

Considering the magnitude of such an undertaking and the practical time constraints of a semester, I have students work in small groups, typically four groups of approximately five students, each group being responsible for a different adaptation proposal. (I do not ask groups to write the whole script.) To keep each group's project distinct, I provide different, and hopefully generative, guidelines: one production must be opulent, on the order of a Disney production; another must be low-budget, designed for a community theater but possibly more experimental than such a production might typically be; another must be set in modern times, with updated political and cultural sensitivities; another must consist of a star-studded cast, with every character played by a living celebrity actor; and so on. I assign the project and the groups before students read *Wyandotté* so that they can keep the project in mind as they work through the novel and relevant scholarship. Each student is responsible for writing, in approximately 1,500 words, about one aspect of their group's proposed production: scripting, set design, casting, directorial vision, costuming and special effects, and so on. After composing their drafts, students work collaboratively on assembling the proposal, cowriting an introduction that argues for the continuing relevance of Cooper's work, provides a coherent vision of their proposed adaptation that incorporates all aspects of the production, and discusses the commercial viability of their production and marketing strategy. (Students often like to design a poster or write a script for a commercial or trailer.) Groups then present their proposals to the class at the semester's end.

Set in upstate New York in the revolutionary period, *Wyandotté* shares much in common with Cooper's Leather-Stocking Tales but is arguably more measured in its pacing, more reflective about its setting, and involves a level of compositional complexity that the earlier novels do not, making it a rewarding novel to teach and better suited to the adaptation project. Once students are about a hundred pages in, I introduce scholarship that helps them identify the novel's five-act structure; Donald Ringe, in "James Fenimore Cooper and Thomas Cole," and Jeffrey Walker, in "Fenimore Cooper's *Wyandotté* and the Cyclic Course of Empire," have identified that the narrative structure of the novel corresponds with *The Course of Empire*, a series of five allegorical paintings—*The Savage State, The Arcadian or Pastoral State, The Consummation of Empire, Destruction,* and *Desolation*—by the American landscape painter and Cooper's personal friend Thomas Cole. (Cole's paintings and Walker's paper are perennial hits with students.) Cole and Cooper inspired each other throughout their careers: Earlier, Cole had painted scenes from *The Last of the Mohicans*, scenes that express a Romantic melancholy over the loss of wilderness—which Cole had termed "American scenery" in an 1836 essay ("Essay")—to industrial development and westward expansion. The same melancholy can be found in both early and late works by Cooper—Cooper even adopts the term "American scenery" at the beginning of *Wyandotté* (5). But in *The Course of Empire*, Cole imagines the fall of an empire, a subject much more dramatic and unsettling than that of his landscape paintings. In the early 1840s, Cooper took his cue from Cole, rejecting a progressive model of American history in *Wyandotté* in favor of a cyclical one, as Walker argues: for Cooper, history followed a pattern of five successive stages, driven by human corruption and violence, not by manifest destiny or the American dream ("Fenimore Cooper's *Wyandotté*").

I point out to students that Cooper warns his readers in his preface that his novel might not be well received by all Americans:

> Although the American revolution was probably as just an effort as was ever made by a people to resist the first inroads of oppression, the cause had its evil aspects, as well as all other human struggles. We have been so much accustomed to hear every thing extolled, of late years, that could be dragged into the remotest connection with that great event, and the principles which led to it, that there is danger of overlooking truth, in pseudo patriotism. (3)

And indeed, *Wyandotté* is the story of a microcosm of American life run amok. The republican spirit of independence is ultimately defeated in the novel, struck down by a betrayal (which I will not spoil here), and the novel ends in a scene like that portrayed in Cole's *Desolation*, with the abandonment of the settlement, a lone hermit occupying the ruins. To help students get a handle on how this cycle works, I ask them to align Cole's paintings with the five stages of the settlement in the novel. This activity can occasion productive discussions about different mediums (painting, writing, dramatic performance) and genres (landscapes, novels, allegory, dramatic tragedy), raising issues students will have to negotiate in their adaptation proposals.

The first issue I address deliberately with students is scenery, a profound concern for Cole and Cooper alike. The two had been friends since the early 1820s; Cole had been among the coterie of "youthful and buoyant" artists and intellectuals known as the Bread and Cheese Club who gathered about Cooper in New York City (Adkins 79). While the club membership was fluid, the members were "all of a liberal turn of mind," with "as much of the Bohemian spirit as any early nineteenth-century American city could have furnished." "Struggling to gain recognition from a world all too practical and too engrossed with humdrum commercial pursuits," the club turned against "the staid and conservative American Academy of the Fine Arts and formed their rival organization, the National Academy of Design," with the aim of inventing a new American identity conceived in relation to uniquely American landscapes (Marckwardt 397).[1]

Yet this new identity was tied to American landscapes that were rapidly disappearing—the expansive and sublime wilderness and frontier settlements were giving way to development. *Wyandotté* is a novel that insistently and tragically ties political and moral character to landscape, and any discerning stage adaptation should address this in a deliberate manner. In "Essay on American Scenery," Cole anticipates the vital loss of American scenery:

> I cannot but express my sorrow that the beauty of such landscapes is quickly passing away—the ravages of the axe are daily increasing—the most noble scenes are made desolate, and oftentimes with a wantonness and barbarism scarcely credible in a civilized nation. The wayside is becoming shadeless, and another generation will behold spots, now rife with beauty, desecrated by what is called improvement; which, as yet, generally destroys Nature's beauty without substituting that of Art. This is a regret rather than a complaint; such is the road society has to travel. (12)

Cole decried the agricultural and industrial development around Cedar Grove, his home in Catskill in the Hudson Valley, and he ranted that the distinctively American landscape was to be found in the "primeval forests, virgin lakes and waterfalls" that American painters had—but were losing—all around them (qtd. in Noble 148). The loss was not just environmental but also spiritual and moral; the wilderness had engendered the American spirit, but as it shrank, so too would the character of Americans. In 1836 Cole wrote his patron Lumen Reed, who had commissioned *The Course of Empire*: "They are cutting down all the trees in the beautiful valley on which I have looked so often with a loving eye" (qtd. in Noble 160–61). Cole asks his friend to "join with [him] in maledictions on all dollar-godded utilitarians." Two days later he apologizes for his tone but ends with sarcasm: "If I live to be old enough, I may sit down under some bush, the last left in the utilitarian world, and feel thankful that intellect in its march has spared one vestige of the ancient forest for me to die by" (161).

In his prospectus for *The Course of Empire*, Cole states his intention for the series of paintings: to "illustrate the history of a natural scene, as well as be an epitome of Man,—showing the natural changes of landscape, and those effected by man in his progress from barbarism to civilization—to luxury—to the vicious state, or state of destruction—and to the state of ruin and desolation." The sequence, Cole continues, "is drawn from the history" not of one empire but of all empires (qtd. in Noble 129)—a project likely inspired by Constantin François de Chassebœuf, comte de Volney, in his widely influential universal history of 1791, *Les ruines, ou méditations sur les révolutions des empires* (*The Ruins; or, A Survey of the Revolutions of Empires*), the English translation of which was begun by Thomas Jefferson and completed by the poet Joel Barlow. Allan Wallach argues that *The Course of Empire* "provides us with a capital record of American Romanticism" (375). It is, he says, the result of Cole's "habitual identification of art with literature," which suggested to him the "serial format that in effect overcame the temporal limitations of individual paintings" (376). Indeed, the sequence of *The Course of Empire* paintings allowed Cole to develop a historical allegory that gave full expression to his philosophical reflection on imperialism and capitalism.

If Cole habitually identified art with literature, then Cooper's *Wyandotté* is similarly ekphrastic, rife with references to landscapes, scenes, pictures, and views. The novel begins with a description of the valley before it is settled, "a picture of solitude" (21), then advances to a description of "the beauty of the landscape" as it is "improved" by agriculture (44), and, later, to "a most picturesque and lovely view" when inhabited (46). After this, however, the descriptions become darker—"Our *picture* would not have been complete, without relating the catastrophe that befel the Hutted Knoll" (358; my emphasis)—and the novel ends in a "closing scene" of desolation (369). This fascination with the visual arts is thematic throughout the novel: characters take in views; they contemplate the knoll from afar, or, conversely, the scenery around it from within its structures (including a cherished painting room); they are seen looking at the scenery, or they conceal themselves within it to spy on "a curious spectacle" (111, 131), "an extraordinary spectacle" (321), or "a sad spectacle" (326). At one point there are even theatrical props tossed about, a "wooden gun" and a "stuffed soldier" to create false scenes (272, 271). I draw students' attention to the metatheatricality of these moments, which students can exploit in their adaptations.

While it is better to have students discover the structure of the novel while reading, here I provide an overview. The first painting in Cole's series, *The Savage State*, depicts a sublime wilderness sparsely inhabited by transient Indians (to borrow the term from the titles of many of Cole's paintings and drawings) who are all but swallowed in the vast expanses of mountains and woods. Cooper's novel tells the story of a retired British soldier and veteran of the French and Indian War, Captain Willoughby, and his American wife, Wilhelmina, who together attempt to establish a settlement beyond "the Colony of New York" in Oneida and Mohawk territory (*Wyandotté* 7). The captain is granted land for his service, and he asks his longtime associate, Saucy Nick, a Tuscarora chief with a history not unlike that of Chingachgook from the Leather-Stocking Tales, to locate rich soil in defensible terrain. Willoughby's goal is to become entirely independent from colonial life, and he embodies the very spirit of the independent republican of the 1770s that the novel celebrates. (It should be noted that the Declaration of Independence is praised no less than six times in the novel.) Familiar with the entire region, Nick identifies a valley that has been dammed by beavers, which pleases the captain greatly; at considerable length, the captain muses on the benefits of beaver lakes: once drained, the land will already be free of trees, the soil will be deep and rich, and the surrounding hills will provide natural protection.

At this moment, however, Cooper invites readers to imagine the prehistory of the region, a nonanthropocentric history in which time is measured in generations of animals: "In the pond, itself, a few 'stubs' alone remained, the water having killed the trees, which had fallen and decayed. This circumstance showed that the stream had long before been dammed, successions of families of beavers having probably occupied the place, and renewed the works, for centuries, at intervals of generations." It is a moment in the novel ripe for ecocritical readings: Cooper suggests that the beavers' recent abandonment of the region was due to the arrival of "their great enemy man" (13), the trade in beaver pelts precipitating the first human impact on the landscape and announcing the arrival of the Anthropocene. Moreover, it is a moment in which the natural world is considered outside the realm of the political, economic, or even moral. Because of the relevance of this moment to current ecological thinking, I encourage students to exploit it in their adaptations. It should be noted, too, that Cooper acknowledges the presence of Indians in this prehistory but dismissively and with casual irony adds that "the Indian right" to the land, like that of the beavers, "was 'extinguished' by means of a few rifles, blankets, kettles and beads" (6). (Along the same lines, of the five mentions of dogs in the novel, four appear in expressions that equate Indians with dogs, and the fifth is that traitors, like dogs, may be shot without moral compunction [98, 244, 261, 308, and 361].) In any case, this prehistoric vision of the valley is brief and soon gives way to the next phase.

The captain breaks ground in the valley after collecting a motley crew of transatlantic laborers in Albany—including a comical but adamantly faithful Irish immigrant from the historically tumultuous County Leitrim, a Scottish mason, a conniving villain from Connecticut who plots against the captain despite serving as the overseer of the settlement, a New England chaplain who ironically becomes a staunch Loyalist in the American Revolution, a retired soldier who had fought under the captain's command, and several African American servants. I find it helpful to review the cast early since there are many characters and most are introduced at the outset of the novel. If one group is working on a star-studded cast adaptation, an early preview of possible actors to play each character can be effective, and it can serve as a counterweight to offset Cooper's use of racial and ethnic stereotypes, particularly of the African American characters. In a matter of pages, the crew discovers the knoll at the center of the soon-drained beaver pond, on which they build first a hut and eventually a more substantial manor home. The valley has changed substantially; at this point the novel moves into "the arcadian or pastoral state," to borrow the title of the second painting in Cole's series.

Soon the agricultural improvement of the land—"the labors of civilization" (Cooper, *Wyandotté* 29)—provides enough to sustain the community and its small industries (a blacksmith, a mill, and a carpentry shop). The captain moves his wife and children from Albany to the settlement, prompting the community to build more housing and fortify the manor home with a palisade—"an indispensable accessory to civilization" (30)—though the captain's family tragically neglects to hang the main gates for most of the novel, a detail so often repeated that it serves as a constant reminder of the family's, and particularly the women's, vulnerability. It should be noted, too, that while the two Willoughby daughters are prominent characters, none of the female characters rise to the level of significant actors in the novel. They watch rather than participate in the improvements. Moreover, the love plot involving the adopted daughter, Maud, perhaps the most compelling of the novel's women characters, is infuriatingly daft: no one understands that Maud, so beloved as a daughter, has fallen in love with her brother, and she cannot bring herself to make the confession lest she seem ungrateful to her parents. Cooper invests much in the subordination of the female characters to the patriarchal order; they are objects of the male gaze and of male desire as well as potential prizes of conquest. (The suicidal flight of a woman who is about to throw herself from a precipice to escape her potential rapist—the focal detail in Cole's *Destruction*—is a fair comparison to Cooper's treatment of female characters.) Just as the captain brings his wife and children to the settlement, so too do his laborers bring their families, who build a community around the manor home and fall into a routine of labor and family life.

Cooper refuses to give a full account of the improvements made to the land, though he suggests such an account would have a "Robinson Crusoe-interest" (12), an allusion that helps explain the narrator's fascination with diet throughout the novel. Just as Daniel Defoe's novel presents agriculture as the initial step toward civilization, and sustenance farming as a means for true independence, the implicit argument of *Wyandotté* is that true independence is won by living off the land and not participating in markets. Independence entails a rigorous investigation of diet, and Defoe spends pages of his novel detailing how Crusoe comes to bake bread. At the outset of his novel, Cooper speaks of the dangers of the "pernicious diet" of his contemporary society (3), and throughout the novel there is a celebration of subsistence agriculture; "Indian corn, oats, pumpkins, peas, potatoes, flax, and several other seeds" are grown in the valley, orchards of apple and pear trees line the valley's sides, and there are swine and free-roaming cattle (14). These are elements of a picturesque landscape, one that stands in contrast to the commercial agricultural landscape Cole decries. Willoughby's plans are not unlike Jefferson's proposal for a republic of yeoman farmers in his 1785 *Notes on the State of Virginia* (171–73); the yield from these operations allows the captain to "live in abundance" as "commander in chief of an isolated establishment" (Cooper, *Wyandotté* 42): "There every thing seemed peaceful and calm, the woods sighing with the airs of their sublime solitude, the genial sun shedding its heats on a grateful and generous soil, vegetation ripening and yielding with all the abundance of a bountiful nature, as in the more tranquil days of peace and hope" (140). Once the settlement is established, its residents are proudly self-sufficient, taking cattle occasionally to market in Albany but, Cooper insists, "nothing else" (42). The identification of food (and the landscape from which it comes) with moral character here is reminiscent of Joel Barlow's 1796 mock-epic poem *The Hasty-Pudding*, in which Barlow celebrates American porridge as emblematic of the vigorous life and moral health of the independent American farmer (6). And yet it must be noted that such passages not only elevate to mythic, if not Edenic, proportions the early American plantation patriarchy but also intimate a fall as inevitable as seasonal change.

Ten years pass, and the settlement has reached the third phase in its history, and what will be its zenith, consummation: the settlement is now peaceful, pastoral, and productive enough to ensure its independence. It is a moment of blissful success: "[I]t suited [Captain Willoughby's] own taste to be the commander in chief of an isolated establishment like this, and he was content to live in abundance, on his flats, feeding his people, his cattle and even his hogs to satiety, and having wherewithal to send away the occasional adventurer, who entered his clearing, contented and happy" (Cooper, *Wyandotté* 42). But this moment does not last. The prodigal son, Major Robert Willoughby of the British army, returns to report to his father about the Battle of Lexington and his anticipation of the Revolutionary War, which will compromise the security of the settlement that was never as isolated as perhaps was hoped. The daughters, Beulah and Maud, fall deeply in love, the former with a neighbor rebel fighter, the latter with the major, her adoptive brother, who returns to service among the British army in Boston. These relationships signify the inevitable connections to the world beyond the settlement that eventually creep in.

As the family and its close associates wrestle with the political controversy, discontent and envy take hold in the settlement, fueling a local conspiracy. The outside threats from Indians and American rebels who might attempt to confiscate Willoughby's property are made real by the conspiracy from within—a man from Connecticut, Joel Strides, conspires to bring Indians, White men disguised as Indians, and shady rebels within the defenses in an attempted coup. Cooper reminds his readers that he is writing a historical novel: "[T]here is scarce an instance of a confiscated estate, during the American revolution, connected with which racy traditions are not to be found, that tell of treachery very similar to this contemplated by the overseer; in some instances of treachery effected by means of kinsmen and false friends" (122). The treachery brings the novel to its climax and presents the penultimate landscape, the destruction of the settlement. Mayhem breaks loose and, in the chaos, the captain and several of his family members are murdered.

Then, in the last few pages, the novel closes with the final landscape, desolation: "[I]t was found that the spirit of destruction, which so widely prevails in the loose state of society that exists in all new countries, had been at work. Every one of the buildings at the falls, had been burnt; probably as much because it was in the power of some reckless wanderer to work mischief, as for any other reason" (369). The survivors disperse. Among them, the Irishman joins the American forces to kill Indians after the war, "laying up scalps on all suitable occasions" (366). (Earlier in the novel, Cooper identifies the "the scalping knife" with American progress: "Such is American History," remarks one character wryly [89]). The chaplain sets himself up as a hermit, occupying the ruins; the surviving children return to England; and the African Americans are provided with enough to secure their independence. For the most part, the valley surrenders to the forces of nature, the cycle ostensibly returning once more to "the savage state," to borrow the title of the first painting in Cole's series. Walker argues, "[J]ust as Cole portrays the rise and fall of civilization in his five paintings by showing how these cycles are immutable, so, too, does Cooper depict in his scenes the history of the Captain's settlement as an apt commentary on the American myth of progress" ("Fenimore Cooper's *Wyandotté*"). This commentary is tempered, however, by Cooper's references to the later history of the region as prosperous; while the microcosm of the settlement comes to an end, Cooper remains ambivalent about the course of American history. What is clear, however, is that Cooper regrets the fall of the kind of paternalistic social relations lionized in the figure of Captain Willoughby, even though Cooper seems critical of the captain's satisfied admissions to having flogged and whipped his subordinates in his younger years (*Wyandotté* 48).

While Walker's reading of the novel suggests that Cooper was moving into an allegorical mode ("Fenimore Cooper's *Wyandotté*"), there is a satirical dimension that other critics have noted. According to James Schramer, much of the drama of the novel has little to do with eighteenth-century issues, including the Revolutionary War, and everything to do "with the Anti-Rent Wars of the 1830s," when tenant farmers collected in revolt against manorial taxes and demanded reform of property rights and land ownership. This widespread political discontent was "fresh in [Cooper's] mind" and entirely defines the character of Joel Strides; Cooper, Schramer argues, was growing more conservative: "He sees the Revolution's rhetoric of egalitarianism as a prelude to unbridled social leveling. His faith in the common man as an untapped reservoir of patriotic virtue has begun to wane. In *Wyandotté*, the lowborn revolutionary is no longer a stoic patriot; he has become a rabble rousing demagogue." Indeed, Cooper denounces demagoguery in his preface, and as John P. McWilliams, Jr., has suggested, the central problem of the novel is not the British but "how to resist the incursion of the [American] demagogue"—an assessment of the novel that leaves us with more questions than answers about Cooper's politics (*Political Justice* 98–99). The tension between allegory and satire, between transcendence and relevance, is the core contention of *Wyandotté*, and in adapting the novel for the stage, students can explore this tension in diverse ways as they consider the present-day relevance of Cooper's story.

To that end, I close the semester with a final discussion on the relation between *Wyandotté* (both the novel and students' adaptations of it) and nationalism. Can *Wyandotté* be understood as a patriotic work, as a work of *American* literature? No class of mine has ever reached a consensus. In a list that serves to structure our discussion, McWilliams surveys the troubling features of a historical novel set during the American Revolution: "[T]here are no glorious battles in *Wyandotté*, no declarations of American progress, no tributes to historical leaders." The novel "has no hero, only a protagonist," and "the villains of *Wyandotté* are Americans" (*Political Justice* 98). And yet students generally agree that the scenery of the novel is definitely and profoundly American and that it is the scenery that makes the novel compelling.

NOTE

[1] For further discussion of Cooper, Cole, and the Bread and Cheese Club, see also Millhouse 17–23.

Cooper's Early Work in a Media History Context

Christopher J. Lukasik

I always experience a certain amount of hesitation—bordering on a foreboding disquiet—before I assign a James Fenimore Cooper novel to one of my English courses. In my teaching experience, the sheer length of Cooper's early novels (that is, anything published before *The Last of the Mohicans*) and the abundance of their descriptive prose often leave students of the *Twitter* generation bored, frustrated, and literally looking elsewhere. Many students, including English majors, confide to me at the end of the semester that novels such as *The Spy*, *The Pioneers*, or even *The Last of the Mohicans* were a struggle to read, let alone finish. Many toss their still crisp, glossy-covered paperbacks aside and give up, complaining that, try as they might, they simply could not make it to the end.

Of course, the easy explanation would be to blame these students for opting out of the hard work of reading a novel from the early nineteenth century. Yet, to do so would be unfair. Lest we forget, no less a reader than the notorious Leslie Fiedler found Cooper's work "unforgivably boring" ("James Fenimore Cooper") during a period when novels did not have to compete with *YouTube*, *Instagram*, or *Snapchat*, let alone a smoldering Daniel Day-Lewis as Natty Bumppo. It's no wonder the popular film critic Roger Ebert praised Michael Mann's 1992 cinematic adaptation of *The Last of the Mohicans* for being a significant upgrade over "Cooper's all but unreadable book." As the appraisals by Fiedler and Ebert suggest, the dissatisfaction that many students experience while leafing through Cooper's novels is hardly theirs alone. Even a cursory glance at the digital repositories of contemporary reader reception—*LibraryThing*, *Goodreads*, *Reddit*, and countless blogs—confirms what many of my students have been trying to tell me. Cooper's novels just aren't as binge-worthy as they used to be.

As much as we, as instructors, may enjoy reading Cooper—and even that's up for debate, as I know many colleagues who do not—I have come to accept that for generations raised in a different media context, one littered with the visual images of film, television, and the Internet, Cooper's novels can be a bit ponderous. This generational difference isn't a slight on our students, I think, so much as a change in our media environment and our reading practices. As one reader writing under the name amerynth sarcastically muses in a *LibraryThing* review of *The Last of the Mohicans*: "[W]hy describe a man as tall and thin when you can spend pages describing every feature from their eyebrows to their toes? Nary a drop of water nor a tree gets by without a vivid, unneeded description." Amerynth describes struggling to get past Cooper's writing style to enjoy the novel and suggests that a "movie version" would be better than "the book." Amerynth's impatience with Cooper's "vivid, unneeded description" and the reader's preference for a film adaptation are telling, because amerynth intuitively points to this change in the media environment. By questioning the necessity of meticulous textual pictures in a twenty-first-century media context in which visual, not verbal, images are often used to convey similar information far more quickly, amerynth wryly connects readerly impatience with the question of medium. To put it another way, Cooper's seemingly endless pages of verbal description can be tiresome, not so much because they lack a purpose (as Mark Twain famously complained in "Fenimore Cooper's Literary Offenses"), but because they strike many modern readers as not being needed. I return to this point below, but I believe that one of the keys to teaching Cooper's novels today is recognizing that the very features that made the novels so popular during Cooper's day might be the same ones that make them unbearable for our students now: their images.

Does this difficulty with reading Cooper's novels make the decision to assign them to students misguided? Not at all. As this volume attests, Cooper's fiction engages a whole range of thought-provoking issues still sparking conversation today: from the environment and racial identity to the scope of individual rights (such as freedom, privacy, and property) in American democracy. However, this difficulty does make the matter of addressing Cooper's images a pressing one. How might instructors pedagogically intervene and address the challenge students face when encountering Cooper's images? How might we persuade the so-called distracted generation to put down their phones rather than the novels? I don't know if I have an answer to the second question, for Cooper is hardly the only nineteenth-century novelist vying for attention in our vast contemporary media environment, but what I do know is that after years of teaching Cooper's early novels to undergraduate and graduate students, I have come to the conclusion that rather than avoiding, defending, or apologizing for "the cumulative dullness" of Cooper's lengthy verbal descriptions (Fiedler, *Love* 180), it is more productive to acknowledge their difficulty and situate them in terms of media history. Although this approach rarely eradicates students' impatience with Cooper's prose style, it does allow students to consider whether their initial reaction to the prose—one usually framed in terms of aesthetic failure or unbridgeable historical distance—might be historically structured by their own media environment.

There are many reasons to teach Cooper's novels from a media history context, but perhaps the most compelling one is simply to equip students with ways to confront and work through the images that so often impede their reading experience. Obviously, if students fail to read Cooper's novels then they will never be in a position to fully comprehend, let alone discuss, the novels' treatment of subjects that have fascinated and frustrated Cooper's readers for nearly two centuries—from race, ethnicity, gender, and class to democracy, liberalism, nationalism, imperialism, and the environment. Yet, no matter what students decide Cooper's novels have to say about those subjects, a media history approach also enables them to understand that the novels' positions might depend as much on *how* Cooper's images represent as on *what* they represent. The question of what *The Pioneers* has to say about race, for instance, can be pursued not only by analyzing how Native or African Americans are depicted in the novel but also by considering how Cooper's images, to borrow a phrase from Jacques Rancière, distribute the sensible,[1] how they determine what can be seen and what can be said. Thus, a second advantage of a media history approach to Cooper's novels is that it can offer instructors another avenue toward helping students understand those issues of long-standing interest and debate, one that empowers students to consider the larger system of visibility to which the novel belongs and from which the visible and invisible are constituted for readers.

A media history approach to Cooper's novels also supplies instructors with a more recent theoretical framework from which to discuss Cooper's images and connect them to our own media environment. While there have been many important critical studies on Cooper's literary pictorialism over the years (e.g., Callow; Ringe, *Pictorial Mode*; and Nevius), their methods are dated and often trade in a notion of media purity that belies the intense intermediality of both nineteenth-century print culture and our digital present. When students learn to think of Cooper's images as residing in early media, they are better positioned to discuss the subsequent transposition of those images into different media (from nineteenth-century engravings and paintings to twentieth-century films, comic books, and television shows) in a process known as remediation. This pedagogical approach has the additional advantage of expanding Cooper's relevance beyond the syllabi of American literature courses. One can easily imagine how *The Spy*, *The Pioneers*, or *The Last of the Mohicans* and their respective remediations might constitute a unit in any number of humanities courses in which the media history of images in novels and their meanings might be as important to course objectives as Cooper's novels and their meanings are. Finally, the wealth of print and optical media available on the Internet and in digital databases makes a media history approach to Cooper's work now more accessible than ever, and these materials can provide instructors with the opportunity not only to integrate multiple media forms into their classrooms but also to ask students to consider how nineteenth- and twenty-first-century media might be historically and dialectically linked.

To this end, the remainder of this essay discusses how instructors might situate Cooper's images in a more general media history so that students might not only read and hopefully finish Cooper's novels but also better understand the relation between nineteenth-century literature and their own media landscape. But first I should make it clear that when I refer to media history, I don't have a single field or critical methodology in mind, but rather a loose assemblage of three related but distinct ways of thinking about media: recent theories of the image, particularly in the work of W. J. T. Mitchell and of Rancière (*Future*); the kind of historically inflected media studies associated with the work of Lisa Gitelman and of Erkki Huhtamo; and intermedial and media theory, especially as it concerns medial transposition or remediation (as in Rajewsky; Bolter and Grusin). These three ways of thinking about media can be used in conjunction with any number of historical materials related to Cooper's novels, including the verbal images in Cooper's novels as well as their nineteenth-century reception, the nineteenth-century media combinations (in illustrated editions) and medial transpositions (such as paintings and dramatizations) generated by Cooper's images, and the twentieth- and twenty-first-century remediations of Cooper's images into various media (such as comic books, film, television, graphic novels, and even an opera). It is unlikely that any single course will have time to fit all these media contexts into its discussion of Cooper's work. Instructors can, however, decide which materials best suit their unit or course objectives and whether that material is best conveyed through lecture summation or directed lines of questioning or assigned directly to students as supplementary reading, viewing, or listening.

To give a more specific sense of how this approach might work in the classroom, let's consider how recent theories of the image, to take one example, might help students better contextualize and understand Cooper's verbal images, their nineteenth-century reception, and their subsequent remediations. Recent theories of the image can be used to encourage students not only to consider literature's place in media history but, more important for the purposes of addressing Cooper's images, to conceive of images in terms other than the technical properties of the medium (that is, as something not necessarily optical). In doing so, students are challenged to discuss literary images without using the received historical frameworks that have differentiated word and image on the basis of their technical medium (verbal or visual), sensory organ (ear or eye), or mode of meaning production (semiotic or sensory). Instructors can use Mitchell's *What Do Pictures Want* and Rancière's *The Future of the Image* to demonstrate how an image is more than its visible or textual equivalent and is instead a nuanced relation between them, an intermedial environment in which the seeable and the sayable coalesce and operate. Rancière's insistence that "the image is not exclusive to the visible" should prompt students to think about what an image is, how it means, and in what ways reading and seeing might or might not be considered equivalent practices (7). Similarly, Mitchell's claim that "literature involves 'virtual' or 'imaginative' experiences of space and vision that are no less real for being indirectly conveyed through language" can be used to introduce how the early nineteenth century thought about verbal images as well as to discuss how much literary pictorialism and readerly visualization still matter to twenty-first-century readers (350).

Mitchell's position, in fact, dovetails nicely with both Cooper's position and the other positions held on the subject in Cooper's period. Like Mitchell, Cooper understood that reading novels would create an imaginative experience similar to seeing. In his most explicit theory of the novel, he describes how the moral force of a novel is best attained through the production of "one of those popular pictures which find their way into every library, and which, whilst they have attractions for the feeblest intellects, are not often rejected by the strongest" (*Letter* 13–14). Cooper grounded the moral force of a novel in its pictures because he believed in the presumed veracity as well as the supposed immediacy and universality of the visual image. As scholars have long noted, Cooper expected his readers "to read descriptive passages as one might view a painting" and "above all to visualize the scene described" (Ringe, *Pictorial Mode* 15). The capacity of literature, particularly novels, to produce such images in the minds of readers was "one of the most significant criteria for determining a text's literary and moral value in post-revolutionary America" (Lukasik 78). Framing Cooper's position on images—as well as other positions held during his period—within the context of recent theories of the image encourages students to move beyond comparing his verbal images to those found in visual media. Instead, students learn to think about how Cooper's images operate in generating what Mitchell calls that virtual experience of the world for readers (350).

Instructors can also use any number of contemporary reviews from *The Spy*, *The Pioneers*, or *The Last of the Mohicans* to show students how nineteenth-century readers received and valued novels in precisely the way that Cooper did: by the effects of their images. *The Pioneers*, for example, was praised for its "almost visual effect" and for how the process of reading was similar to advancing from "one of his paintings to another" ("*The Pioneers*" [*Album*] 165, 158). This kind of historical contextualization can help students understand that optical media were not the only, let alone preferred, form for circulating images in the early nineteenth century. To be sure, there were paintings, engravings, and illustrations, but the kind of mass visual culture that we now inhabit was only beginning to take shape during this time. A media historical perspective also allows instructors to remind students that Cooper's early novels were published at a particular historical moment, one in which the images being circulated in print culture were beginning to shift from verbal to visual images.

For this reason, Cooper's novels from the 1820s are significant for showing how the rising medium for images in print culture (illustration) might have already been nested within the older medium (literature and its verbal images). Instructors can use nineteenth-century reviews of Cooper's early novels to illustrate this point. The *Port Folio* suggested this point in 1823 when it noted in its review of *The Pioneers* that "the scene in which Elizabeth is saved from the panther" would make "a fine subject for the painter" and should "excite the pencil of some one" ("*The Pioneers*" [*Port Folio*] 243). And it did. A few months later, the *Port Folio* reported that *The Pioneers* had "excited a sensation among the artists, altogether unprecedented in the history of our domestic literature" ("Literary Intelligence" 520). Like *The Spy* before it, *The Pioneers* inspired an unprecedented amount of visual material, including illustrations, engravings, and paintings, during the 1820s and 1830s. Instructors can use illustrations by artists such as Henry Inman, Tony Johannot, William Dunlap, Gideon Fairman, Tompkins Matteson, Robert Farrier, John Quidor, F. O. C. Darley, and George Loring Brown—who all depicted scenes from *The Pioneers*—to address issues of medium and remediation as well as to encourage students to consider how later optical media (in the case of *The Pioneers*, illustration, film, and television) might be understood as extensions of rather than replacements for literature.

The integration into a course of subsequent remediations of Cooper's novels — illustrations, paintings, comic books, films, or television series — also enables instructors and students to focus on how the medium shapes the message. Instructors, especially if they are integrating twentieth-century remediations of Cooper's works into their courses, can ask students whether the medium in which images appear or how they are consumed (such as by reading words or looking at visual images) matters. For example, does the historical shift from Cooper's verbal images to Mann's cinematic ones in *The Last of the Mohicans* matter? If so, in what ways? Does the medium diminish or enlarge any of the values that Cooper's or our students' generation assign to the practice of reading a novel or that our students' generation assigns to watching a film (such as improving the attention, observation, comprehension, or imagination of the reader)? In the case of the capacities of the individual imagination, students might be asked to weigh the advantages and disadvantages of visualizing a scene for themselves as opposed to having someone else do it for them through optical media such as paintings, film, or television. One concrete way to make this point is to ask students whether they first encountered *Harry Potter and the Sorcerer's Stone*, or another popular novel, through the book or the film adaptation. Those who first read the book (and there should be many) should then be asked whether the bespectacled actor Daniel Radcliffe was the image for Harry Potter they had in mind when they first read the book. And they should be asked, furthermore, what might be gained or lost intellectually and creatively from not being able to picture things for themselves. Besides injecting some lively discussion into the classroom, these questions often help students begin to conceive of Cooper's images, however cumbersome they might appear initially, in a new light.

Recent theories of the image, such as Rancière's, can also encourage students to address the familiar problem of the politics of literary representation in new ways that are particularly relevant for Cooper's works. Students can be encouraged to think about what Cooper's images make visible, how they do so, and to what ends. The opening chapter of *The Spy* and that of *The Pioneers* are especially fruitful in this regard. Each foregrounds the practice of looking by detailing how characters look at each other and how readers, in turn, come to see or visualize them. These chapters can provide occasions for discussing the ways in which people become visible or remain invisible and the discourses by which they become recognizable and thus socially legible or illegible. These chapters — and there are many like them throughout Cooper's early novels — also create opportunities to examine how detailed verbal description and narrative focalization can command readerly attention and model for readers actual ways of looking, or what Rob Burnett refers to as "vantage points" (13). Students can then be invited to consider how the media forms they are most familiar with shape the way they perceive the world.

I hope this essay on approaching Cooper's novels from a media history perspective invites instructors to reconsider how they think about images and their relation to texts and prompts instructors to reassess how they teach the novels of Cooper in particular and nineteenth-century American literature in general. In my mind, this matter is all the more urgent given the ubiquity of the image in our culture today as well as the current debates within the field concerning the relation between literary and media studies. "The exclusion of literature from the disciplinary formation of media studies was a mistake," John Guillory has recently argued, "damaging both to media studies and literary studies. . . . Undoing this institutional segregation in fact as well as in theory will likely prove difficult, but the vitality of both sets of disciplines depends on it." For this reason, Guillory believes that a renewal of the cultural disciplines (which we could all use) will depend on how well we can account for "the relation between literature and later technical media without granting to literature the privilege of cultural seniority or to later media the palm of victorious successor" (361). It has been my intention to demonstrate how the image—when discussed in all its senses (verbal, visual, and mental)—might provide us with an opportunity to account for this relation by situating Cooper's early novels in the wider nineteenth-century media landscape, of which they were undoubtedly a part, and in the twenty-first-century media landscape in which readers now encounter them.

NOTE

[1] See Rancière, *Politics* 12–45 for a discussion of the "distribution of the sensible" (12).

The Social Power of Sentimental Lament: The Last of the Mohicans and Mann's Film Adaptation

Paul Gutjahr

When James Fenimore Cooper's *The Last of the Mohicans* calls for our attention today, it is often because scholars point to it as the book that first introduced readers of American literature to such terms as *totem, white man,* and *red skins* and that offered hugely influential early renditions of the lone, heroic frontiersman through Natty Bumppo and the stereotype of the noble savage through Chingachgook and his son, Uncas (Franklin, *James Fenimore Cooper: The Early Years* 474).[1] What is easily missed in such broad characterizations of *The Last of the Mohicans* is how the work stood not only as a fountain of key elements in our mythology of the American West but as a fountain of blood as well. One scholar has gone so far as to note that the words *blood* or *bloody* appear in the text no less than ninety-five times (Philbrick 29). The novel is so steeped in carnage, conflict, and extermination that it is little wonder that many scholars treat it as a sort of urtext for the myth of the vanishing American Indian. For Cooper, however, the novel was more than an exercise in exploring what would become the mythos of the American West; it was a heartfelt personal exploration of his own ambivalence toward Native Americans and his family's complicity in their marginalization in American society.

The Last of the Mohicans was Cooper's sixth book, and for a time, because of illness and financial troubles, Cooper thought it might be his last (Franklin, *James Fenimore Cooper: The Early Years* 514–15). Thus, he approached it with a seriousness and skill not only born of crafting a number of previously successful novels but also driven by the fear that he might not have another chance to convey to readers his own thinking about the cost of the nation's westward movement in the opening decades of the nineteenth century. For Cooper, *The Last of the Mohicans* became his most extended and profound treatise on what it meant for different societies and races to be thrown together in a colonial environment and to battle for survival and, ultimately, ascendancy.

At its core, Cooper's story concerns two worlds—the world of European settlement and the indigenous world of the Native Americans—locked in mortal combat as White settlers moved west. When Cooper composed *The Last of the Mohicans* in the mid-1820s, the United States was experiencing a period of unprecedented growth. The population of the western state of Ohio, for example, had grown almost fivefold since 1810 to nearly a million, while Indiana's population had leapt from less than 25,000 White settlers in 1810 to over 340,000 in 1830 (Rohrbaugh 130). Such massive population shifts put incredible pressure on government officials to make land available for settlement. In his annual address to Congress in 1824, President James Monroe hinted at his intention to develop a relocation policy for Native Americans that would free up new land for White settlers: "unless the tribes be civilized, they can never be incorporated into our system in any form whatever" (218). Monroe then proceeded to advocate policies that clearly treated Native American nations not as independent sovereignties, as they had been by the United States government since the revolution, but as subservient groups under American federal control. In the main, Monroe attempted to put in place more equitable policies of coexistence with Native Americans, but his policies laid the groundwork for President Andrew Jackson's later, more aggressive Indian Removal strategies, which resulted in such mass forced migrations as the Trail of Tears.[2]

One senses throughout *The Last of the Mohicans* Cooper's own conflicted attitude toward American westward expansion, as Cooper witnessed its terribly high price for the continent's indigenous populations. A portion of his ambivalence may well have been rooted in a complicity he felt in the declining fortunes of Native Americans because of his own family history. His father, William Cooper, had been one of the country's first great land barons. The elder Cooper had acquired thousands of acres of land over the course of his lifetime, much of it carved from traditional tribal lands in what has become upstate New York (Taylor 33–40). Remembered now almost entirely for the founding of Cooperstown, the home of the National Baseball Hall of Fame, William Cooper exercised great economic and political power during his lifetime. He became a pivotal figure in the nation's expansion westward by selling much of the land he had acquired to some forty thousand settlers and boasting that he had helped settle "more acres than any man in America" (Banner 466).[3] In the end, William Cooper may have distributed as much as 750,000 acres of land to Whites who were moving west, and his land sales made him, at the time of his death, one of the wealthiest men in America.

William Cooper's vast land holdings probably provided yet another, more personal, reason behind the doubts James Fenimore Cooper harbored about the legitimacy of Native American dispossession. When he died in 1809, William Cooper left significant inheritances to his five sons, of whom James was the youngest. By 1820, this youngest Cooper was the sole surviving heir, but the fifty thousand dollars his father had left him in both cash and property was exhausted. He had lost the majority of his inheritance to plunging land values and his own spending habits. In truth, his inheritance had always been worth more on paper than it was worth in reality. Not only did Cooper lose thousands of acres of land he was forced to sell to settle debts; eventually his financial situation deteriorated to such an extent that he lost his family's mansion in Cooperstown as well as his own home there (Franklin, *James Fenimore Cooper: The Early Years* 4, 303–34). Cooper's experience losing long-held family property may thus have made him more sympathetic to the removal of Native Americans from their lands.

In *The Last of the Mohicans*, Cooper ultimately crafted a novel that served as a blood-soaked, sentimental lament commemorating the ascendancy of a new

White nation built on the ruins of once powerful indigenous populations.[4] *Sentimental* is used here in the same sense as it is employed by the literary scholar Shirley Samuels, who identifies sentimental writing in Cooper's period as pieces focused on activating the sympathy of readers in such a way that they are driven to right moral action (*Culture* 4–6). Cooper penned his novel, with its carefully and elaborately drawn Native American characters, as a heartfelt sentimental rumination on the disappearance of once great tribes that might call his readers to see and treat Native Americans as profoundly human and humane figures (Franklin, *James Fenimore Cooper: The Early Years* 471–72). The novel's sentimental lamentation reaches its apex in the final funeral scene, where the death of the potentially messianic figure of Uncas is mourned and where the aged Delaware chief Tamenund laments that "the pale-faces are masters of the earth" and that Native Americans have nothing to look forward to but the darkness of night (Cooper, *Last* 350).[5]

Mapping Cooper's Novel and Mann's Film Adaptation

To help my students appreciate how Cooper inflected *The Last of the Mohicans* with an air not only of lament but also of moral sympathy and protest, I turn to Michael Mann's 1992 film adaptation of Cooper's novel. Several different film adaptations of *The Last of the Mohicans* have been made, of which Mann's is the most recent (Gutjahr, "Selected Bibliography" 458). Although Mann made use of the screenplay for George Seitz's 1936 adaptation, Mann's production stands apart from all previous adaptations in how it shares Cooper's agenda not only for lament but also for at least a mild form of social protest.

As I have my students approach Mann's film, I work to add complexity to the notion held by so many of them that the best film adaptations of a literary work are those that remain truest to the work in their content and structure. Such a view is only one of many ways of judging the quality of a film adaptation.[6] I wish to have my students move beyond a simple formal equivalence of a novel to its movie incarnation by pushing them to analyze the film as a work unto itself. Although a film adaptation may be based on a writer's original idea, screenwriters, directors, and even actors bring their own interpretations of the original work to the film. To create some separation between Cooper's novel and Mann's reinterpretation of that novel, I have my students analyze first the novel and then the film by using a detailed correlation—or mapping—exercise.

First, I have my students create a list of what they think are the elements in Cooper's novel that most clearly signal what they believe to be the writer's cultural values and beliefs. I make no pretension that we can know for certain what Cooper thought when he wrote the novel, but I do ask students to make arguments from evidence for why they believe he might take certain positions on various culturally important issues of his day. Thus, I have them use this mapping exercise to link moments in the novel to arguments they wish to make about what they believe Cooper might have meant by his representations of events, persons, relationships, places, and objects.

This mapping exercise can lead to any number of results, and the discussions that ensue about whether an event or a character supports a certain line of argumentation are just one of the benefits for students wishing to carefully consider Cooper's text. Although there are dozens of textual touch points that might be mined through this exercise, I will mention just four aspects (all linked to race) that often arise when students argue for what Cooper might have thought or valued as he crafted *The Last of the Mohicans*:

> *Element in the novel*: Hawk-eye proclaims he is a man without a cross in his blood (35).
>
> *Possible interpretation*: Such proclamations are undercut by the fact that Hawk-eye is often represented as having both red (or dark) and white skin in the novel. Students may argue that although Cooper gives lip service in the novel to the importance of racial purity, Hawk-eye, the novel's most recognized White character, is blended almost to the point of obscurity with his Native American companions.
>
> *Element in the novel*: Cora is mixed race, European and Creole.
>
> *Possible interpretation*: Like Hawk-eye, Cora is a character who bridges different races. Her liminal quality, however, and her gender do not keep her from being represented as one of the strongest and smartest characters in the novel. (For example, when the men have little idea of what to do at Glen's Falls, Cora is the one who gives direction to the group [77–80].) Once again, students might argue that Cooper does not prize racial purity as much as suggested by his seemingly ubiquitous comments about his characters having no cross in their blood, or mixed ancestry.
>
> *Element in the novel*: In its second half, the novel features costume changes, disguises, and cases of mistaken identity, such as when characters pretend to be, for example, doctors, bears, and beavers.
>
> *Possible interpretation*: Students might argue that such a pronounced emphasis on identity fluidity signals Cooper's view that purity of identity, racial or otherwise, is a matter of extreme complexity and that one finds the best chance of navigating a incredibly hostile world in accepting identities that shift depending on circumstances and perspective.
>
> *Element in the novel*: Uncas and Cora die, while Alice and Duncan survive.
>
> *Possible interpretation*: Through the fates of his characters, Cooper offers a glimpse of the future diminishment of Native Americans and the ascendency of their White counterparts in the United States. Given

Cooper's often positive emphasis on racial hybridity in the novel, one must wonder if Cooper is simply offering what he considers to be the inevitable effect of European settlement, rather than a statement about racial preference.

Once my students have been able to distill what they believe to be their strongest arguments about Cooper's values as they manifest themselves in the text, I have them turn to analyze Mann's screenplay and directorial decisions in the same light. What might Mann value and what messages might he wish to convey through his particular redactions, rearrangement, and visual representation of Cooper's text? When it comes to issues of race and European imperialism, I encourage students to examine how Mann's decisions at times resonate with Cooper's own conflicted attitudes and at other times complicate—and even work against—the themes students see embedded in Cooper's novel. Once again, I confine my discussion to aspects of Mann's film that address the same moments touched upon in the mapping exercise mentioned above. It is also helpful to note that one of the most effective means of assessing these mapping exercises comes when students map the same event, place, relationship, or other point of study in both the book and the movie and then provide effective lines of argumentation that arise—often quite differently—when the book and film version are placed in this type of juxtaposition.

> *Element in the film*: At no point does Hawk-eye (Nathaniel) proclaim that he is a man without a cross, a statement repeated in the novel.
>
> *Possible interpretation*: Nathaniel is clearly the movie's protagonist, and he is just as clearly associated with the Native American characters in the movie. He has a knowledge of White culture but little affinity for it and thus identifies more with the Native American characters.
>
> *Element in the film*: Cora is not of mixed race in the movie. (Both she and her sister, Alice, are clearly coded as White.)
>
> *Possible interpretation*: Mann deemphasizes any preference for White culture not just through Nathaniel but also through Cora, who moves over time to align herself with the Native American cultures featured in the film through her romance with Hawk-eye and her newfound appreciation for Native American beliefs and practices.
>
> *Element in the film*: The film features none of the costume changes, exercises in disguise, or cases of mistaken identity that are so plentiful in the book.
>
> *Possible interpretation*: Characters in the film make their values known not through their appearances but through their actions.

Element in the film: Alice and Duncan are killed at the end of the movie, while Cora and Nathaniel survive.

Possible interpretation: Whereas Cooper chose to leave Alice and Duncan firmly in charge of a White destiny for the United States, Mann shows a distaste for certain aspects of American imperialism by killing off both Alice and Duncan. Mann gives over the nation's future to Hawk-eye and Cora, who will presumably bear children who are more likely to bring a stronger commitment to Native American cultures.

Students most often argue that Mann shows a pronounced preference for themes linked to Native American empowerment. Such views are bolstered by the end of the film, where the White characters with the fewest ties to Native American cultures (Duncan and Alice) die and where White characters with pronounced sympathies for Native Americans survive. My students have also argued that Mann's commitment to Native American empowerment is further emphasized in the film by the decision to have Chingachgook kill the story's chief villain, Magua, whereas in the novel Hawk-eye kills Magua.

Sentimental Lament in Mann's Film Adaptation

On issues of race, Mann — like the screenwriters and directors of previous adaptations of *The Last of the Mohicans* — reinterpreted key moments of Cooper's text to emphasize his own priorities and values. But his choice to cast Russell Means as Chingachgook is what makes his film categorically different from other cinematic adaptations of Cooper's novel and is perhaps the clearest indicator of just how strongly Mann sympathized with Cooper's agenda of sentimental lament verging on moral protest about the treatment of Native Americans.

To help students appreciate the significance of Mann's casting of Means, I spend time in class familiarizing them with the emergence of the American Indian movement (AIM) in the late 1960s and early 1970s.[7] AIM sought to harness some of the energy and focus of the African American civil rights movement by bringing greater attention to the poor treatment of Native Americans by the American government in particular and large segments of American society more generally. AIM gained such attention through a series of high-profile protests. From 1969 to 1971, AIM protesters participated in the occupation of the abandoned federal prison of Alcatraz in San Francisco Bay (Smith and Warrior 18–35). On Thanksgiving Day 1970, protesters seized a replica of the *Mayflower* ship anchored in Boston Harbor, a ceremonial prop to commemorate the 350th anniversary of the landing of the Pilgrims at Plymouth Rock. A year later they occupied the top of Mount Rushmore for a few days, proclaiming the sculptures there a sacrilegious monument that glorifies hundreds of years of White oppression and that is situated on land the Lakota Sioux had long considered sacred (88–89). In 1972, AIM protesters worked with other Native American groups to mount a protest march in Washington, DC, known as the Trail of Broken Treaties. Thousands of Native Americans traveled to Washington, where they occupied the Bureau of Indian Affairs building for six weeks and then submitted a detailed proposal to the United States government on issues for which they sought redress (149–68). Perhaps AIM's most famous protest moment came in 1973 when several protesters seized a group of buildings at Wounded Knee on the Pine Ridge Indian Reservation, the site of an infamous massacre of Native Americans in 1891. The ensuing standoff garnered national media attention for over a month and resulted in several deaths and woundings (194–268).

A key player in each of these protests was Means, a founding participant in AIM.[8] By the early 1970s, Means had established himself as one of AIM's principal leaders and one of its most recognizable spokespersons. In ensuing decades, he not only came to be closely associated with matters of Native American rights advocacy but grew to become an internationally recognized leader for the rights of indigenous people, doing work in both Central and South America. In the 1990s, *The Washington Post* described Means as "[o]ne of the biggest, baddest, meanest, angriest, most famous American Indian activists of the late twentieth century" (qtd. in Means, front cover).

As Mann was putting together what would become his 1992 adaptation of *The Last of the Mohicans*, he worked with a casting agency to seek out Means to play the character of Chingachgook. Although Means would later go on to a prolific acting career in both film and television, he had never acted prior to being cast in Mann's movie. Mann pursued Means not because he knew he could act — although Means does a credible job throughout the film — but for what Means symbolized as a warrior for Native American rights. The casting of Means as Chingachgook could be likened to casting Martin Luther King, Jr., in a film version of a slave narrative.

Means states in his autobiography that he was drawn to acting in Mann's film because he so identified with being the last of a tribe (Means 510–17). The years he had spent in Native American rights advocacy that seemingly had so little effect seem to echo the life and efforts of Cooper's lonely, last Mohican. Mann embedded profound layers of moral protest in his film by casting an unknown actor but decidedly well-traveled Native American activist. Taken together, Mann's choice of thematic development, his commitment to fully realized Native American characterization, and his casting of Means give the film an emphasis on Native American rights. In the film's sympathies and its pathos, one can argue that it has much in common with the sentimental lament one finds so pervasive in Cooper's novel.

The tensions explored by Cooper and by Mann as Native American and White cultures interact in their respective works ultimately allow me to lead students into discussions about more contemporary Native American and White cultural interactions since the height of AIM's activism in the 1960s and 1970s. The questions of morality and action that emerge from beneath the surface of Cooper's novel and Mann's film provide a basis for students to study more current debates on the place of Native Americans in contemporary American culture. The United States government may no longer have the same overt policies of Indian Removal that it had in Cooper's day, but these policies have deep resonances with how American society continues to ignore, marginalize, and vanish Native American populations today, a truth Mann readily hints at in his film.

In this section of my course I often allow students to pursue longer research projects that are rooted in Cooper's novel. Such projects can address a wide range of more contemporary topics: issues of Native American political sovereignty, the disputes over removing human bones from tribal lands, the use of Native American symbols in American advertising and sports, the language still used in mainstream American culture to describe Native American populations, the intertribal conflicts in casino and land development ventures, Native American alcohol abuse, and changing representations of Native Americans in literary works and school curricula.[9]

Given the numerous editions of Cooper's novel still in print and its various film adaptations over the past century, *The Last of the Mohicans* demonstrates a remarkable ability to capture the American imagination nearly two hundred years after the novel's first appearance. A thoughtful examination of the novel in the context of Mann's film adaptation provides an opportunity to analyze not only the continuing currency of the novel's themes but also how artistic works provide a means of lament, protest, and advocacy regarding aspects of our society that cry out for attention and change.

NOTES

[1] The image of the lone frontiersman and the so-called noble savage in relation to *The Last of the Mohicans* has been explored in a number of places, including Berkhofer 86–104 and H. Smith 59–70.

[2] For treatments of the United States government's Indian Removal policies and activities, see Ammon 474–75, 536–40; Dunbar-Ortiz 95–116; Bowes 18–77.

[3] For a longer discussion of William Cooper's settlement practices see Taylor 7–73, 86–101.

[4] An illuminating discussion of this connection between Cooper's loss and that of Native American tribes is found in Peck 141–45.

[5] Citations of Cooper's *The Last of the Mohicans* refer to the edition published by the State University of New York Press and edited by Sappenfield and Feltskog. The importance of Uncas as the true hero of the novel is convincingly argued in Darnell.

[6] For helpful discussions of various ways to approach cinematic adaptations of literary works, see Cahir 13–71 and Leitch, "Adaptation."

[7] The best single-volume treatment of this period of AIM's development is Smith and Warrior. A good photographic history of AIM can be found in Bancroft and Wittstock.

[8] A good introduction to AIM can be found in the film *Incident at Oglala*. In telling the story of the Native American activist Leonard Peltier, the director, Michael Apted,

includes compelling, succinct explanations of AIM as the film recounts the occupation of Wounded Knee. I often show select clips from this movie to my classes, who get a good sense for both AIM and a young Means, who is shown giving an interview where he states he is willing to die for his convictions. Another film that sheds helpful light on aspects of AIM and some of its principal actors is *A Good Day to Die*.

[9] A bibliography that gives helpful references for works on many of these topics can be found in Dunbar-Ortiz 240–44.

Teaching *The Last of the Mohicans* through Cinematic Adaptation

David W. Hartwig

As educators, we know our students consume much more visual than print media, yet we might overlook visual media as a productive locus of study, especially for encouraging critical thought in general education courses. In this essay, I recount my teaching of James Fenimore Cooper's *The Last of the Mohicans* alongside its cinematic adaptations, especially Michael Mann's 1992 film of the same name. This pedagogical approach is effective since Cooper's novel is often challenging to students because of the author's archaic writing style, students' lack of familiarity with Cooper's works, and the ambivalent romanticism with which Cooper addresses the dispossession and diminution of Native Americans. I begin by introducing fidelity discourse as a useful pedagogical tool; I then discuss class exercises and assignments to foster better understanding of Cooper's work and its cinematic offshoots; finally, I share student projects that resulted from this pedagogical approach to support the argument that teaching Cooper's novel alongside its cinematic descendants fosters creative and critical thinking.

Fidelity Discourse in the Classroom

In a general education course titled Literature in the American Experience, I spend the first three weeks on Cooper's novel and about two weeks on its adaptations. In addition to Mann's 1992 epic film, students analyze selected scenes from both Maurice Tourneur and Clarence L. Brown's 1920 silent film and George Seitz's 1936 blockbuster, both also titled *The Last of the Mohicans*, the latter of which was the basis for Mann's script. While Cooper's novel serves as the source for these adaptations, they all depart from it in meaningful ways and differ significantly from one another. Students naturally ask how one source can yield so many variations, thus raising questions about fidelity to the source; this way of thinking about adaptations is known as fidelity discourse. While fidelity discourse in adaptation studies is a problematic mode of study, it proves quite useful in the classroom. The notion of faithfulness to an original novel is reductive and limits the critical discourse to a dialogue between two works—original and adaptation—thereby eliding medium, genre, and cultural connotation, at minimum. Sarah Cardwell argues that "comparison leads us to false expectations about the film's intentions and form, blinding us to what it itself is trying to achieve and allowing us to be biased against the adaptation" (52). Thus, strict comparison of novel and adaptation leads to commonplace and unproductive evaluations such as that the book was better.

Fidelity discourse's pedagogical utility requires that instructors lead students away from such simplistic evaluations and toward the explication and interpretation of a film's adaptive choices. Dudley Andrew and Robert Stam, two of the most widely published and reprinted adaptation scholars, agree on this point. Andrew notes in *What Cinema Is!*, "Fidelity . . . nourishes the judgments of ordinary viewers as they comment on what are effectively aesthetic" values, and he further argues that "if we tuned in on these discussions we might find ourselves listening to a vernacular version of comparative media semiotics" (127). Like Andrew's "ordinary viewers," general education students are not film scholars and typically have limited knowledge of cinema's critical traditions and how they differ from literary study. While students consume more cinema than literature, their years of education have made them more accustomed to studying literature. For this reason, student responses about the relation between a novel and an adaptation tend to work from a simplified narratological perspective. This is what Stam notes when he writes, "Fidelity discourse asks questions about the filmic recreation of the setting, plot, characters, themes, and style of the novel" (14). Rather than resist students' tendency to focus on fidelity and simplified narratology, I harness this discourse.

My approach was partly inspired by two collections of essays: *The Pedagogy of Adaptation* and *Redefining Adaptation Studies*, both edited by Dennis Cutchins, Laurence Raw, and James M. Welsh. While both collections push beyond fidelity discourse, the specter of fidelity is apparent in many of the essays published therein. The editors note in the introduction to *Pedagogy*: "Any adequate pedagogy of adaptation must, in short, explain not [only] the 'whats' and the 'hows' of adaptations, but must also approach the 'whys' of any particular adaptation" (xvii). In my course, therefore, I encourage students to focus not on categorizing the changes made to Cooper's story in the film adaptations, nor on whether they prefer the novel or one of the films, but rather on the possible meanings of those changes. Thus, my approach begins by harnessing fidelity discourse so students can identify the alterations made by cinematic adaptations, and it then proceeds toward an exploration of narratology in order to direct student attention to differences in the novel and its adaptations in terms of media, genre, audience, characters, themes, and contexts—with the goal of inspiring critical and analytical thinking about these subjects.

Pedagogy

This course satisfies general education requirements for writing and social diversity. The module covering *The Last of the Mohicans* is the first chronologically in the course and thus serves as an introduction to the various discourses to which the class will attend. We begin with background reading on James Fenimore Cooper and proceed to a hermeneutic examination of the novel. Students read several secondary texts before we proceed to examining several cinematic adaptations. At the end of the module, students write and present a paper on a topic of their choice.

In class, we discuss the need to have specific knowledge about a medium (in this case film) to effectively write about it. Students are generally comfortable with studying texts; they have done so with varying degrees of success all their academic lives. They are also comfortable with watching a film adaptation to supplement, or supplant, their study of a literary work. Rarely have they been asked to read a film adaptation as intensively as they do a novel. Cutchins recounts an assignment that reverses the novel-to-film adaptation process by novelizing a scene from a film. He writes that in doing this assignment students "come to realize that a filmmaker can communicate a great deal with a color, a glance, a bit of editing, an asynchronous sound, or a snippet of music" (92). Students perform similar exercises in class, especially focusing on the interpretation of visual imagery: students write out the opening hunting montage from Mann's film, and analyze the meaning behind individual visual elements like Daniel Day-Lewis's depiction of Hawk-eye (named Nathaniel Poe in the film), shirtless and toting his long rifle, or the placement of the familial triad of Hawk-eye, Chingachgook, and Uncas during both the chase and Chingachgook's prayer over the dead deer. Students begin to recognize that the cinematic medium can be just as interpretable as a literary text, with just as many layers of meaning. After this exercise, students often ask how the opening scene can be both a celebration of Native American culture and a reinforcement of its subjugation by White European cultures. This tension runs throughout Mann's film, as well as Cooper's novel, and most students find that it is never sufficiently resolved. In furthering the discourse around race and identity in the film adaptations, the class examines why none of them preserve Cora's ethnic heritage. There is also critical discussion of stereotypes of Native Americans and the ways in which the film adaptations uphold them, consciously or not.

Hawk-eye's role as hero is questioned in class discussion, and students pay special attention to how our notion of a hero has changed since Cooper wrote *The Last of the Mohicans*. Informed by secondary readings and our own cultural perceptions, students and I collaborate on a working definition of *hero*, and the definition varies slightly with each group of students. Students are particularly critical of what they perceive as the racism of Hawk-eye in the novel and his seeming unwillingness to sacrifice himself in chapter 30. After Tamenund passes judgment and Magua prepares to depart with Cora as his prisoner, Hawk-eye offers himself in trade, but not to be a victim of Magua's knife. Cooper's hero states, "It would be an unequal exchange, to give a warrior, in the prime of his age and usefulness, for the best woman on the frontiers."[1] Only after numerous negotiations—about a temporary imprisonment for Hawk-eye, his giving up his rifle "Killdeer" (354), and his offering to train Magua's men—does Hawk-eye consent to forfeit his life as a trade for Cora's. Cooper's hero is reluctant to sacrifice himself for another. Turning to Mann's adaptation, we discuss the ways in which Hawk-eye has changed as a character, and specifically why Mann made those changes. Mann created the love triangle between Hawk-eye, Cora, and Heyward (building on Seitz's love triangle between Hawk-eye, Alice, and Heyward). Subsequent discussion focuses on the reasons this romantic plot takes center stage in the narrative, including a discussion of historical drama as a film genre in which romance is a necessary element. The class watches and analyzes the scene from Mann's adaptation in which Magua takes the Munro sisters before a sachem (1:33:15–41:14), which Cooper's novel narrates in chapters 28 and 29 (*Last* 330–45); in the film scene Hawk-eye immediately offers himself as a trade for the sisters only to be outdone by Heyward's redemptive sacrifice. Students respond well to this narratological form of inquiry, producing many insightful comments regarding the concept of heroism in contemporary cinema. Several students have even noted that Heyward's character (more negatively portrayed in the film versions than in Cooper's novel) redeems himself with this sacrifice in much the same way that David Gamut in the novel is willing to sacrifice himself so that Uncas may escape from captivity (309). This recognition demonstrates students' ability to read intertextually, as these moments occur in analogous plot points in the novel and the film.

In contrast to our discussion of Hawk-eye as hero, we also examine both Cooper's and the film adaptations' depictions of Magua as villain. Students are quick to point out that at the climax of the first capture-rescue cycle in the novel, Magua reveals his motivation for wanting to marry Cora (116–19), and Cooper creates a modicum of pathos for his villain. That said, the consistent depiction of Magua as pure evil, even the biblical allusion to Magua as "Prince of Darkness" (321), moderates any compassion students have for Cooper's antagonist. We compare Magua's depiction in the novel to the depiction of Magua and the other Huron characters in the film versions. In Tourneur and Brown's silent film, Magua (played by a White actor in redface) is bloodthirsty and has no redemptive backstory. Similarly, in Seitz's film the Native American characters are portrayed as drunken and wild. Magua is slightly more sophisticated in Seitz's film, but students found that the character did not evoke pathos. Given that most of the named Native American characters are played by White actors in redface, students see these racist depictions as harnessing the worst possible elements of Cooper's narrative. We even discuss *Leather Stocking*, D. W. Griffith's deeply racist cinematic rendering of the novel. Only in Mann's version—replete with the director's desire to recuperate Cooper's novel—did students find Magua a more sympathetic character than in Cooper. They acknowledge that he remains the villain but understand that late-twentieth-century racial attitudes required Mann to rehabilitate Magua somewhat while retaining him as the antagonist.

All these discussions question why adapters change certain things, and given the course's emphasis on American social diversity, our conversation regularly turns toward cultural values. In this respect, I found it helpful to refer to Natalie Jones Loper's "rhetorical triangle"—occasion, audience, and purpose. In her pedagogical piece, Loper writes, "The rhetorical triangle helps students understand that all texts are built around a unique set of circumstances and that recognizing these circumstances can provide deeper insight and more concrete analysis" (41). Loper's model is particularly helpful in framing fruitful discussions about rhetorical studies, particularly on questions of purpose. Students read John McWilliams's introduction to the novel (Cooper, *Last* ix–xvi), as well as Cooper's own 1826 preface and 1831 introduction (3–6, 7–11), in order to establish a working model for the rhetorical triangle, and I also assign Gary Edgerton's essay on cinematic adaptation of *The Last of the Mohicans*, "A Breed Apart." This helps students to better understand the level of detail necessary for a film analysis as well as to establish some of the important cultural circumstances surrounding Mann's film in 1992. As a corollary, an optional secondary reading is M. Elise Marubbio's "Celebrating with *The Last of the Mohicans*," which draws further attention to the film's cultural circumstances relating to the five hundredth anniversary of Columbus's voyage and to neocolonial cinema. I point out several changes Mann made to the story, leaving students room to focus on the whys, or the purposes (in Loper's model), for the changes made. I am careful to bring discussion of rhetorical purpose back to narratological analysis of the film adaptation, pointing out the ways in which adaptation and novel remain in dialogue with each other and with student's interpretations.

This dialogic approach leads students to develop what Cutchins calls "double-mindedness." He argues, "Studying adaptations requires students to adopt an essential and persistent double-mindedness . . . hold[ing] at least two texts in their minds at once" (88). As evidenced in the classroom, though, this double-mindedness is not solely in service of the work of literary analysis but is rather a recursive and cyclical process for analyzing any cultural text. In class, we discuss the various genres Cooper draws upon: adventure tale, captivity narrative, and historical fiction. For the first two genres, we discuss Cooper's use of popular tales from his time, like the story of Daniel Boone's daughter's capture and the story that inspired John Vanderlyn's painting *The Death of Jane McCrea* (Blackmon 60; Starbuck). Students keep those stories in mind and see resonances of them in the novel, especially during the hilltop battle that serves as the climax of the novel's first capture-recovery plot cycle: particularly during the surprise attack in chapter 11 and in the imagery of Cora's brush with death in chapter 12 (125–26, 129). Students are required to research and report on historical accounts of the massacre at Fort William Henry to inform their reading of Cooper's dramatization of the massacre in chapter 17 (198–203), which helps them understand the novel as historical fiction. And, of course, the sheer number of adaptations of *The Last of the Mohicans* makes this type of thinking more fruitful.

In class, we extend our discussion of the rhetorical triangle to the filmmaker. We specifically address Mann's film both through the lens of Mann's statements regarding his purposes and within the cultural context of 1992. Discussions focus on Mann's attention to historical detail in the costumes, weapons, and scenery; his employment of Native Americans as named major characters (the first adaptation to do so) and as unnamed extras; and Mann's use of a Native American language for some of the dialogue. These discussions point us toward the idea that Mann's purpose for the film was not solely to entertain audiences but to make a political statement as well. We address and problematize Mann's purpose in more nuanced ways as we examine the portrayal of Chingachgook in particular. Russell Means had long been a leader in the American Indian movement, and the film's press kit quotes Means's positive view of the film and his character: "The screenplay when I first read it, I loved it. It creates cinematic history. Now my character is three dimensional, has all the positive attributes of a human being. . . . This film is a definite plus for Indian people, and Indian and white relationships" (qtd. in Edgerton 7). However, students quite presciently note that Chingachgook's final words, some of the most poignant in the film, are spoken in English. Perhaps, several argue, this is to allow the speech to have maximum emotional effect on Mann's English-speaking audience, but others question the cultural ramifications of Mann's linguistic choice.

We also discuss the cultural ramifications of other changes in Mann's film: the villainizing of the British in keeping with late-twentieth-century American cinematic tradition, the alteration of the love stories, and particularly the centralizing of Hawk-eye and the creation of a new ethnic heritage for him. When discussing the novel, students are often put off by Hawk-eye's "repeated retreat to a cult of origins" (Murray 486). They may point out that in the novel Hurons are all bad, Native Americans always kill their enemies, and Hawk-eye is a "man without a cross" (Cooper, *Last* 130). This epithet, repeated ad nauseam in Cooper's novel, is often cited by students as a particular barrier to developing pathos for Cooper's hero. In Mann's film, Hawk-eye is a cultural hybrid. His parents were killed when he was young, and he was adopted by Chingachgook and raised as a brother to Uncas. The two, he tells Cora, were educated at Reverend Wheelock's school (00:31:27–32), although the school was founded just three years before the story takes place. Hawk-eye considers himself to be a Mohican, as revealed during the scene outside the burial ground when he refers to Chingachgook as "my father" (00:29:44). The issue, of course, is that Mann depicts a White man who has appropriated characteristics of Native Americans and has thus become a cultural hybrid. In effect, Mann positions Hawk-eye as the ideal for future White Americans as distinct from their British forebears. This authorizes, in a way, the marginalization of Native American cultures that happened in the decades after Cooper wrote his novel. Nevertheless, students feel more sympathetic to the depiction of Hawk-eye as a hero in the film than in the novel, revealing the purpose behind some of Mann's changes, but also the problems inherent therein.

Assessing Student Learning

As this class is in the general education curriculum, the emphasis is always on writing about the subjects we study. In his essay "How to Teach Film Adaptations," Thomas Leitch argues that because adaptations are a pervasive form of writing, "courses in adaptation are by definition courses in composition" (11).

He goes on to set out four goals for courses on adaptation: "recovering the sense of adaptations as adaptations" (12), "analyzing adaptations as necessary, contingent, and incessant writings" (13), writing adaptations as a means of analyzing textual precursors (14), and making a film out of an adapted screenplay (15). All but the last are part of the assessment for the *Last of the Mohicans* module in my course. Once we have completed our study of the novel and three of its film adaptations, students then devise a topic and write a five-to-seven-minute presentation and a five-to-six-page paper on that topic. For the paper, students can write an analytical essay focusing on a point of interest from the novel or film, an analytical essay on a point of adaptation from novel to film, or their own adaptation of Cooper's story. For the third option, I encourage students to think about moving the story to a medium other than film or to focus on explaining how their adaptations to film would differ from the ones we studied and the reasons for their interpretive choices.

As of this writing, 142 students have taken the course over five semesters. Of those, eighty-two students wrote analytical essays on topics like the depictions of ethnicity in the novel or the role of women in the film, forty-eight students wrote about issues relating to the adaptation of some aspect of the novel to the cinematic medium, and eleven students chose to construct their own adaptations of Cooper's story. These data suggest that at an early point in the semester nearly half of the students were sufficiently engaged with issues of adaptation to write about them or to try their hands at writing their own adaptations; this is a fairly successful rate for the first module of a general education course. An even greater sign of success was that none of the students who wrote about issues of adaptation slipped into an evaluative mode; the discourse of fidelity was only utilized for analytical or interpretive means, not to advocate for one medium over another.

Given that the course did not include a creative writing module, I was impressed with the ways students chose to adapt Cooper's work into other media. Five students chose to adapt the story into films—writing summaries, dialogue, and explanations of specific scenes. Most chose to adapt their cinematic narratives more in line with Cooper's work, intentionally working against the other cinematic works we studied. However, they also focused on issues of ethnic and gender identity in their adaptations and did so in a way that was informed by twenty-first-century cultural attitudes (i.e., by changing the characters and themes in Cooper's novel). The implication is that the study of the cinematic adaptations enhanced these students' readings of *The Last of the Mohicans*. One student, who grew up in Syria, saw parallels between Cooper's novel and Syria's colonial history. This student planned a film utilizing some of Cooper's themes and ideas and the novel's cyclical plot structure, but with characters and settings drawn from the film *Lawrence of Arabia* and from Syrian colonial history. Thus, the student engaged in a dual adaptation that was very interesting and yielded, for the student, a fruitful means of telling a colonial narrative.

Several students chose to adapt the story to video games, but interestingly, they all opted for different video game genres for their adaptations. One was an open-world game in which players could move around and explore quite freely; the game blended strategy and action and gave players the option of choosing to play as any of the major characters from the novel. Another student designed a more structured first-person shooter game. Yet another chose to cast the player as Duncan Heyward in a narrative-driven learning and strategy game. Two students strayed from traditionally narrative media: one created a theme-park ride based on the novel, and another a themed obstacle course race similar to Tough Mudder. The students who chose to write their own adaptations universally agreed that adapting required a strong interpretive point: without that, it would have been impossible for them to decide which narrative elements of *The Last of the Mohicans* were valuable and which were expendable. Given the demands of adapting Cooper's work, students who did so met the required general education goals for composition because of the ways in which they synthesized the threads of the course.

Teaching a work of literature with its cinematic adaptations can be highly productive. Students can begin to see adaptation as a process that often involves the tasks we ask of them — namely, the analysis or evaluation of literary subjects. The mediation of a literary text by a more contemporary screenwriter and director gives students a sense of the original text as a product of a culture driven by artistic and economic forces and as having its own purpose. The methods I have outlined here can help students better understand the media they consume on a regular basis, and the influence of literature on those media. Understanding the interplay between the literary precursor and its cinematic adaptations can help students see texts not as intransigent artifacts, but as narratives that continue to be reimagined for new audiences. Furthermore, as indicated by my assessment of student work, those students who were most attuned to the study of adaptations recognized the importance of close analysis of Cooper's novel in the study or creation of an adaptation.

NOTE

[1] Citations to Cooper's *The Last of the Mohicans* refer to the Oxford edition edited by McWilliams.

Cooper and Adaptation as Layered Cultural History

Todd Nathan Thompson

One of my most enduring memories from college is that of my panicked roommate watching Michael Mann's 1992 film *The Last of the Mohicans* at 2:00 a.m. as he wrote a paper—due, of course, later that morning—about James Fenimore Cooper's 1826 novel, which he had not finished reading. Twenty-five years later, whenever we say goodbye to each other, we still recite Hawk-eye's iconic line to Cora in the movie: "You stay alive, no matter what occurs! I will find you. No matter how long it takes, no matter how far, I will find you!" (01:27:26).

My roommate and I did not know then what became painfully obvious to me once I began teaching Cooper's novel to undergraduate and graduate students (and what was no doubt obvious to my roommate's instructor in 1994): that the novel and Mann's movie are very different. Indeed, those who teach Cooper's *The Last of the Mohicans* tend to have a fraught relation with Mann's film adaptation. When one student raises their hand in class to comment on how Hawk-eye was Chingachgook's adopted son, or when another writes in their paper about the significance of Alice's and Duncan's deaths at the end, an instructor knows that a student has watched the movie but not read the novel. Many instructors denigrate or simply avoid showing or discussing the film because of these and other key departures from Cooper's original plot and vision.

According to recent adaptation theory, however, closer attention to these changes—to the when and the why of adaptation in addition to the what—offers an important educational opportunity. Adaptation studies has, in the last decade, moved away from notions of fidelity—that is, away from judging an adaptation solely based on how closely it hews to its source material—and "towards more malleable and productive concepts of creativity" (Sanders, Introduction). Linda Hutcheon explains that "the morally loaded discourse of fidelity is based on the implied assumption that adapters aim simply to reproduce the adapted text" This, of course, is not true, especially in film versions of *The Last of the Mohicans* that radically rewrite the novel's plot and shift its focus. Instead, Hutcheon asserts, if we think of adaptation as "repetition, but repetition without replication," we can productively consider the "many different possible intentions behind the act of adaptation" (7). Hutcheon also urges scholars to rethink the "criteria of success" for an adaptation, stressing instead of fidelity such factors as "popularity, persistence, or even the diversity and extent of dissemination" (xxvi).

Elsewhere, the biologist Gary Bartolotti and Hutcheon employ a biological conception of adaptation that reconceives cultural adaptation as the joint product of a narrative idea and its cultural-historical environment. Narratives, in this view, are replicators, much like genes, and can spread and change in the manner of memes, a concept eminently digestible to today's students. In this way, the same story can be adapted to speak to different issues in different historical moments (447–49). Such considerations tend to quell a common objection to teaching adaptations in the classroom—namely, that studying a nineteenth-century text alongside a modern adaptation of it risks flattening history, thus eliding the source text's historical otherness. An instructor who does not judge an adaptation based on its proximity to the original encourages students to perform multiple historicizations and to consider the cultural work a story did and still does, both then and now. Instructors can ask students to consider how an original work and its adaptation each spoke to its own time and to develop close readings of an adaptation to determine how its creator or creators updated a previous work for new sociohistorical circumstances. This not only reminds students of the similarities and, just as important, the differences of historical periods but also highlights the importance of nineteenth-century literature to students' own lives. As Russ Castronovo puts it, scholars and students must "make sense of the ways in which dusty texts quicken ethical sensibilities and energize political longings" ("Disciplinary Panic" 488). Teaching adaptation lays bare for students how stories speak to the urgent ethical and political questions of different eras in different but nevertheless meaningful ways.

Reading Cooper's *The Last of the Mohicans* alongside George Seitz's 1936 adaptation and Mann's 1992 adaptation prods students to historicize four discrete moments in American history: the era in which the novel was set, the era in which it was written, and the two eras in which it was adapted to film. Such comparative history surfaces issues that are key to any study of *The Last of the Mohicans*: race relations and racializing depictions, the uses of history, and national identity as imagined by artists telling the same story in and for four very different moments in American history.

The Last of the Mohicans makes for a complicated adaptation study for a couple of reasons. First, the novel was published in 1826, its action is set in 1757, and the story hints at the founding moments of American independence and nation formation that occurred between those two dates. In this way, the novel layers multiple historical moments. Second, Cooper's novel has been adapted a great number of times over the years, in many different formats—from (at least fourteen) films to television programs to plays to cartoons to comic books to advertisements. An appendix to Martin Barker and Roger Sabin's *The Lasting of the Mohicans: History of an American Myth* lists twenty-five American stage, film, TV, and radio versions of the story and eighteen American comic book and picture-book versions (205–08). Julie Sanders describes such proliferation as inherent to adaptations in general, highlighting "the reproductive capacity of both adaptations and the study of adaptation and appropriation." Sanders writes, "Texts feed off each other and create other texts, as well as other critical studies; literature creates more literature, art creates more art" (Introduction). Speaking more specifically about *The Last of the Mohicans*, Jacquelyn Kilpatrick explains the story's cultural ubiquity as deriving from a combination of three factors:

Cooper's construction of an American mythology, developing and using uniquely American symbols which still resonate; his adherence to the Romantic tradition, which happened to fit his subject matter nicely and provided a kind of pattern with which readers could identify; and his working the first two elements into a framework which fits its own complex, or perhaps confused, political views. It is this last trait, the complex and even contradictory nature of Cooper's ideas, that has made the story so adaptable by filmmakers and others who have made the story their own.

("Keeping" 71)

These are, at least in part, the same reasons why instructors continue to teach the novel in high school and college classrooms: it is a handbook of foundational myths that continue to animate the conceptions Americans have of themselves and their conflicted, often confusing histories. This is why it is important to study adaptations of Cooper's novel as well; when taught together, the novel and its adaptations reveal how each generation of Americans retells and revises these myths based on how that generation chooses to see itself in relation to its past.

Choosing which adaptations of *The Last of the Mohicans* to teach depends entirely on pedagogical goals. It would be fascinating and productive, for instance, to compare multiple comic book versions with one another and with the novel, with a particular eye toward the portrayal of the Native American and White characters.[1] For my own undergraduate and graduate courses, however, I choose to teach Mann's and Seitz's films, the two most commercially successful film adaptations of *The Last of the Mohicans*, each of which tells a story not only of the mid–eighteenth century but also of and to its own time. (And of course, to complicate matters further, Mann's film is as much an adaptation of Seitz's film as it is of Cooper's novel.) Seitz's film, a major Hollywood production shot during the Great Depression, is interesting in part because of the changes it makes to Cooper's story. If the novel itself prefigured the modern western, Seitz's film is decidedly a western, starring the leading man Randolph Scott as Hawk-eye. As Barker and Sabin point out, the film virtually eliminates Cooper's wilderness and ignores the titular plot about the fate of Native American tribes (83). It highlights instead antagonisms between Britain and an emergent America, particularly as portrayed through the conflict between the American frontiersman Hawk-eye and Duncan Heyward (who in the movie is not a Virginian but a British officer). The film's celebration of American exceptionalism mirrored mid-1930s American isolationism amid concerns about Europe's fate.

Mann's version, which instructors and students are more likely familiar with, makes many of the same plot changes as Seitz's version does but is much more invested in the importance of the wilderness to the story and its themes. Even more important for class discussion is the film's revisionist foundational myth of colonial America as a multicultural contact zone in which Native Americans and frontier settlers live together amicably, sharing friendships, food, and families.

This fantasy offers up an American dream for the 1990s in which White viewers are absolved of guilt for their ancestors' settler colonialism; indeed, the villains in this film are the Europeans who destroy this harmony as a consequence of geopolitical squabbles that neither the White settlers nor the Native Americans understand. These two film versions largely share a script but tell very different stories about how America was founded — and who counts as an American — for audiences of different eras.

In teaching these two adaptations and Cooper's novel, I seek to foreground both the timelessness and the continuing timeliness of *The Last of the Mohicans* as a quintessential American narrative. Though based on my own teaching experiences in an undergraduate pre-1900 American literature survey course and a graduate seminar titled Adapting the American Renaissance, my recommendations are intended to be general enough that they are scalable for any level, from high school to graduate school. I leave some of the details to individual instructors, who can adapt these recommendations to their own pedagogical and institutional contexts.

Before teaching the film versions of *The Last of the Mohicans*, I introduce Cooper's novel in its own historical contexts. I begin by situating the novel within contemporary discourses about the relocation of Native Americans from their lands, a process known as Indian Removal. *The Last of the Mohicans* was published two years after James Monroe presented a formal plan of relocation to Congress and four years before Andrew Jackson signed the Indian Removal Act into law. With this context in mind, I have students read the 1830 law (United States 411–12). Depending on the level of the course, I may also ask students to give presentations on two key concepts that have undergirded the novel and readers' reception of it since 1826 — the trope of the noble savage and the myth of the vanishing Indian.[2]

When students are about halfway through the novel, I break them into small groups and ask each group to conduct a targeted analysis of a major character. In their analyses, students are asked to identify the character's traits; explain how the character is described, acts, and speaks; articulate the character's role and purpose in the book; and, finally, present a claim about what the character represents or about Cooper's use of the character as part of a larger cultural project. In ensuing class sessions we also discuss the form and politics of the genre of historical romance, the structural role of captivity narratives in the plot, the persistent theme of racial mixing, the prevalence of masquerades in the second half of the novel, and the dialogue between disparate epistemologies articulated by Hawk-eye and Chingachgook. But instructors might choose different approaches based on student population and curricular goals.[3] My aim in teaching the novel is to ensure that students are a "knowing" audience by the time they watch the films — that is, that students are familiar with the text that the films adapt. The difference between "knowing" and "unknowing" audiences matters (Hutcheon 120) in the study of adaptations because, as Hutcheon explains,

> [i]f we do not know that what we are experiencing actually *is* an adaptation or if we are not familiar with the particular work that it adapts, we simply experience the adaptation as we would any other work. To experience it *as an adaptation* . . . we need to recognize it as such and to know its adapted text, thus allowing the latter to oscillate in our memories with what we are experiencing. (120–21)

My college roommate, then, was arguably an "unknowing audience" (120); he knew that the film was an adaptation of the novel (indeed, that was his reason for watching it) because of its title and the acknowledgments in the opening credits, but he did not really "know its adapted text," at least not well enough for it to "oscillate" in his memory as he watched the film (Hutcheon 121).

To maximize such productive oscillation between film and text, I diverge from the standard operating procedure of showing movies in literature classes. That is, I do not, as one might expect, show Seitz's film, then ask students to make comparisons between the film and novel, then repeat the process with Mann's film. Instead, I show short (fifteen- to twenty-minute) parallel segments or scenes of Seitz's and Mann's films, after which we discuss the differences between the book and the two films with respect to those scenes. After this discussion we move on to another set of parallel scenes and discuss again. I do this for two reasons. First, it is difficult for students (and instructors) to remember all the details of a long novel and its film adaptation, much less two adaptations. Breaking the films into shorter segments allows students to make more detailed comparisons and to cite particular passages in the novel. This, of course, does require some preparation on the part of the instructor in identifying which scenes to show, at what time stamps they stop and start, and so on. But such curation pays off in the intricate comparative work that students do in class. Both times that I have taken this approach, students have made connections or noted details that I had not previously considered.

The second reason I choose to show shorter scenes is because I have always been wary about what happens when I dim the lights and hit play on a movie during class time, no matter how relevant the movie is to the course material. Today's students are, of course, experienced consumers of visual media, but their tendency when watching movies is to shift away from the actively engaged, critical thinking they had just been doing in wrestling with the books on their desks and to instead become passive viewers. Students (and instructors) sometimes act more like they are on their couches than in the classroom when watching a film. In short, they stop analyzing and start watching. Breaking the films up into parallel clips interspersed with discussion is an attempt to short-circuit that passivity.

To guide students' responses and to remind them of their roles in comparing these films and the novel, I also create a worksheet with several open-ended questions and space for students to compile their notes as they watch. This, too, discourages passive viewing and makes the ensuing discussion more specific and targeted. Below is the text from my worksheet, though instructors could just as easily write their own prompts:

> Note the plot differences between Cooper's novel, Seitz's film, and Mann's film. What do the adaptations cut, add, or alter? How do those changes affect, among other things, the story's focus, themes, and tone?
>
> Note the differences in characterization between Cooper's novel, Seitz's film, and Mann's film. What characters are missing, added, or markedly different? What character traits are emphasized in the film adaptations? To what ends?
>
> Attempt to account historically for these differences in plot and characterization. How do these differences allow Seitz's and Mann's films to speak to American audiences in 1936 and 1992, respectively? What social changes or trends do these differences reflect?
>
> List some of the filmic devices (i.e., music, titles, camera shots and angles, editing decisions, etc.) that Seitz's and Mann's films use to tell the story. How do these devices help advance the story? How do they influence, among other things, the story's emphases, tone, and themes?

After watching clips from the two films over multiple class sessions, students share their observations and insights, building on one another's interpretations and drawing connections to the novel, its form and themes, and especially its sociopolitical context. I then ask students to take their favorite observation from their comparative work on the films and novel and to craft it into a short claim (no more than a few sentences) about the adaptations, which they then share with the rest of the class.

In my fall 2018 graduate course on adaptation, over the three weeks that we dealt with *The Last of the Mohicans* on page and screen, I added other readings, assignments, and in-class activities focused on adaptation. I began the first week with a discussion of the novel without reference to adaptations of it, focusing on the trope of the noble savage and the myth of the vanishing Indian. At the end of the week we watched a segment of both Seitz's and Mann's films (00:00:00–20:00 for Seitz's film and 00:00:00–35:00 for Mann's film) and discussed them with respect to these tropes.

In the second week I assigned readings from our two adaptation theory texts—Hutcheon's *A Theory of Adaptation* (141–53) and Sanders's *Adaptation and Appropriation* (chs. 7 and 8)—and asked students to write response papers that applied adaptation theory to the particular case of *The Last of the Mohicans* and the two films. The prompts for these response papers were as follows:

> Sanders argues that "the Victorian era [specifically 1837–1900] proves ripe for appropriation because it highlights many of the overriding concerns of the postmodern era: questions of identity; of environmental and genetic conditioning; of repressed and oppressed modes of sexuality; of

criminality and violence; of an interest in urbanism and the potentials and possibilities of new technology; of law and authority; of science and religion; and of the postcolonial legacies of empire" (ch. 7). But Sanders's approach is decidedly Anglocentric, since all her examples are British. To what extent can we apply her analysis to nineteenth-century American works and history?

Hutcheon writes that part of the "context" we must consider in adaptation includes such things as "buzz" and the actors cast to play roles in film versions (142). What role might the star power of Randolph Scott in Seitz's film and of Daniel Day-Lewis in Mann's film play in terms of whether Heyward or Hawk-eye is portrayed as a model American?

Hutcheon writes, "Sometimes adapters purge an earlier text of elements that their particular cultures in time or place might find difficult or controversial; at other times, the adaptation 'de-represses' an earlier adapted text's politics. . . . Even within a single culture, the changes can be so great that they can in fact be considered transcultural, on a micro- rather than macrolevel" (144). Do you see this type of "purg[ing]" or "de-repress[ing]" at work in either Seitz's or Mann's film? Why or why not?

Class discussion was structured around students' responses to these questions. In the second week we also watched, took notes on, and discussed another segment of each film, chosen according to which topics students addressed in their responses.

In the third week we began by watching and discussing segments of each film, again chosen according to students' interests, after which students crafted argumentative claims based on their observations. To make students feel like scholars who were actively engaged in critical debates about adaptation, I added several other in-class activities. First, I asked students to complete an exercise that allowed them to reflect on the anatomy of a scholarly article by identifying the structure, thesis, approach, claims, and evidence of an article or book chapter about film adaptations of *The Last of the Mohicans*. I then split the class into small groups, asking each group to create a study guide combining quotations from the following sources: criticism we had read on *The Last of the Mohicans* and its adaptations, the response papers that students had written about those adaptations, and claims that students had crafted after our discussion. A deliverable like this, in which graduate students see their own names and arguments alongside those of the critics they read, helps them see themselves less as students and more as emergent scholars. After reviewing these study guides together, students compared their own readings of *The Last of the Mohicans* adaptations with critics' readings. The purpose of this discussion was for students to see how they could add to the critical conversation by noting things that critics may have missed, mistaken, or ignored. A logical next step in a graduate course would be to use this critical conversation to identify research topics and questions for the entire class or individuals to follow up on in the form of articles or conference papers.

Of course, other instructors might use this general approach to adaptations of *The Last of the Mohicans* but achieve their pedagogical goals through different learning activities that align with their own course topics and student populations. For instance, an instructor could assign groups of students to research and present on the contexts in each of the overlapping historical moments invoked by the novel and its filmic adaptations: 1757, 1826, 1936, and 1992. A more creative learning activity might ask students to imagine, plan for, and, if a film, speculatively cast a new adaptation of *The Last of the Mohicans* that speaks to their current sociopolitical moment. Students could, and likely would, incorporate various genres and social issues, everything from manga to MAGA (the presidential campaign slogan "Make America great again"), as they planned their adaptations. Asking students to explain their thinking and justify their adaptation choices would deepen their understanding of Cooper's novel and the cultural uses to which its myths have been and could continue to be put. In this way, studying adaptations as adaptations teaches students not just which stories we choose to retell again and again but also how and why we change them in the retelling. Learning about the simultaneous staying power and malleability of narratives empowers students as they unpack American cultural history in a way that assures them that they can rewrite their own, and their society's, future.

NOTES

[1] For a rundown and analysis of comic book versions of *The Last of the Mohicans*, see Barker and Sabin 146–80.

[2] On the noble savage trope, see Berkhofer; Deloria. On captivity narratives and the novel, see Haberly.

[3] For other potential discussion topics, see the essays in the "History and Culture" section in part 2 of this volume.

NOTES ON CONTRIBUTORS

Stephen Carl Arch is professor of English at Michigan State University. He is the associate lead editor of The Writings of James Fenimore Cooper and the volume editor of the forthcoming edition of Cooper's 1838 novel, *Home as Found* (State U of New York P). He is editing Edith Wharton's short stories published between 1904 and 1914 for *The Complete Works of Edith Wharton* (Oxford UP).

Robert Daly is SUNY Distinguished Teaching Professor of English and Comparative Literature at the University at Buffalo, State University of New York. He has won the Chancellor's Award for Excellence in Teaching, the Student Association Teaching Award, and the Marshall Mentoring Award from the Northeastern Association of Graduate Schools. He has received a Leverhulme Fellowship, a Guggenheim Fellowship, and grants from the National Endowment for the Humanities; held visiting appointments at the University of Essex, Cambridge University, Cornell University, and Chapman University; and lectured at universities in the United States, England, Hungary, Denmark, and Norway. His seventy-some publications include a Cooper conference keynote address (2005) and the introduction to an edition of *The Pioneers* (Harvard UP, 2011).

Michael Demson is associate professor of English and director of the MA program in English at Sam Houston State University, where he teaches classes in Romanticism, literary theory, and world literature. His research explores the intersections of transatlantic radical political culture and Romantic literature. He has published widely on issues ranging from agricultural and labor history to print media and graphic narratives to the history of satire. His recent publications include *Romantic Automata: Exhibits, Figures, and Organisms*, coedited with Christoper Clason (2020); *Commemorating Peterloo: Violence, Resilience, and Claim-Making in the Romantic Era*, coedited with Regina Hewitt (2019); and *Transatlanticism and* The Blithedale Romance, a special issue of the *Nathaniel Hawthorne Review* coedited with Derek Pacheco (2017). In addition, he published a nonfictional graphic novel, *Masks of Anarchy: The History of a Radical Poem, from Percy Shelley to the Triangle Factory Fire* (2013), and collaborated with Helena Halmari on a translation of a Finnish graphic novel, *Me, Mikko, and Annikki* (2019).

Betty Booth Donohue (Cherokee Nation) is an independent scholar who publishes on Indigenous American and early American literature. Among her publications are "Alexander Posey," in *Native American Writers of the United States*, volume 75 of *Dictionary of Literary Biography*; "Oktahutchee's Song: Reflections on Teaching Nineteenth-Century American Indian Poetry," in *Approaches to Teaching Nineteenth-Century American Poetry*; and "Native Poetics in Edward Johnson's *Wonder-Working Providence of Sions Saviour in New England*," in *American Literature and the New Puritan Studies*.

Elaina Anne Frulla is a doctoral candidate in the English department at the University at Albany, State University of New York, where she teaches courses in American literature, analytical writing, and film studies. Her dissertation is on representations of foreign and accented speech in early American literature. A section of her first chapter was published as an article titled "Noah Webster and the Standardization of Sound."

NOTES ON CONTRIBUTORS

Paul Gutjahr is Ruth N. Halls Professor of English at Indiana University, Bloomington. He is the author of *An American Bible: A History of the Good Book in the United States, 1777–1880* (1999), *Charles Hodge: Guardian of American Orthodoxy* (2011), *The Book of Mormon: A Biography* (2012), and numerous articles and book chapters. In addition, he has edited two major anthologies: one on American popular literature of the nineteenth century and the other on American bestsellers in the nineteenth century. He also served as the sole editor of the *Oxford Handbook of the Bible in America* (2017).

David W. Hartwig is assistant professor and graduate program director in English at Weber State University in Ogden, Utah. His primary research interests are adaptation studies and Shakespeare, and he regularly teaches courses on Shakespeare, film adaptation, and performance studies. Hartwig's work has recently appeared in *Shakespeare Bulletin* and *The Journal of the Wooden O*.

Joseph J. Letter is associate professor of English and writing and director of the Academic Writing Program at the University of Tampa. His work primarily focuses on representations of revolution in early American historical fiction, and his research has appeared in numerous journals, including *American Literature*, *Early American Literature*, *American Periodicals*, *Studies in American Fiction*, *College English*, and *Pedagogy*.

Christopher J. Lukasik is a Provost Fellow and associate professor of English and American studies at Purdue University. He has received over twenty-five fellowships, including long-term awards from the Rockwell Center for American Visual Studies, the National Endowment for the Humanities, and the Fulbright Scholar Program. He is the author of *Discerning Characters: The Culture of Appearance in Early America* (2011) and is currently completing a book project entitled "The Image in the Text: Intermediality, Illustration, and Nineteenth-Century American Literature."

Barbara Alice Mann, professor in the Jesup Scott Honors College of the University of Toledo, has written fourteen books, including *President by Massacre* (2019), *Spirits of Blood, Spirits of Breath* (2016), *The Tainted Gift* (2009), *George Washington's War on Native America* (2005), and *Iroquoian Women* (2000), as well as over four hundred articles. She applies her historical and ethnographic understandings to literature, particularly the works of James Fenimore Cooper. Mann's *The Cooper Connection: The Influence of Jane Austen on James Fenimore Cooper* (2014) is forthcoming in a new edition by the University of Toledo Press.

Keat Murray is associate professor of English at Pennsylvania Western University, California, where he teaches early American, Native American, and environmental literatures. He specializes in the writings of James Fenimore Cooper and is preparing scholarly editions of two of Cooper's novels for The Writings of James Fenimore Cooper. His work has been published in *Early American Literature*, *Journal of the Early Republic*, *Journal of American Culture*, and *Oxford Bibliographies*.

Donna Richardson is professor emerita at St. Mary's College of Maryland, where she taught for thirty-three years. Her primary fields are poetry pedagogy and British Romanticism. She is the author of a book, *Visual Paraphrasing of Poetry*; several articles on Percy Bysshe Shelley; and articles on A. E. Housman, Joseph Conrad, Gerard Manley Hopkins, William Wordsworth, Sylvia Plath, and James Fenimore Cooper.

Anna Scannavini is associate professor of American literature in the Department of Human Studies at the University of L'Aquila, Italy. She has written books and essays on the strategies of inclusion of foreign and nonmainstream languages in American literature, including *Per una poetica del bilinguismo: Lo spagnolo nella letteratura portoricana in inglese* (*Bilinguism Poetics: Spanish in Puerto Rican Literature in English*), *Giochi di giochi: Parole e lingua nella letteratura angloamericana* (*Games of Games: Words and Language in American Literature*), and, with Anna Scacchi and Sara Antonelli, *La babele Americana: Lingue e identità negli Stati Uniti di oggi* (*American Babel: Language and Identity in Contemporary United States*). She has worked and published extensively on James Fenimore Cooper, particularly on his Italian writings. With Lance Schachterle she coedited *The Wing-and-Wing* (2019) for The Writings of James Fenimore Cooper.

Sarah Sillin is assistant professor of transnational American literature at Central Washington University. Her research on the role of feeling in defining nineteenth-century Americans' ties to the world has appeared in *African American Review*, *Journal of American Studies*, *Early American Literature*, *Literature of the Early American Republic*, and *MELUS*.

Matthew Wynn Sivils is Liberal Arts and Sciences Dean's Professor at Iowa State University, where he teaches courses on nineteenth-century American literature and the environmental humanities. He has written or edited nine books, most recently a critical edition of Harriet Prescott Spofford's 1859 novel, *Sir Rohan's Ghost* (2020), and coedited, with Dawn Keetley, *Ecogothic in Nineteenth-Century American Literature* (2017).

Todd Nathan Thompson is professor of English at Indiana University of Pennsylvania. He is also treasurer-secretary of the American Humor Studies Association. He is the author of *The National Joker: Abraham Lincoln and the Politics of Satire* (2015). He has earned research fellowships through the Center for Mark Twain Studies, the American Antiquarian Society, the Library Company of Philadelphia, and the Lilly Library. His work on political satire and pre-1900 American literature has also appeared in *Scholarly Editing*, *Early American Literature*, *ESQ*, *Nineteenth-Century Prose*, *Studies in American Humor*, *Teaching American Literature*, and elsewhere. He currently is at work on a forthcoming book entitled *Imperial Laughter, Comic Contact: Nineteenth-Century American Humor and Empire in the Pacific World*.

Lisa West is professor at Drake University, where she teaches courses on American literature before 1900 and on the environmental humanities. She has published on James Fenimore Cooper, Susan Fenimore Cooper, Catharine Maria Sedgwick, Susanna Rowson, Lydia Maria Child, and other late-eighteenth- and early-nineteenth-century writers. She is invested in the recovery of early American women writers and their approaches to domestic and natural spaces.

Rochelle Raineri Zuck is associate professor of English at Iowa State University. Her research and teaching interests include early American literature, African American literature, American Indian literature, and print culture. She is the author of *Divided Sovereignties: Race, Nationhood, and Citizenship in Nineteenth-Century America* (2016), and some of her most recent articles have appeared in scholarly journals such as *American Periodicals*, *Journal of American Studies*, and *Studies in American Indian Literatures*.

SURVEY PARTICIPANTS

Melissa Adams-Campbell, *Northern Illinois University*
Pat Bradley, *Middle Tennessee State University*
Matthew Steven Bruen, *Young Harris College*
David Callahan, *University of Aveiro*
Richard Carr, *University of Alaska, Fairbanks*
Russ Castronovo, *University of Wisconsin, Madison*
Schuyler J. Chapman, *University of Pittsburgh*
Robert Clark, *University of East Anglia*
Teresa Coronado, *University of Wisconsin, Parkside*
Robert Daly, *University at Buffalo, State University of New York*
Michael Demson, *Sam Houston State University*
Mary M. Evans, *Hudson Valley Community College*
Robert Franciosi, *Grand Valley State University*
Elaina Anne Frulla, *University at Albany, State University of New York*
Theresa Gaul, *Texas Christian University*
Paul Gutjahr, *Indiana University, Bloomington*
Richard Hancuff, *Misericordia University*
Wendy Harding, *University of Toulouse, Jean Jaurès*
Steven P. Harthorn, *University of Northwestern, St. Paul*
David W. Hartwig, *Weber State University*
John C. Havard, *Auburn University at Montgomery*
John Hay, *University of Nevada, Las Vegas*
Roger Hecht, *State University of New York, Oneonta*
Melissa Homestead, *University of Nebraska, Lincoln*
Jeffry Hotz, *East Stroudsburg University*
Alisa Iannucci, *Independent scholar*
Luis A. Iglesias, *University of Southern Mississippi*
Philip Kadish, *Hunter College, City University of New York*
Christina Katopodis, *Graduate Center, City University of New York*
Lisa Logan, *University of Central Florida*
Carol Loranger, *Wright State University*
Christopher J. Lukasik, *Purdue University*
Robert D. Madison, *University of Arkansas, Fayetteville*
Barbara Alice Mann, *University of Toledo*
Kristopher Mecholsky, *Louisiana State University*
John David Miles, *Louisiana State University*
Jeff Miller, *Gonzaga University*
Richard Millington, *Smith College*
Nicholas Mohlmann, *Silver Lake College of the Holy Family*
Leland S. Person, *University of Cincinnati*
Jillian Sayre, *Rutgers University, Camden*
Anna Scannavini, *University of L'Aquila*
Lance Schachterle, *Worcester Polytechnic University*

Jodi Schorb, *University of Florida*
James Joseph Schramer, *Youngstown State University*
Christopher Stampone, *Southern Methodist University*
Timothy Sweet, *West Virginia University*
Robert T. Tally, Jr., *Texas State University*
Randi Tanglen, *Austin College*
Paul Thifault, *Springfield College*
Todd Nathan Thompson, *Indiana University of Pennsylvania*
Jana Tigchelaar, *Marshall University*
Rita C. Tobin, *Hunter College, City University of New York*
Colleen Tremonte, *Michigan State University*
Marina Trninic, *Prairie View A&M*
Marilyn Walker, *Monroe Community College*
Michael Weisenburg, *University of South Carolina*
Lisa West, *Drake University*
Randall Wilhelm, *Anderson University*

WORKS CITED

Abbey, Edward. *Desert Solitaire: A Season in the Wilderness*. Simon and Schuster, 1968.

"About." *Sedgwick Stories: The Periodical Writings of Catharine Maria Sedgwick*, sedgwickstories.omeka.net/about. Accessed 24 Feb. 2022.

Adkins, Nelson F. "James Fenimore Cooper and the Bread and Cheese Club." *Modern Language Notes*, vol. 47, no. 2, 1932, pp. 71–79.

Alewyn, Richard. "Origin of the Detective Novel." 1974. *The Poetics of Murder: Detective Fiction and Literary Theory*, edited by Glen W. Most and William W. Stowe, Harcourt Brace Jovanovich, 1983, pp. 62–78.

Allen, Paula Gunn. *Grandmothers of the Light: A Medicine Woman's Sourcebook*. Beacon, 1991.

Aloha. Directed by Cameron Crowe, Columbia Pictures, 2015.

"American Indian and Alaskan Native Documents in the Congressional Serial Set, 1817–1899." *The University of Oklahoma College of Law Digital Commons*, digitalcommons.law.ou.edu/indianserialset/.

Amerynth. Review of *The Last of the Mohicans*. *LibraryThing*, 19 July 2019, librarything.com/work/4599771/reviews.

Ammon, Harry. *James Monroe: The Quest for a National Identity*. U of Virginia P, 1990.

Anderson, Benedict. *Imagined Communities: Reflections on the Origin and Spread of Nationalism*. Verso Books, 1991.

Anderson, Virginia DeJohn. *Creatures of Empire: How Domestic Animals Transformed Early America*. Oxford UP, 2004.

Andrew, Dudley. *What Cinema Is! Bazin's Quest and Its Charge*. Wiley-Blackwell, 2010.

Apess, William. *Indian Nullification of the Unconstitutional Laws of Massachusetts*. Jonathan Howe, 1835.

Armstrong, Nancy, and Leonard Tennenhouse. "Recalling Cora: Family Resemblances in *The Last of the Mohicans*." *American Literary History*, vol. 28, no. 2, 2016, 223–45.

Armstrong, Philip. *What Animals Mean in the Fiction of Modernity*. Routledge, 2008.

Arnold, Gary. "Indian Actors Cheering on the Bad Guy." *The Washington Times*, 28 Sept. 1992, p. D1.

Atwood, Margaret. *Oryx and Crake*. Anchor Books, 2003.

Axelrad, Allan M. "*The Last of the Mohicans*, Race Mixing, and America's Destiny." Walker, *Leather-stocking Redux*, pp. 33–56.

Axtell, James. "Babel of Tongues: Communicating with the Indians in Eastern North America." Gray and Fiering, pp. 15–60.

Bailyn, Bernard. *The Ideological Origins of the American Revolution*. Belknap Press, 1967.

Bakhtin, M. M. *Rabelais and His World*. Translated by Helene Iswolsky, Indiana UP, 1984.

Bancroft, Dick, and Laura Waterman Wittstock. *We Are Still Here: A Photographic History of the American Indian Movement*. Minnesota Historical Society Press, 2013.

Banner, James M., Jr. "William Cooper." *American National Biography*, edited by John A. Garraty and Mark C. Carnes, vol. 5, Oxford UP, 1999, pp. 466–67.

Barker, Martin, and Roger Sabin. *The Lasting of the Mohicans: History of an American Myth*. UP of Mississippi, 1995.

Barlow, Joel. *The Hasty-Pudding: A Poem, in Three Cantos, by Joel Barlow, Written in Germany, in Savoy, January, 1793*. New York, 1796.

Barnum, H. L. *The Spy Unmasked; or, Memoirs of Enoch Crosby, Alias Harvey Birch, the Hero of Mr. Cooper's Tale of the Neutral Ground*. J. and J. Harper, 1828.

Bartolotti, Gary R., and Linda Hutcheon. "On the Origin of Adaptations: Rethinking Fidelity Discourse and 'Success'—Biologically." *New Literary History*, vol. 38, no. 3, 2007, pp. 443–58.

Bartram, William. *William Bartram: Travels and Other Writings*. Edited by Thomas Slaughter, Library of America, 1996.

Baym, Nina. "The Women of Cooper's Leatherstocking Tales." *American Quarterly*, vol. 23, no. 5, 1971, pp. 696–709.

Beard, James Franklin. Introduction. Cooper, *Last of the Mohicans: A Narrative* [Sappenfield and Feltskog], pp. xv–xlviii.

Begg, Leah A. "'I See Nothing but Land and Water; and a Lovely Scene It Is': Nature's Enchantment in *The Last of the Mohicans*." *James Fenimore Cooper Society*, 2019, jfcoopersociety.org/articles/ala/2019ala-begg.html.

Bellin, Joshua David. *The Demon of the Continent and the Shaping of American Literature*. U of Pennsylvania P, 2001.

Benson, Etienne. "Animal Writes: Historiography, Disciplinarity, and the Animal Trace." *Making Animal Meaning*, edited by Linda Kalof and Georgina Montgomery, Michigan State UP, 2011, pp. 3–16.

Bercovitch, Sacvan. *The Rites of Assent: Transformations in the Symbolic Construction of America*. Routledge, 1992.

Berger, Jason. *Antebellum at Sea: Maritime Fantasies in Nineteenth-Century America*. U of Minnesota P, 2012.

Berkhofer, Robert. *The White Man's Indian: Images of the American Indian from Columbus to the Present*. Vintage Books, 1979.

Best, Stephen, and Sharon Marcus. "Surface Reading: An Introduction." *Representations*, no. 108, fall 2009, pp. 1–21.

Bhabha, Homi K. *The Location of Culture*. Routledge, 1994.

Bigelow, Allison. *Mining Language: Racial Thinking, Indigenous Knowledge, and Colonial Metallurgy in the Early Modern Iberian World*. Omohundro Institute of Early American History and Culture / U of North Carolina P, 2020.

Bird, Robert Montgomery. *Nick of the Woods; or, The Jibbenainosay*. Carey, Lea, and Blanchard, 1837. 2 vols.

Blackmon, Richard D. *Dark and Bloody Ground*. Westholme Publishing, 2012.

Blumenberg, Hans. *Shipwreck with Spectator: Paradigm of a Metaphor for Existence*. Translated by Steven Rendall, MIT Press, 1997.

Boes, Tobias. "On the Nature of the *Bildungsroman*." *PMLA*, vol. 124, no. 5, Mar. 2009, pp. 647–59.

Boggs, Colleen Glenney. *Transnationalism and American Literature: Literary Transitions, 1773–1892*. Routledge, 2007.

Bolter, Jay David, and Richard Grusin. *Remediation: Understanding New Media*. MIT Press, 1999.

Bowes, John P. *Land Too Good for Indians: Northern Indian Removal*. U of Oklahoma P, 2016.

Bragdon, Kathleen J. *The Columbia Guide to American Indians of the Northeast*. Columbia UP, 2001.

Brantlinger, Patrick. "Forgetting Genocide; or, The Last of *The Last of the Mohicans*." *Colonial Studies*, vol. 12, no. 1, 1998, pp. 15–30.

Brantz, Dorothee. *Beastly Natures: Animals, Humans, and the Study of History*. U of Virginia P, 2010.

Bray, Kingsley M. *Crazy Horse: A Lakota Life*. Oklahoma UP, 2006.

Bronstein, Michaela. "Taking the Future into Account: Today's Novels for Tomorrow's Readers." *PMLA*, vol. 134, no. 1, Jan. 2019, pp. 121–36.

Brooks, Cleanth. *The Well Wrought Urn*. Harcourt, 1975.

Brown, Charles Brockden. *Wieland; or The Transformation: With Related Texts*. Edited by Philip Barnard and Stephen Shapiro, Hackett Publishing Company, 2009.

Buell, Lawrence. *The Environmental Imagination: Thoreau, Nature Writing, and the Formation of American Culture*. Harvard UP, 1995.

Buffon, Georges-Louis Le Clerc, Comte de. *Natural History, General and Particular*. Translated by William Smellie, 3rd ed., vol. 5, Strahan and Cadell, 1791.

Burnett, Rob. *How Images Think*. MIT Press, 2004.

Cahir, Linda Costanzo. *Literature into Film: Theory and Practical Approaches*. McFarland, 2006.

Callow, James. *Kindred Spirits: Knickerbocker Writers and American Artists, 1807–1855*. U of North Carolina P, 1967.

Cardwell, Sarah. "Adaptation Studies Revisited: Purposes, Perspectives, and Inspiration." *The Literature/Film Reader: Issues of Adaptation*, edited by James M. Welsh and Peter Lev, Scarecrow Press, 2007, pp. 51–64.

Carson, Rachel. *Silent Spring*. Houghton Mifflin, 2002.

Cass, Lewis. "Structure of the Indian Languages." *North American Review*, vol. 26, no. 59, Apr. 1828, pp. 357–403.

Cassuto, Leonard, et al., editors. *The Cambridge History of the American Novel*. Cambridge UP, 2011.

Castronovo, Russ. "Disciplinary Panic: A Response to Ed White and Michael Drexler." *Early American Literature*, vol. 45, no. 2, 2010, pp. 485–90.

———. "James Fenimore Cooper and the NSA: Security, Property, Liberalism." *American Literary History*, vol. 28, 2016, pp. 677–701.

WORKS CITED

"Chamber Sponsors 'Mohicans' Opening." *The Film Daily*, 3 Sept. 1936, p. 12.

Chesnutt, Charles. *The House behind the Cedars*. 1900. Penguin, 1993.

Child, Lydia Maria. *Hobomok*. Hobomok *and Other Writings on Indians*, edited by Carolyn L. Karcher, Rutgers, 1986, pp. 1–150.

Chiles, Katy L. *Transformable Race: Surprising Metamorphoses in the Literature of Early America*. Oxford UP, 2014.

Chopin, Kate. *The Awakening*. Edited by Nancy A. Walker, 2nd ed., Bedford/St. Martin's Press, 2000.

Christophersen, Bill. *Resurrecting Leather-Stocking: Pathfinding in Jacksonian America*. U of South Carolina P, 2019.

Cole, Thomas. *The Course of Empire: Desolation*. 1836. New-York Historical Society Museum and Library, emuseum.nyhistory.org/objects/21572/the-course-of-empire-desolation?ctx=19fc85ac0eac663391b8d648385f06068b431888&idx=3.

———. *The Course of Empire: Destruction*. 1836. New-York Historical Society Museum and Library, emuseum.nyhistory.org/objects/41597/the-course-of-empire-destruction?ctx=19fc85ac0eac663391b8d648385f06068b431888&idx=4.

———. *The Course of Empire: The Arcadian or Pastoral State*. 1834. New-York Historical Society Museum and Library, emuseum.nyhistory.org/objects/56323/the-course-of-empire-the-arcadian-or-pastoral-state?ctx=19fc85ac0eac663391b8d648385f06068b431888&idx=2.

———. *The Course of Empire: The Consummation of Empire*. 1835–36. New-York Historical Society Museum and Library, emuseum.nyhistory.org/objects/54911/the-course-of-empire-the-consummation-of-empire?ctx=9cda288704c466dfd1fb05fd9b28bec3697629d1&idx=0.

———. *The Course of Empire: The Savage State*. 1834. New-York Historical Society Museum and Library, emuseum.nyhistory.org/objects/54879/the-course-of-empire-the-savage-state?ctx=19fc85ac0eac663391b8d648385f06068b431888&idx=5.

———. "Essay on American Scenery." *The American Monthly Magazine*, vol. 1, Jan. 1836, pp. 1–12.

———. *Landscape with Figures: Scene from "The Last of the Mohicans."* 1826. Private collection.

———. *Scene from "The Last of the Mohicans": Cora Kneeling at the Feet of Tamenund*. 1827. Wadsworth Atheneum, Hartford.

Coleridge, Samuel Taylor. *Biographia Literaria; or, Biographical Sketches of My Literary Life and Opinions*. Edited by J. Shawcross, vol. 2, Oxford UP, 1954.

Collins, Wilkie. *The Moonstone*. 1868. Wordsworth Editions, 1993.

———. *The Woman in White*. 1860. Broadview Editions, 2006.

Conron, John, and Constance Ayers Denne. "Historical Introduction." Cooper, *Gleanings*, pp. xix–xlvi.

Cooper, James Fenimore. *Afloat and Ashore; or, The Adventures of Miles Wallingford*. 1844. Edited by Thomas Philbrick and Marianne Philbrick, AMS Press, 2002–04. 2 vols.

———. *The American Democrat*. Liberty Classics, 1981.

———. The American Democrat *and Other Political Writings*. Edited by Bradley J. Birzer and John Willson, Regnery Publishing, 2001.

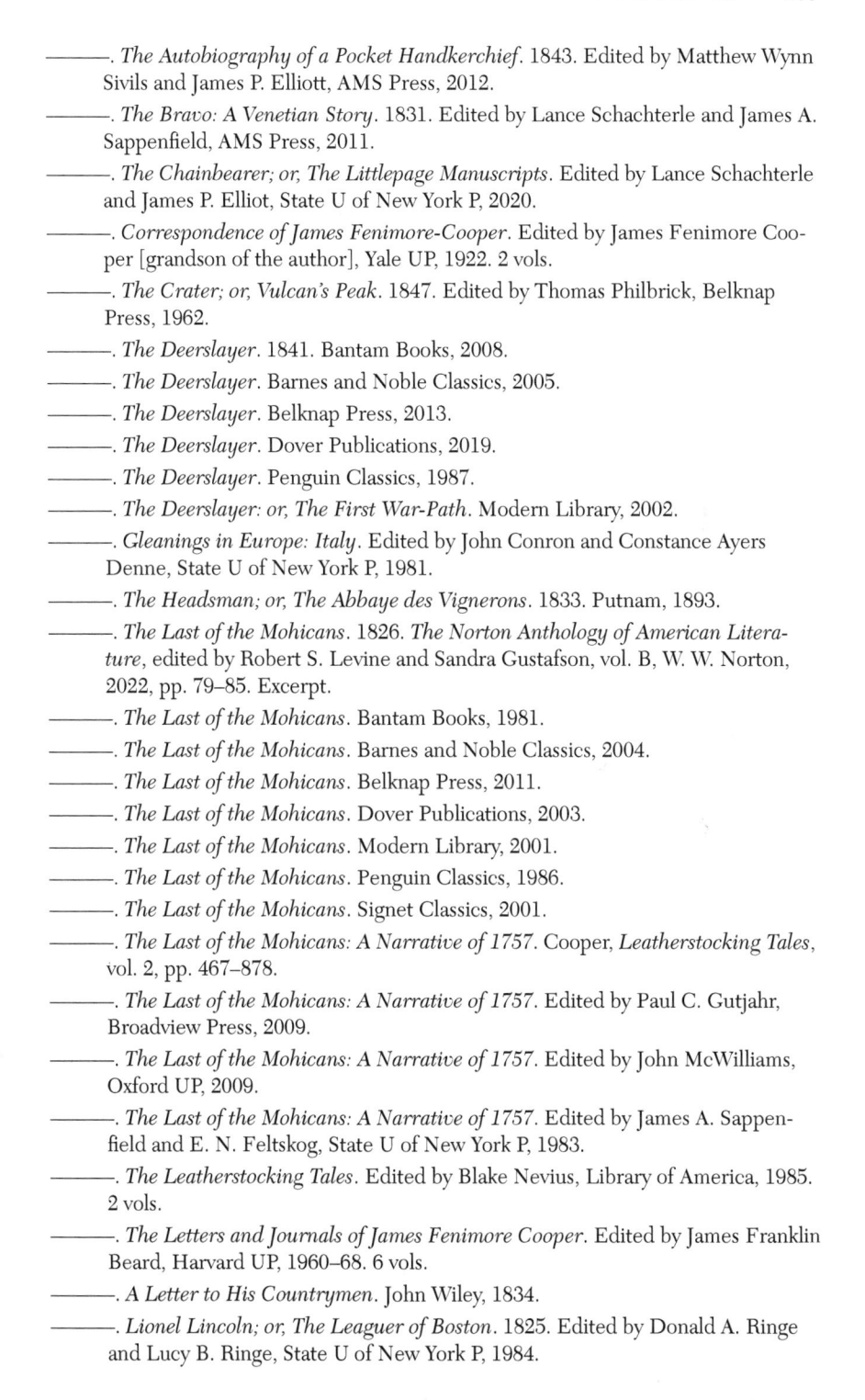

———. *The Autobiography of a Pocket Handkerchief.* 1843. Edited by Matthew Wynn Sivils and James P. Elliott, AMS Press, 2012.

———. *The Bravo: A Venetian Story.* 1831. Edited by Lance Schachterle and James A. Sappenfield, AMS Press, 2011.

———. *The Chainbearer; or, The Littlepage Manuscripts.* Edited by Lance Schachterle and James P. Elliot, State U of New York P, 2020.

———. *Correspondence of James Fenimore-Cooper.* Edited by James Fenimore Cooper [grandson of the author], Yale UP, 1922. 2 vols.

———. *The Crater; or, Vulcan's Peak.* 1847. Edited by Thomas Philbrick, Belknap Press, 1962.

———. *The Deerslayer.* 1841. Bantam Books, 2008.

———. *The Deerslayer.* Barnes and Noble Classics, 2005.

———. *The Deerslayer.* Belknap Press, 2013.

———. *The Deerslayer.* Dover Publications, 2019.

———. *The Deerslayer.* Penguin Classics, 1987.

———. *The Deerslayer: or, The First War-Path.* Modern Library, 2002.

———. *Gleanings in Europe: Italy.* Edited by John Conron and Constance Ayers Denne, State U of New York P, 1981.

———. *The Headsman; or, The Abbaye des Vignerons.* 1833. Putnam, 1893.

———. *The Last of the Mohicans.* 1826. *The Norton Anthology of American Literature*, edited by Robert S. Levine and Sandra Gustafson, vol. B, W. W. Norton, 2022, pp. 79–85. Excerpt.

———. *The Last of the Mohicans.* Bantam Books, 1981.

———. *The Last of the Mohicans.* Barnes and Noble Classics, 2004.

———. *The Last of the Mohicans.* Belknap Press, 2011.

———. *The Last of the Mohicans.* Dover Publications, 2003.

———. *The Last of the Mohicans.* Modern Library, 2001.

———. *The Last of the Mohicans.* Penguin Classics, 1986.

———. *The Last of the Mohicans.* Signet Classics, 2001.

———. *The Last of the Mohicans: A Narrative of 1757.* Cooper, *Leatherstocking Tales*, vol. 2, pp. 467–878.

———. *The Last of the Mohicans: A Narrative of 1757.* Edited by Paul C. Gutjahr, Broadview Press, 2009.

———. *The Last of the Mohicans: A Narrative of 1757.* Edited by John McWilliams, Oxford UP, 2009.

———. *The Last of the Mohicans: A Narrative of 1757.* Edited by James A. Sappenfield and E. N. Feltskog, State U of New York P, 1983.

———. *The Leatherstocking Tales.* Edited by Blake Nevius, Library of America, 1985. 2 vols.

———. *The Letters and Journals of James Fenimore Cooper.* Edited by James Franklin Beard, Harvard UP, 1960–68. 6 vols.

———. *A Letter to His Countrymen.* John Wiley, 1834.

———. *Lionel Lincoln; or, The Leaguer of Boston.* 1825. Edited by Donald A. Ringe and Lucy B. Ringe, State U of New York P, 1984.

———. *The Oak Openings; or, The Bee-Hunter*. 1848. Putnam, 1893.

———. *The Pathfinder*. 1840. Barnes and Noble Classics, 2005.

———. *The Pathfinder*. Belknap Press, 2015.

———. *The Pathfinder*. Signet Classics, 2006.

———. *The Pathfinder; or, The Inland Sea*. Penguin Classics, 1989.

———. *The Pilot: A Tale of the Sea*. 1824. Edited by Kay Seymour House, State U of New York P, 1986.

———. *The Pioneers*. 1823. *The Norton Anthology of American Literature*, edited by Robert S. Levine and Sandra Gustafson, vol. B, W. W. Norton, 2022, pp. 62–78. Excerpt.

———. *The Pioneers*. Belknap Press, 2011.

———. *The Pioneers*. Library of America, 2012.

———. *The Pioneers*. Penguin Classics, 1988.

———. *The Pioneers*. Signet Classics, 2007.

———. *The Pioneers; or, The Sources of the Susquehanna: A Descriptive Tale*. Edited by James Franklin Beard et al., State U of New York P, 1980.

———. *The Prairie*. 1827. Cooper, *Leatherstocking Tales*, vol. 2, pp. 879–1317.

———. *The Prairie*. Belknap Press, 2014.

———. *The Prairie*. Penguin Classics, 1987.

———. *The Prairie: A Tale*. Edited by James P. Elliott, State U of New York P, 1985.

———. *The Red Rover: A Tale*. 1828. Edited by Thomas Philbrick and Marianne Philbrick, State U of New York P, 1991.

———. *Satanstoe; or The Littlepage Manuscripts: A Tale of the Colony*. 1845. Edited by Kay Seymour House and Constance Ayers Denne, State U of New York P, 1990.

———. *The Sea Lions; or, The Lost Sealers*. 1849. Putnam, 1893.

———. *Sea Tales:* The Pilot, The Red Rover. Library of America, 1991.

———. *The Spy: A Tale of the Neutral Ground*. 1821. Edited by Wayne Franklin, Penguin Classics, 1997.

———. *The Spy: A Tale of the Neutral Ground*. AMS Press, 2002.

———. *The Spy: A Tale of the Neutral Ground*. State U of New York P, 2020.

———. *The Two Admirals: A Tale*. 1842. Edited by Donald Ringe et al., State U of New York P, 1990.

———. *Two Novels of the American Revolution:* The Spy *and* Lionel Lincoln. Edited by Alan Taylor, Library of America, 2019.

———. *The Water-Witch; or, The Skimmer of the Seas*. 1830. Edited by Thomas Philbrick and Marianne Philbrick, AMS Press, 2007.

———. *The Ways of the Hour: A Tale*. 1850. W. A. Townsend, 1861.

———. *The Wept of Wish-ton-Wish*. 1829. Putnam, 1893.

———. *The Wing-and-Wing; or, Le Feu-Follet: A Tale*. 1842. Edited by Lance Schachterle and Anna Scannavini, State U of New York P, 2019.

———. *Wyandotté; or, The Hutted Knoll: A Tale*. 1843. Edited by Thomas Philbrick

and Marianne Philbrick, State U of New York P, 1982.
Cordell, Ryan, et al. "Kaleidoscopic Pedagogy in the Classroom Laboratory." Travis and DeSpain, pp. 3–23.
Costaguta, Lorenzo, and Virginia Pignagnoli. "Teaching American Studies in Europe: Perspectives and New Directions for the Twenty-First Century." *RSA Journal*, no. 29, 2018, pp. 159–94.
Cowell, Pattie. "Figuring Multicultural Practice in Early American Literature Classrooms." *Teaching the Literatures of Early America*, edited by Carla Mulford, Modern Language Association of America, 2000, pp. 63–74.
Cutchins, Dennis. "Why Adaptations Matter to Your Literature Students." Cutchins et al., *Pedagogy*, pp. 87–95.
Cutchins, Dennis, et al. Introduction. Cutchins et al., *Pedagogy*, pp. xi–xix.
———, editors. *The Pedagogy of Adaptation*. Scarecrow Press, 2010.
———, editors. *Redefining Adaptation Studies*. Scarecrow Press, 2010.
Dances with Wolves. Directed by Kevin Costner, Orion Pictures, 1990.
Darnell, Donald. "Uncas as Hero: The *Ubi Sunt* Formula in *The Last of the Mohicans*." *American Literature*, vol. 37, no. 3, Nov. 1965, pp. 259–66.
Darwin, Charles. *The Expression of the Emotions in Man and Animals*. John Murray, 1872.
Davis, Randall C. "Fire-Water in the Frontier Romance: James Fenimore Cooper." *Studies in American Fiction*, vol. 22, no. 2, autumn 1994, pp. 215–31.
Dekker, George. *The American Historical Romance*. Cambridge UP, 1987.
Deloria, Philip J. *Playing Indian*. Yale UP, 1998.
DeMello, Margo. *Animals and Society: An Introduction to Human-Animal Studies*. Columbia UP, 2012.
Descartes, Rene. "Letter to Henry More, 5 February 1649." *Philosophical Letters*, translated by Anthony Kenny, U of Minnesota P, 1970, pp. 237–45.
Dibble, Charles, and Arthur Anderson, translators. *Florentine Codex*. By Bernardino Sahagun, Utah UP, 2012. 13 vols.
Donald, Ralph, and Karen MacDonald. *Women in War Films: From Helpless Heroine to G.I. Jane*. Rowman and Littlefield, 2014.
Donohue, Betty Booth (Cherokee Nation). *Bradford's Indian Book: Being the True Roote and Rise of American Letters as Revealed by the Native Text Embedded in Of Plimoth Plantation*. UP of Florida, 2011.
———. "Remembering Muskrat: Native Poetics and the Oral Tradition." *The Cambridge History of American Poetry*, edited by Alfred Bendixen and Stephen Burt, Cambridge UP, 2015.
Doolen, Andy. *Territories of Empire: U.S. Writing from the Louisiana Purchase to Mexican Independence*. Oxford UP, 2014.
Dooling, D. M., and Paul Jordan-Smith, editors. *I Become Part of It: Sacred Dimensions in Native American Life*. Parabola Books, 1989.
Dreamkeeper. Directed by Steve Barron, ABC, 2003.
Dunbar-Ortiz, Roxanne. *An Indigenous Peoples' History of the United States*. Beacon Press, 2014.

Dunne, Philip. *Take Two: A Life in Movies and Politics*. Limelight, 1992.
Easterlin, Nancy. *A Biocultural Approach to Literary Theory and Interpretation*. Johns Hopkins UP, 2012.
———. "The Functions of Literature and the Evolution of Extended Mind." *New Literary History*, vol. 44, no. 4, autumn 2013, pp. 661–82.
Ebert, Roger. "*The Last of the Mohicans*." 25 Sept. 1992. *RogerEbert.com*, rogerebert.com/reviews/the-last-of-the-mohicans-1992.
Edgerton, Gary. "'A Breed Apart': Hollywood, Racial Stereotyping, and the Promise of Revisionism in *The Last of the Mohicans*." *Journal of American Culture*, vol. 17, no. 2, 1994, pp. 1–20.
Edwards, Peter. "Nature Bridled: The Treatment and Training of Horses in Early Modern England." Brantz, pp. 155–75.
Ellet, Elizabeth Fries Lummis. "Cardillac the Jeweler: A Tale from the German of Hoffmann." *The United States Magazine and Democratic Review*, new series, vol. 13, Aug. 1843, pp. 157–84.
Empson, William. *Seven Types of Ambiguity*. Chatto and Windus, 1949.
Everson, William K. *American Silent Film*. Oxford UP, 1978.
Faherty, Duncan, and Ed White. "What We've Learned (about Recovery) through the *Just Teach One* Project." Travis and DeSpain, pp. 105–16.
Fiedler, Leslie. "James Fenimore Cooper: The Problem of the Good Bad Writer." 1979. *James Fenimore Cooper Society*, jfcoopersociety.org/articles/suny/1979suny-fiedler.html.
———. *Love and Death in the American Novel*. Criterion, 1962.
Fire, John, and Richard Erdoes. *Lame Deer: Seeker of Visions*. Simon and Schuster, 1972.
Fisher, Philip. *Hard Facts: Setting and Form in the American Novel*. Oxford UP, 1985.
Flint, Kate. *The Transatlantic Indian, 1776–1930*. Princeton UP, 2008.
Franklin, Wayne. "James Fenimore Cooper and American Artists in Europe: Art, Religion, Politics." *Transatlantic Romanticism: British and American Art and Literature, 1790–1860*, edited by Andrew Hemingway and Alan Wallach, U of Massachusetts P, 2015, pp. 144–68.
———. "James Fenimore Cooper: Beyond Leather-Stocking." Kennedy and Person, pp. 247–61.
———. *James Fenimore Cooper: The Early Years*. Yale UP, 2007.
———. *James Fenimore Cooper: The Later Years*. Yale UP, 2017.
Freneau, Philip. "The Pilgrim, No. Nineteen." *The Prose Works of Philip Freneau*, edited by Philip M. Marsh, Scarecrow Press, 1955, pp. 68–72.
"The Friendship Turbulence." *The Big Bang Theory*, performance by Kaley Cuoco, season 7, episode 17, CBS, 2014.
Fudge, Erica. *Brutal Reasoning: Animals, Rationality, and Humanity in Early Modern England*. Cornell UP, 2006.
Ganter, Granville. "Battles of Rhetoric: Oratory and Identity in Cooper's *Last of the Mohicans*." 1997. *James Fenimore Cooper Society*, jfcoopersociety.org/articles/ala/1997ala-ganter.html.

Garforth, Lisa. "Green Utopias: Beyond Apocalypse, Progress, and Pastoral." *Utopian Studies*, vol. 16, no. 3, 2005, pp. 393–427.

Garrard, Greg, editor. *The Oxford Handbook of Ecocriticism*. Oxford UP, 2014.

Gasché, Rodolphe. *Persuasion, Reflection, Judgment: Ancillae Vitae*. Indiana UP, 2017.

Gaul, Theresa Strouth. "Romance and the 'Genuine Indian': Cooper's Politics of Genre." *ESQ*, vol. 48, 2002, pp. 159–86.

Gemme, Paola. *Domesticating Foreign Struggles: The Italian Risorgimento and Antebellum American Identity*. U of Georgia P, 2005.

Gitelman, Lisa. *Always Already New: Media, History and the Data of Culture*. MIT Press, 2006.

Goble, Alan, editor. *The Complete Index to Literary Sources in Film*. Bowker-Saur, 1999.

Goddard, Ives. "'I Am a Redskin': The Adoption of a Native American Expression (1796–1826)." *European Review of Native American Studies*, vol. 19, no. 2, 2005, pp. 1–20.

Godeanu-Kenworthy, Oana. "Creole Frontiers: Imperial Ambiguities in John Richardson's and James Fenimore Cooper's Fiction." *Early American Literature*, vol. 49, no. 3, 2014, pp. 741–70.

A Good Day to Die: Dennis Banks and The American Indian Movement. Directed by David Mueller and Lynn Salt, Kino Lorber, 2011.

Graff, Gerald. "Disliking Books at an Early Age." *Falling into Theory: Conflicting Views on Reading Literature*, edited by David H. Richter, Macmillan, 2000, pp. 36–44.

Graff, Gerald, and Cathy Birkenstein. *They Say / I Say: The Moves That Matter in Academic Writing*. 3rd ed., W. W. Norton, 2010.

Gray, Edward G., and Norman Fiering, editors. *The Language Encounter in the Americas, 1492–1800*. Berghahn Books, 2000.

Grinde, Donald A., and Bruce E. Johansen. *Exemplar of Liberty: Native America and the Evolution of Democracy*. American Indian Studies Center, 1991.

Grossman, James. *James Fenimore Cooper*. Stanford UP, 1949.

Guillory, John. "Genesis of the Media Concept." *Critical Inquiry*, vol. 36, no. 2, winter 2010, pp. 321–62.

Gustafson, Sandra M. "Cooper and the Idea of the Indian." Cassuto et al., pp. 103–16.

———. *Imagining Deliberative Democracy in the Early American Republic*. Chicago UP, 2011.

Gutjahr, Paul C. Introduction. Cooper, *Last of the Mohicans: A Narrative* [Gutjahr], pp. 13–26.

———. "Selected Bibliography." Cooper, *Last of the Mohicans: A Narrative* [Gutjahr], pp. 455–58.

Haberly, David T. "Women and Indians: *The Last of the Mohicans* and the Captivity Tradition." *American Quarterly*, vol. 28, no. 4, 1976, pp. 431–44.

Haile, Berard. *Legend of the Ghostway Ritual in the Male Branch of Shootingway, Part 1: Suckingway: Its Legend and Practice, Part 2*. St. Michaels Press, 1950.

Hamilton: An American Musical. Written by Lin-Manuel Miranda, Atlantic Records, 2015.

Hamilton's America: A Documentary Film. Directed by Alex Horwitz, PBS, 2016.

Harper, Judith E. "New York Married Women's Property Acts." *Women's Rights in the United States: A Comprehensive Encyclopedia of Issues, Events, and People*, edited by Tiffany K. Wayne and Lois Banner, ABC-CLIO, 2015, pp. 138–39.

Harrington, Ellen. "Failed Detectives and Dangerous Females: Wilkie Collins, Arthur Conan Doyle, and the Detective Short Story." *Journal of the Short Story in English*, vol. 45, autumn 2005, pp. 13–28.

Harris, Edward. "Cooper on Film." *James Fenimore Cooper Society*, jfcoopersociety.org/drama/film.html.

Hawthorne, Nathaniel. *The Scarlet Letter*. The Scarlet Letter *and Other Writings*, edited by Leland S. Person, 2nd Norton Critical Edition, W. W. Norton, 2017, pp. 1–155.

Hay, John. *Postapocalyptic Fantasies in Antebellum American Literature*. Cambridge UP, 2017.

Haywood, Ian. *Bloody Romanticism: Spectacular Violence and the Politics of Representation, 1776–1832*. Palgrave MacMillan, 2006.

Heckewelder, John. *History, Manners, and Customs of the Indian Nations*. 1819. *Memoirs of the Historical Society of Pennsylvania*, vol. 12, Historical Society of Pennsylvania, 1876.

Herrero, Ana, editor. *El indio dividido: Fracturas de conciencia en el Perú colonial: Edición crítica y estudio de los "Coloquios de la verdad" de Pedro de Quiroga*. Iberoamericana, 2009.

Hinds, Janie. "Dr. Rush and Mr. Peale: The Figure of the Animal in Late Eighteenth-Century Medical Discourse." *Early American Literature*, vol. 48, no. 3, 2013, pp. 641–70.

Hoffman, Charles Fenno. *Greyslaer: A Romance of the Mohawk*. Harper and Brothers, 1840. 2 vols.

Hoffmann, Ernst Theodor Amadeus. *Das Fräulein von Scuderi: Erzählung aus dem Zeitalter Ludwig des Vierzehnten*. 1819. Hamburg-Grossborstel Verlag der Deutschen Dichter-Gedächtnis-Stiftung, 1905.

———. *Tales of Hoffmann*. Translated by R. J. Hollingdale, Penguin Classics, 1982.

"The Hofstadter Insufficiency." *The Big Bang Theory*, performance by Kaley Cuoco, season 7, episode 1, CBS, 2013.

"Home." The Wide, Wide World *Digital Edition*, Southern Illinois University, Edwardsville, widewideworlddigitaledition.siue.edu/. Accessed 24 Feb. 2022.

Horak, Jan-Christopher. "Maurice Tourneur's Tragic Romance." *The Classic American Novel and the Movies*, edited by Gerald Peary and Roger Shatzkin, Frederick Ungar, 1977, pp. 4–19.

Horner, Avril. "Apocalypses Now: Collective Trauma, Globalisation and the New Gothic Sublime." *Trauma in Contemporary Literature Narrative and Representation*, edited by Marita Nadal and Mónica Calvo, Routledge, 2014, pp. 35–50.

House, Kay Seymour. *Cooper's Americans*. Ohio State UP, 1965.

———. "Historical Introduction." Cooper, *Satanstoe*, pp. xiii–xxxiii.

Howe, Daniel Walker. *What Hath God Wrought: The Transformation of America, 1815–1848.* Oxford UP, 2007.

Huet, Marie-Hélène. *The Culture of Disaster.* U of Chicago P, 2012.

Huhtamo, Errki. *Illusions in Motion: Media Archaeology and the Moving Panorama and Related Spectacles.* MIT Press, 2013.

Hutcheon, Linda. *A Theory of Adaptation.* 2nd edition, Routledge, 2013.

Incident at Oglala: The Leonard Peltier Story. Directed by Michael Apted, Miramax Films / Spanish Fork Motion Picture Company, 1991.

"Indian Removal Act: Primary Documents in American History." *Library of Congress*, guides.loc.gov/indian-removal-act.

Insko, Jeffrey. "The Logic of Left Alone: *The Pioneers* and the Conditions of U.S. Privacy." *American Literature*, vol. 81, 2009, pp. 659–85.

"Jack Chalman's 'Mohicans' Campaign." *The Film Daily*, 12 Oct. 1936, p. 6.

"James Fenimore Cooper." *Transatlantic Romanticism: An Anthology of British, American, and Canadian Literature*, edited by Lance Newman et al., Pearson Education, 2006, p. 649.

Jefferson, Thomas. *Notes on the State of Virginia.* Lilly and Wait, 1832.

J. T. M. Review of *The Last of the Mohicans*, by James Fenimore Cooper. 3 Sept. 1936. *The New York Times Film Reviews, 1913–1968*, vol. 2, New York Times, 1970, pp. 1315–16.

Kauth, Jean-Marie. "Post-apocalyptic Storytelling as Global Society's Environmental Unconscious." *Interdisciplinary Essays on Environment and Culture: One Planet, One Humanity, and the Media*, edited by Luigi Manca and Kauth, Lexington Books, 2015, pp. 283–303.

Keating, Patrick. *The Drama of Light: Hollywood Lighting from the Silent Era to Film Noir.* Columbia UP, 2010.

Kennedy, J. Gerald, and Leland Person, editors. *The American Novel to 1870.* Oxford UP, 2014. Vol. 5 of *The Oxford History of the Novel in English*.

Kilpatrick, Jacquelyn. *Celluloid Indians: Native Americans and Film.* U of Nebraska P, 1999.

———. "Keeping the Carcass in Motion: Adaptation and Transmutations of the National in *The Last of the Mohicans.*" *Literature and Film: A Guide to the Theory and Practice of Film Adaptation*, edited by Robert Stam and Alessandra Raengo, Blackwell, 2005, pp. 71–85.

King, Dennis. "*The Last of the Mohicans*: Oklahoman Plays Key Role in Film of Cooper's Novel." *Tulsa World*, 20 Sept. 1992.

Kornhaber, Spencer. "*Hamilton's America* Has Its Eyes on History." *The Atlantic*, 20 Oct. 2016, www.theatlantic.com/entertainment/archive/2016/10/hamiltons-america-pbs-documentary-lin-manuel-miranda-history/504527/.

Kovach, Margaret (Plains Cree and Saulteaux). *Indigenous Methodologies: Characteristics, Conversations, and Contexts.* Toronto UP, 2009.

Lacey, Theresa Jensen. *The Pawnee.* Chelsea House, 2006.

"The Last of the Mohicans." *Variety*, 9 Sept. 1936, p. 16, variety.com/1935/film/reviews/the-last-of-the-mohicans-1200411143/.

The Last of the Mohicans. Directed by Michael Mann, performances by Daniel Day-Lewis, Russell Means, Madeleine Stowe, and Wes Studi, Warner Brothers, 1992.
The Last of the Mohicans. Directed by George B. Seitz, performances by Randolph Scott, Binnie Barnes, Henry Wilcoxon, and Bruce Cabot, United Artists, 1936.
The Last of the Mohicans. Directed by Maurice Tourneur and Clarence L. Brown, performances by Wallace Beery, Barbara Bedford, Lillian Hall, and Alan Roscoe, Associated Producers, 1920.
"*The Last of the Mohicans* (1936)." *AFI Catalog of Feature Films*, American Film Institute, 2019, catalog.afi.com/Catalog/MovieDetails/985.
"*The Last of the Mohicans* Press Kit." Twentieth Century Fox, 1992.
Lawrence, D. H. *Studies in Classic American Literature*. Thomas Seltzer, 1923.
Lawson-Peebles, Robert. "The Lesson of the Massacre of Fort William Henry." *New Essays on* The Last of the Mohicans, Cambridge UP, 1992, pp. 115–38.
Leather Stocking. Directed by David Wark Griffith, Biograph Studios, 1909.
Le Guin, Ursula K. *Always Coming Home*. U of California P, 1985.
Leitch, Thomas. "Adaptation and Intertextuality; or, What Isn't an Adaptation, and What Does It Matter?" *A Companion to Literature, Film, and Adaptation*, edited by Deborah Cartmell, Wiley Blackwell, 2014, pp. 87–104.
———. "How to Teach Film Adaptations, and Why." Cutchins et al., *Pedagogy*, pp. 1–20.
Leopold, Aldo. *A Sand County Almanac*. Oxford UP, 1987.
Letter, Joseph J. "Past Presentisms: Suffering Soldiers, Benjaminian Ruins, and the Discursive Foundations of Early U.S. Historical Novels." *American Literature*, vol. 82, no. 1, 2010, pp. 29–55.
Levine, Robert S. "Temporality, Race, and Empire in Cooper's *The Deerslayer*: The Beginning of the End." *The Oxford Handbook of Nineteenth-Century American Literature*, edited by Russ Castronovo, Oxford UP, 2012, pp. 163–78.
Lewis, Jane Johnson. "1848: Married Women Win Property Rights." *ThoughtCo*, 1 Dec. 2017, thoughtco.com/1848-married-women-win-property-rights-3529577.
"Literary Intelligence: *The Pioneers*." *The Port Folio*, vol. 15, 5th series, June 1823, p. 520.
Little Big Man. Directed by Arthur Penn, Cinema Center Films, 1970.
Long, Robert Emmet. *James Fenimore Cooper*. Continuum, 1990.
Loper, Natalie Jones. "Adapting Composition, Arguing Adaptation: Using Adaptation in the Composition Classroom." Cutchins et al., *Pedagogy*, pp. 35–52.
Lounsbury, Thomas R. *James Fenimore Cooper*. Houghton Mifflin, 1896.
Lukasik, Christopher. *Discerning Characters: The Culture of Appearance in Early America*. U of Pennsylvania P, 2011.
Lynch, Deidre Shauna, and Evelyne Ender. "Introduction—Time for Reading." *PMLA*, vol. 133, no. 5, Oct. 2018, pp. 1073–82.
A Man Called Horse. Directed by Elliott Silverstein, Cinema Center Films / Sandy Howards Production, 1970.
Mani, B. Venkat. "Rights, Permissions, Claims: World Literature and the Borders of Reading." *PMLA*, vol. 134, no. 1, Jan. 2019, pp. 144–49.

Mann, Barbara Alice. *The Cooper Connection: The Influence of Jane Austen on James Fenimore Cooper*. AMS Press, 2014.

———. "Man with a Cross: Hawk-Eye was a 'Half-Breed.'" *James Fenimore Cooper Society Miscellaneous Papers*, no. 10, 1998, pp. 1–8.

———. "Maria Monk, Samuel Morse, and James Fenimore Cooper's *Ways of the Hour*." *Four Score*, U of Toledo P, 2020, pp. 149–71.

Marckwardt, Albert H. "The Chronology and Personnel of the Bread and Cheese Club." *American Literature*, vol. 6, no. 4, Jan. 1935, pp. 389–99.

"Martin Burnett's 'Mohicans' Campaign." *The Film Daily*, 1 Oct. 1936, p. 11.

Marubbio, M. Elise. "Celebrating with *The Last of the Mohicans*: The Columbus Quincentenary and Neocolonialism in Hollywood Film." *The Journal of American and Comparative Culture*, vol. 25, nos. 1–2, 2002, pp. 139–54.

Maslin, Janet. "*The Last of the Mohicans*." 25 Sept. 1992. *The New York Times Film Reviews, 1991–1992*, Times Books / Garland Publishing, 1993, p. 422.

May, Chad. "The Romance of America: Trauma, National Identity, and the Leather-Stocking Tales." *Early American Studies*, vol. 9, no. 1, 2011, pp. 167–86.

McCarthy, Cormac. *The Road*. Vintage, 2006.

McGann, Jerome. "Fenimore Cooper's Anti-Aesthetic and the Representation of Conflicted History." *Modern Language Quarterly*, vol. 73, no. 2, 2012, pp. 123–55.

McHugh, Susan. *Animal Stories: Narrating across Species Lines*. U of Minnesota P, 2011.

McShane, Clay, and Joel A. Tarr. "The Horse in the Nineteenth-Century American City." Brantz, pp. 227–45.

McWilliams, John P. "*The Pioneers*: Stumps in Clearing the Classroom Forest." Walker, *Reading*, pp. 32–45.

———. *Political Justice in a Republic: James Fenimore Cooper's America*. U of California P, 1972.

Means, Russell, with Marvin J. Wolf. *Where White Men Fear to Tread: The Autobiography of Russell Means*. St. Martin's Press, 1995.

Meek, Barbra A. "And the Injun Goes 'How!': Representations of American Indian English in White Public Space." *Language in Society*, vol. 35, no. 1, Feb. 2006, pp. 93–128.

Melville, Herman. *The Confidence-Man: His Masquerade*. 1857. Edited by Hershel Parker and Mark Niemeyer, W. W. Norton, 2006.

———. *Moby-Dick; or, The Whale*. 1851. W. W. Norton, 2002.

Millhouse, Barbara Babcock. *American Wilderness: The Story of the Hudson River School of Painting*. Black Dome Press, 2007.

Mitchell, W. J. T. *What Do Pictures Want? The Lives and Loves of Images*. U of Chicago P, 2005.

Momaday, N. Scott. "The Native Voice." *Columbia Literary History of the United States*, edited by Emory Elliott, Columbia UP, 1988, pp. 5–15.

Monroe, James. "Eighth Annual Message, Dec. 7, 1824." *The Addresses and Messages of the Presidents of the United States, Complete in One Volume*, Charles Lohman, 1837, pp. 209–19.

Montaigne, Michel de. *The Complete Essays of Montaigne*. Translated by Donald M. Frame, Stanford UP, 1958.

Monteiro, Lyra D. "Race-Conscious Casting and the Erasure of the Black Past in Lin-Manuel Miranda's *Hamilton*." *The Public Historian*, vol. 38, no. 1, Feb. 2016, pp. 89–98.

Mooney, James. *James Mooney's History, Myths, and Sacred Formulas of the Cherokees*. Bright Mountain Books, 1992.

Moretti, Franco. *Signs Taken for Wonders: Essays in the Sociology of Literary Forms*. Translated by Susan A. Fischer et al., rev. ed., Verso, 1988.

Morrison, Toni. *Playing in the Dark: Whiteness and the Literary Imagination*. Harvard UP, 1992.

Murray, Keat. "'The Unhappiest Idea Possible' in James Fenimore Cooper's Leather-Stocking Tales." *Early American Literature*, vol. 51, no. 2, 2016, pp. 477–99.

Muszynska-Wallace, E. Soteris. "The Sources of *The Prairie*." *American Literature*, vol. 21, no. 2, 1949, pp. 191–200.

Nagel, Rebecca. "The Ruling." *This Land*, season 1, episode 10, Crooked Media, 16 July 2020.

———. "The Treaty." *This Land*, season 1, episode 4, Crooked Media, 24 June 2019.

Nash, Gary B. *The Unknown American Revolution: The Unruly Birth of Democracy and the Struggle to Create America*. Penguin Books, 2005.

Nathan, Ian. "*Last of the Mohicans* Review." *Empire*, 1 Jan. 2000, empireonline.com/movies/reviews/last-mohicans-review/.

Nelson, Dana. "Cooper's Leatherstocking Conversations: Identity, Friendship, and Democracy in the New Nation." Person, *Historical Guide*, pp. 123–54.

Nevius, Blake. *Cooper's Landscapes: An Essay on the Picturesque Vision*. U of California P, 1976.

Noble, Louis Legrand. *The Life and Works of Thomas Cole*. Edited by Elliot S. Vesell, Belknap Press, 1964.

O Pioneers! Directed by Glenn Jordan, Hallmark, 1992.

Österberg, Bertil O. *Colonial America on Film and Television: A Filmography*. McFarland, 2001.

Pawelczak, Andy. "The Last of the Mohicans." *Films in Review*, vol. 43, Nov.-Dec. 1992, pp. 403–04.

Pearson, Susan J., and Mary Weismantel. "'Does the Animal Exist?': Toward a Theory of Social Life with Animals." Brantz, pp. 17–37.

Pease, Donald E., and Robyn Wiegman, editors. *The Futures of American Studies*. Duke UP, 2002.

Peck, H. Daniel. *A World by Itself: The Pastoral Moment in Cooper's Fiction*. Yale UP, 1977.

Person, Leland S., editor. *A Historical Guide to James Fenimore Cooper*. Oxford UP, 2007.

Peters, Richard, ed. *The Case of the Cherokee Nation against the State of Georgia: Argued and Determined at the Supreme Court of the United States, January Term 1831*. John Grigg, 1831.

Philbrick, Thomas. "*The Last of the Mohicans* and the Sounds of Discord." *American Literature*, vol. 43, no. 11, Mar. 1971, pp. 25–41.

"*The Pioneers.*" *Album*, vol. 3, May 1823, pp. 155–78.

"*The Pioneers.*" *Port Folio*, vol. 15, 5th series, Mar. 1823, pp. 230–48.

Pitts, Michael R. *Western Movies: A Guide to 5,105 Feature Films*. 2nd ed., McFarland, 2013.

Plant, John. *The Plains Indian Clowns, Their Contraries and Related Phenomena*. 2010. anjol.de/documents/100802_heyoka_neu.pdf.

Poe, Edgar Allan. "J. Fenimore Cooper." 1845. Poe, *Works*, vol. 3, pp. 380–92.

———. "The Murders in the Rue Morgue." Poe, *Works*, vol. 1, pp. 178–212.

———. *The Works of the Late Edgar Allan Poe: The Literati*. Edited by Rufus Wilmot Griswold et al., Blakeman and Mason, 1859. 4 vols.

Port, Cynthia. "Rereading the Future." *PMLA*, vol. 133, no. 3, May 2018, pp. 640–46.

Railton, Stephen. *James Fenimore Cooper: A Study of His Life and Imagination*. Princeton UP, 1978.

———. "James Fenimore Cooper (15 September 1789–14 September 1851)." *Antebellum Writers in New York and the South*, edited by Joel Myerson, Gale, 1979, pp. 74–93.

Rajewsky, Irina. "Intermediality, Intertextuality, and Remediation: A Literary Perspective on Intermediality." *Intermédialitiés*, vol. 6, autumn 2005, pp. 43–64.

Rancière, Jacques. *The Future of the Image*. Verso, 2007.

———. *The Politics of Aesthetics: The Distribution of the Sensible*. Edited and translated by Gabriel Rockhill, Continuum, 2004.

Rans, Geoffrey. *Cooper's Leather-stocking Novels: A Secular Reading*. U of North Carolina P, 1991.

Ratner-Rosenhagen, Jennifer. *The Ideas That Made America: A Brief History*. Oxford UP, 2019.

Rayner, Jonathan. "Endangering the Domestic: *Manhunter*, *The Last of the Mohicans*, *The Insider*." *The Cinema of Michael Mann: Vice and Vindication*, Wallflower Press, 2013, pp. 93–126.

Register, Seeley [Metta Victoria Fuller Victor]. *The Dead Letter: An American Romance*. Beadle and Company, 1866.

Review of *The Last of the Mohicans*, by James Fenimore Cooper. 3 Jan. 1921. *The New York Times Film Reviews, 1913–1968*, vol. 1, New York Times, 1970, p. 87.

Richardson, Donna. "Cooper's Revision of *Paradise Lost* and of Romantic Satanism in *The Last of the Mohicans*." *Literature in the Early American Republic*, vol. 6, 2014, pp. 217–44.

Rifkin, Mark. *When Did Indians Become Straight? Kinship, the History of Sexuality, and Native Sovereignty*. Oxford UP, 2011.

Ringe, Donald A. *James Fenimore Cooper*. Twayne, 1962.

———. "James Fenimore Cooper and Thomas Cole: An Analogous Technique." *American Literature*, vol. 30, no. 1, 1958, pp. 26–36.

———. *The Pictorial Mode: Space and Time in the Art of Bryant, Irving, and Cooper.* UP of Kentucky, 1971.

Ringe, Donald A., and Lucy B. Ringe. "Historical Introduction." Cooper, *Lionel Lincoln*, pp. xv–xl.

Röder, Birgit. *A Study of the Major Novellas of E. T. A. Hoffmann.* Camden House, 2003.

Rohrbaugh, Malcolm J. *The Trans-Appalachian Frontier: People, Societies, and Institutions, 1775–1850.* Wadsworth, 1990.

Romero, Lora. *Home Fronts: Domesticity and Its Critics in the United States.* Duke UP, 1997.

Rosenwald, Lawrence. "*The Last of the Mohicans* and the Languages of America." *College English*, vol. 60, no. 1, 1998, pp. 9–30.

———. *Multilingual America: Language and the Making of American Literature.* Cambridge UP, 2008.

Roylance, Patricia Jane. *Eclipse of Empires: World History in Nineteenth-Century U.S. Literature and Culture.* U of Alabama P, 2013.

Ruiz de Burton, María Amparo. *Who Would Have Thought It?* 1872. Edited and translated by Rosaura Sánchez and Beatrice Pita, Arte Público Press, 1995.

Russell, Steve. "What Gen. Washington Learned from Native Warriors: Indians and the Colonial Army." *Indian Country Today*, 13 Sept. 2018, indiancountrytoday.com/archive/what-gen-washington-learned-from-native-warriors-indians-and-the-colonial-army.

Ryan, Susan M. *The Moral Economies of American Authorship: Reputation, Scandal, and the Nineteenth-Century Literary Marketplace.* Oxford UP, 2016.

Samuels, Shirley, editor. *The Culture of Sentiment: Race, Gender, and Sentimentality in Nineteenth-Century America.* Oxford UP, 1992.

———. *Romances of the Republic: Women, the Family, and Violence in the Literature of the Early American Nation.* Oxford UP, 1996.

———. "Women, Blood, and Contract." *American Literary History*, vol. 20, no. 1, 2008, pp. 57–75.

Sanborn, Geoffrey. "James Fenimore Cooper and the Invention of the Passing Novel." *American Literature*, vol. 84, no. 1, 2012, pp. 1–29.

———. *Whipscars and Tattoos:* The Last of the Mohicans, Moby-Dick, *and the Maori.* Oxford UP, 2011.

Sand, George. "Fenimore Cooper." *Fenimore Cooper: The Critical Heritage*, edited by George Dekker and John P. Williams, Routledge, 2013, pp. 261–69.

Sanders, Julie. *Adaptation and Appropriation.* 2nd ed., e-book ed., Routledge, 2016.

Sansay, Leonora. *Laura.* Secret History; or, The Horrors of St. Domingo *and* Laura, edited by Michael Drexler, Broadview, 2008, pp. 155–221.

———. *Secret History; or, The Horrors of St. Domingo.* Secret History; or, The Horrors of St. Domingo *and* Laura, edited by Michael Drexler, Broadview, 2008, pp. 59–153.

Scannavini, Anna. "Cooper's Italian Seas." *James Fenimore Cooper Society Miscellaneous Papers*, no. 31, 2015, pp. 24–27.

Schachterle, Lance. "James Fenimore Cooper on the Languages of the Americans: A Note on the Author's Footnotes." *Nineteenth-Century Literature*, vol. 66, no. 1, 2011, pp. 37–68.

Scheckel, Susan. *The Insistence of the Indian: Race and Nationalism in Nineteenth-Century American Culture*. Princeton UP, 1998.

Schramer, James J. "Shaping the American Political Landscape: James Fenimore Cooper's and Susan Cooper's Perspectives on Property and Polity." *James Fenimore Cooper Society*, Aug. 2009, jfcoopersociety.org/articles/suny/2007suny-schramer.html.

Sedgwick, Catharine Maria. *Hope Leslie; or, Early Times in the Massachusetts*. 1827. Penguin Books, 1998.

Shakespeare, William. *Much Ado about Nothing*. *The Complete Plays and Poems of William Shakespeare*, edited by William Allan Neilson and Charles Jarvis Hill, New Cambridge Edition, Riverside Press / Houghton Mifflin, 1942, pp. 179–210.

Shell, Marc. *American Babel: Literatures of the United States from Abnaki to Zuni*. Harvard UP, 2002.

———. "Babel in America; or, The Politics of Language Diversity in the United States." *Critical Inquiry*, vol. 20, no, 1, 1993, pp. 103–27.

Shelley, Mary. *Frankenstein; or, The Modern Prometheus*. 1818. Edited by Joanna M. Smith, Bedford Books, 1992.

Silko, Leslie Marmon. *Ceremony*. Penguin Books, 2006.

Simon, John. "Return of the Native." *National Review*, 16 Nov. 1992, pp. 61–62.

Sivils, Matthew Wynn. *American Environmental Fiction, 1782–1847*. Ashgate, 2014.

Smith, Gavin. "Mann Hunters." *Film Comment*, vol. 28, no. 6, Nov.-Dec. 1992, pp. 72–77.

Smith, Henry Nash. *Virgin Land: The American West as Symbol and Myth*. Harvard UP, 1978.

Smith, Paul Chaat, and Robert Allen Warrior. *Like a Hurricane: The Indian Movement from Alcatraz to Wounded Knee*. The New Press, 1996.

Somerville, William. *The Chace: A Poem*. Hawkins, 1735.

Spiller, Robert E. *Fenimore Cooper: Critic of His Times*. Minton, Balch, 1931.

Spratt, Danielle, and Bridget Draxler. "Pride and Presentism: On the Necessity of the Public Humanities for Literary Historians." *Profession*, spring 2019, profession.mla.org/pride-and-presentism-on-the-necessity-of-the-public-humanities-for-literary-historians/.

Sragow, Michael. "Michael Mann's *The Last of the Mohicans*." *Library of America*, 27 Jan. 2016, loa.org/news-and-views/1115-michael-manns-_the-last-of-the-mohicans.

Stam, Robert. "Introduction: The Theory and Practice of Adaptation." *A Guide to the Theory and Practice of Film Adaptation*, edited by Stam and Alessandra Raengo, Blackwell, 2005, pp. 1–52.

Starbuck, David R. "The Mystery of the Second Body: A Forensic Investigation of Jane McCrea's Final Resting Place." *Plymouth Magazine*, vol. 28, no. 1, 2006, plymouth.edu/magazine/uncategorized/the-mystery-of-the-second-body/.

Steele, Ian K. "The Last of the Mohicans." *Journal of American History*, Dec. 1993, pp. 1179–81.

Steinberg, Theodore. "What Is a Natural Disaster?" *Literature and Medicine*, vol. 15, no. 1, 1996, pp. 33–47.

Sterritt, David. "The Last of the Mohicans (1920)." *Turner Classic Movies*, 14 Mar. 2012, www.tcm.com/tcmdb/title/308184/the-last-of-the-mohicans/#articles-reviews?articleId=480765.

Straub, Kristina. "The Suspicious Reader Surprised; or, What I Learned from 'Surface Reading.'" *The Eighteenth Century*, vol. 54, no. 1, spring 2013, pp. 139–43.

Sullam Calimani, Anna-Vera. *Il primo dei mohicani: L'elemento americano nelle traduzioni dei romanzi di J. F. Cooper*. Istituti Editoriali e Poligrafici Internazionali, 1995.

Sundquist, Eric J. "The Literature of Expansion and Race." *The Cambridge History of American Literature*, edited by Sacvan Bercovitch, vol. 2, Cambridge UP, 1995, pp. 125–337.

Tawil, Ezra. *The Making of Racial Sentiment: Slavery and the Birth of the Frontier Romance*. Cambridge UP, 2006.

Taylor, Alan. *William Cooper's Town: Power and Persuasion on the Frontier of the Early American Republic*. Alfred A. Knopf, 1995.

Tompkins, Jane. *Sensational Designs: The Cultural Work of American Fiction, 1790–1860*. Oxford UP, 1985.

Travers, Peter. "The Last of the Mohicans." *Rolling Stone*, 25 Sept. 1992, rollingstone.com/movies/movie-reviews/the-last-of-the-mohicans-124648/.

Travis, Jennifer, and Jessica DeSpain, editors. *Teaching with Digital Humanities*. U of Illinois P, 2018.

Trocchio, Rachel. "Memory's Ends: Thinking as Grace in Thomas Hooker's New England." *American Literature*, vol. 90, no. 4, 2018, pp. 693–722.

Twain, Mark. *The Adventures of Huckleberry Finn*. Penguin Books, 2002.

———. "Fenimore Cooper's Literary Offenses." *North American Review*, vol. 161, no. 464, July 1895, pp. 1–12.

Underhill, Harriette. "The Last of the Mohicans." *New-York Tribune*, 3 Jan. 1921. *Chronicling America: Historic American Newspapers*, Library of Congress, chroniclingamerica.loc.gov/lccn/sn83030214/1921-01-03/ed-1/seq-8/.

United States, Congress. *United States Statutes at Large*. 21st Congress, 1st session, 1830. *Library of Congress*, memory.loc.gov/cgi-bin/ampage?collId=llsl&fileName=004/llsl004.db&recNum=458.

Vonnegut, Kurt. *Galápagos*. Dial, 2009.

Walker, Jeffrey. "Deconstructing an American Myth: Hollywood and *The Last of the Mohicans*." *Film and History*, vol. 23, nos. 1–4, pp. 103–16.

———. "Fenimore Cooper's *Wyandotté* and the Cyclic Course of Empire." 1987. *James Fenimore Cooper Society*, jfcoopersociety.org/articles/suny/1986suny-walker.html.

———, editor. *Leather-stocking Redux; or, Old Tales, New Essays*. AMS Press, 2011.

———, editor. *Reading Cooper, Teaching Cooper*. AMS Press, 2007.

Walker, Warren, editor. *Plots and Characters in the Fiction of James Fenimore Cooper*. Archon Books, 1978.

Wallach, Alan P. "Cole, Byron, and the Course of Empire." *The Art Bulletin*, vol. 50, no. 4, 1968, pp. 375–79.

Walters, Kerry. "The 'Peaceable Disposition' of Animals: William Bartram on the Moral Sensibility of Brute Creation." *Pennsylvania History*, vol. 56, no. 3, July 1989, pp. 157–76.

Weaver, Erica. "Premodern and Postcritical: Medieval Enigmata and the Hermeneutic Style." *New Literary History*, vol. 50, no. 1, winter 2019, pp. 43–64.

Wegener, Signe O. *James Fenimore Cooper versus the Cult of Domesticity: Progressive Themes of Femininity and Family in the Novels*. McFarland, 2005.

———. "Marmaduke Temple: James Fenimore Cooper's Portrait of a Man of Leisure." Walker, *Leather-Stocking Redux*, pp. 103–23.

Weltfish, Gene. *The Lost Universe: Pawnee Life and Culture*. 1965. Rev. ed., U of Nebraska P, 1990.

Wilentz, Sean. *The Rise of American Democracy: Jefferson to Lincoln*. W. W. Norton, 2005.

Wilson, Jeffrey R. "Historicizing Presentism: Toward the Creation of a Journal of the Public Humanities." *Profession*, spring 2019, profession.mla.org/historicizing-presentism-toward-the-creation-of-a-journal-of-the-public-humanities/.

Woidat, Caroline M. "Teaching the Politics and Practice of Textual Recovery with DIY Critical Editions." Travis and DeSpain, pp. 133–50.

Wolloch, Nathaniel. "Animals in Enlightenment Historiography." *Huntington Library Quarterly*, vol. 75, no. 1, Mar. 2012, pp. 53–68.

Wood, Gordon S. *The Creation of the American Republic, 1776–1787*. U of North Carolina P, 1969.

Woolfolk, Alan. "Natural Man, Natural Rights, and Eros: Conflicting Visions of Nature, Society, and Love in *The Last of the Mohicans*." *The Philosophy of Michael Mann*, edited by Steven Sanders et al., UP of Kentucky, 2014, pp. 215–26.

Woolman, John. "The Journal of John Woolman." *The Heath Anthology of American Literature*, edited by Paul Lauter, 7th ed., vol. A., Houghton Mifflin, 2013, pp. 749–64.

Wyman, Leland C. *Beautyway: A Navajo Ceremonial*. Pantheon, 1957.

Yingling, Charlton W. "No One Who Reads the History of Hayti Can Doubt the Capacity of Colored Men: Racial Formation and Atlantic Rehabilitation in New York City's Early Black Press, 1827–1841." *Early American Studies*, vol. 11, no. 2, 2013, pp. 314–48.

Younging, Gregory (Opsakwayak Cree). *Elements of Indigenous Style: A Guide for Writing by and about Indigenous Peoples*. Brush, 2018.